Sixth Edition

PROCESS & PRACTICE

COMPOSITION FOR CANADIAN STUDENTS

Sixth Edition
PROCESS & PRACTICE
COMPOSITION FOR CANADIAN STUDENTS

Ronald Conrad

McGraw-Hill
Ryerson

McGraw-Hill Ryerson Limited

Toronto Montreal Boston Burr Ridge IL Dubuque IA Madison VT New York
San Francisco St. Louis Bangkok Bogotá Caracas Kuala Lumpur Lisbon London
Madrid Mexico City Milan New Delhi Santiago Seoul Singapore Sydney Taipei

McGraw-Hill
Ryerson Limited

A Subsidiary of The **McGraw·Hill** Companies

Process and Practice
Composition for Canadian Students
Sixth Edition

ISBN: 0-07-086499-3

1 2 3 4 5 6 7 8 9 10 MP 0 9 8 7 6 5 4 3 2 1

Printed and bound in Canada

Care has been taken to trace ownership of copyright material contained in this text; however, the publisher will welcome any information that enables them to rectify any reference or credit for subsequent editions.

VICE PRESIDENT AND EDITORIAL DIRECTOR: Pat Ferrier
SENIOR SPONSORING EDITOR: Veronica Visentin
ASSOCIATE SPONSORING EDITOR: Marianne Minaker
MARKETING MANAGER: Ralph Courtney
SENIOR SUPERVISING EDITOR: Margaret Henderson
PRODUCTION EDITOR: Rodney Rawlings
PRODUCTION COORDINATOR: Sue Penny
DESIGN AND COMPOSITION: Lynda Powell
COVER DESIGN: Greg Devitt
COVER IMAGE: Adrian Duey / The Image Bank
PRINTER: Maracle Press

Canadian Cataloguing in Publication Data

Conrad, Ronald, 1941 –
    Process & practice : composition for Canadian students

6th ed.
Includes index.
ISBN 0-07-086499-3

1. English language — Rhetoric. 2. English language — Grammar. I. Title.
II. Title: Process and practice.

PE1408.C583 2000   808'.042   C00-932472-0

CONTENTS

The world is changing much faster than ever before. Near the end of this book, our sample research essay examines some of the effects on you and your classmates: in a world transformed by technology, with old categories of jobs falling right and left, how can today's students find success in the new workplace? By improving their writing, suggests one expert we quote, Canadian demographer David Foot. "The decline of literacy," he points out, "has enhanced the value of the small minority who can write well. . . ."

He is right, and if you need some help developing this key skill for the future, you are holding it in your hand. *Process and Practice* is meant to strengthen your writing, showing you techniques, tricks, and strategies to make your work more relevant, better organized, more fully developed, and more polished. Our first section, on "short essays," takes you through the conception and planning stage, into warmups to overcome any writer's block, and through the "discovery draft" of a brand new sample essay based on an adventure in the Canadian North. Then it demonstrates dozens of ways to fine-tune that first draft into more polished versions. Three more new sample essays follow.

Next, the paragraph chapter, with many new worksheets and activities for this edition, teaches how to develop and write different kinds of paragraphs for different purposes. Then begins a large section on editing: that is, on polishing your early versions. This means both troubleshooting errors and also applying useful principles of style, to heighten your power on the page. The exercises in this section are made of examples collected from student essays, so they will "ring true." (By the way, note that answers to many of these exercises are given at the end of the book, so you can check your work, whether you are taking a course or using this book on your own.)

Finally, if your class is also doing a research paper, near the end of the book this more scholarly art is examined, and the full sample essay already mentioned shows how the principles are applied. A new feature of this section, "Researching with Internet Sources," shows how to sharpen your skills on the Web, and examines the issue of judging which information found on the Internet may be reliable enough to put in your essays.

Let's close by looking at our title: *Process and Practice*. Many teachers once believed that writing was planned out all in advance, with a detailed outline functioning something like a blueprint on a construction site. As the world has changed around us, though, so has our view of writing. Current research shows what most good writers have always known in their heart, that writing is a messy business—not a technology of any kind, but an art. When we set out on a writing task, we often don't even know the best ideas we'll end up with by the time we're done. This book recognizes, even celebrates, the reality of *thinking by writing*. That is the "process." The "practice," of course, is what you are about to do. . . .

R. C.

Welcome to the sixth edition of *Process and Practice: Composition for Canadian Students.* Our desire to offer a fully Canadian text continues into the new millennium. This book is written here, edited here, filled with Canadian examples, and unafraid to confront issues that affect Canadian student writers.

What is new in this edition?

- In response to many requests, we have increased the number of sample "short essays" from one to four. All are brand-new in this edition. The first is longer than the others, and has full study apparatus, for classes that have the time. The other three are shorter, in the 500-to-600-word range, to reflect closely the length and scope of essays most often written in composition courses, and to give materials for classes that have less time or that have many other items on their agenda. Both the longer essay and the three short ones have a new feature, concise explanations in the margin next to the things they point out.

- We have dropped the short chapter on computing. As our reviewers advised us, it was once necessary but now most students are so proficient at computing that it is no longer needed. Yet we have kept the concise text boxes throughout, which link particular techniques of computing to specific tasks of writing. (See also the point on new Internet research material below.)

- We have beefed up the paragraph section with several newly created exercises, especially focussing on coherence. For ease of use we have also reorganized the whole section, placing each exercise next to the material to which it relates.

- In the large editing section we have revised most of the exercises, with many items newly collected from actual student writing. We continue to seek examples that both illustrate clearly the matter at hand and are concrete and vivid enough to maintain student interest.

- Our sample research essay, new in the last edition, seems to have struck a chord. The reviewers advised us to keep it. We have made other changes to the research essay section, though. We have recommended many more new electronic sources for student research, and have added a whole new subsection on Internet research. It profiles the most-used search engines, gives concrete techniques for conducting an Internet search, and gives guidance in the new and slippery area of how to select and evaluate materials found on the Web.

- Finally, we have improved the design and format. For example we have summarized more points and marked them with "bullets," for ease of study, and we've used more white space throughout this edition.

If you are new to this book, here are a few overall suggestions:

- The order of chapters suggests a course plan. We advise starting right off with the "Process in Short Essays" chapter, and basing a large part of any composition course on it. Until materials are generated and the actual writing begins, what is there to edit? Writing should be the main and ongoing activity of the course.

  We also know that some teachers prefer to begin with paragraphs, which, like essays, are long enough that they can support the skills of invention, focus, and development. If this is what works best for you, then clearly you should do it, reversing the order of our first two chapters and perhaps drawing on some of the essay chapter material on invention to use with your study of paragraphs.

  We recommend the system of drafts explored in the "Short Essays" chapter. The first draft by your students can be checked but not evaluated, or can be treated in peer editing, or—if class size limits your marking time—can be handed in at the same time as a second draft; you then mark only the second, while briefly checking the first to verify that some real revision has been done.

■ Meanwhile, in the area of style and correctness, as the needs of the students make themselves clear through what you see in their papers, select the appropriate editing materials from wherever they occur in the book (rather than marching a whole class through a prescribed set of activities). Do note that many of these sections have a diagnostic and a progression of two or more levels of exercises, so you can individualize work for different groups. (Answers to those exercises that are not open-ended are in the Answer Key at the end of the book.)

Another approach is to individualize: assign exercises as you mark each person's paper. These can then be done at home, and either checked by the student against the answer key or handed in (the exercises are detachable).

In presenting a large number of editing topics and exercises, we in no way suggest you feel obliged to use everything. One reviewer said that, having required the students to buy the book, he feels compelled to use every exercise. But we view the goal as choice and individualization. If the class or a student in it has serious trouble with pronouns, then you may want to do every exercise in that section. But if your students show no difficulties with parallel form, then do consider passing it over to concentrate on more pressing matters.

By the way, do note a feature one teacher told us he had not discovered till the course was over: on the inside back cover appears the Editing Guide, which in very large print lists the common essay correction symbols, tells what they represent, and directs students to the page where discussion of that matter begins.

We really hope you like *Process and Practice*, sixth edition. I thank our many reviewers, who gave cogent and detailed advice on developing this resource:

Kim Cechetto, Fanshawe College
Gary Corscadden, New Brunswick Community College
Ross Laing, Sir Wilfrid Laurier Secondary School
Sheila Lanthier-O'Connor, Concordia University
Linda Large, Canadore College
Beth Mawhiney, Georgian College
Judy Mussio, Georgian College
Phyllis Schwartz, Lord Byng Secondary School
Robert Wiznura, Grant MacEwan Community College

And the reviewers for the Fifth Edition were:

Janet Baker, St. Mary's University
Barry Fox, St. Mary's University
Carol Fullerton, Mount Royal College
Janet Hill, Acadia University
Gary Lipschutz, Centennial College
Jim Maloney, Seneca College
Sally Nelson, Dawson College
Joan Pilz, Humber College

Another person who deserves at least as much credit is my wife, Mary, whose good judgement has contributed so much to this edition and all the others before it.

R. C.

PART ONE

Process in Short Essays

How do you write? Answers to this question have changed since your parents and grandparents were in school. Some widely believed folklore has been exposed as untrue, while research has more and more clearly shown what really happens when you sit down at the computer or writing desk. Let's examine some theories of the past that no longer make sense.

POPULAR MISCONCEPTIONS ABOUT WRITING

■ *Misconception 1: Writing is just a matter of inspiration: I either hit it or miss it.*

Most ideas, including this one, contain at least a bit of truth. We all hope for inspiration as we write. But now we know good writing doesn't just strike the paper like a lightning bolt, but expands and takes on power through a process of revision. The first try is just a start; the second version is better developed; a third is better developed still. As many good writers have believed all along, "writing is 10 percent inspiration and 90 percent perspiration."

■ *Misconception 2: Writing is almost totally planned in advance.*

Years ago most teachers and students believed (or at least said they believed) that preparing a beautifully reasoned outline was the main task in writing an essay. All the rest was filling in the blanks. But today we know this approach can actually paralyze our thought process. While a short outline usually does help, overplanning is a straitjacket that blocks the many good ideas *that start to come only when we are*

writing. Now we know that the act of writing is only partly planning—the rest is discovery!

You would take a compass to hike or canoe up north, and you would take an outline to travel through your thoughts. But a compass can't predict the hills and valleys, or the wind and waves on the lake, or the bear or moose around the next turn of the trail. If it could, your sense of adventure would vanish. In the same way, an outline can't predict the progression of your thoughts, the surprises that jolt you as one idea leads to the next. Do use an outline, like a compass, especially in longer papers, so you don't get lost, but leave room for discovery. And if your discoveries overpower your outline, then your outline was weak to begin with. Consider changing it, in the light of what you've learned while writing.

■ *Misconception 3: If I just avoid enough errors, then my writing will be good.*

It is easy to see where this idea led in the past: people were so nervous about correctness that they paid too little attention to the main point of writing—the message. Stopping to look at suspicious subjects and verbs in the middle of writing a passage, they lost their train of thought and spent the next 10 minutes chewing their pencil—especially if they believed Misconception 1, that they either "hit it or miss it" the first time.

Writing should be pleasure, not pain. The first draft should go fast. Be free and open. After all, you are exploring: the goal is to get your ideas safely out on paper, without worrying about how "correct" you are. Then *later,* once the pressure is off, you tinker with grammar, spelling and style.

This whole book is organized to encourage writing as a process. The opening chapter deals with the big things:

- getting an idea
- focussing it
- trying the idea out in a quick first draft
- then revising your *thoughts*

The later chapters move on to secondary things:

- paragraphing
- conciseness
- clear sentence structure
- agreement
- clear pronoun reference
- spelling, etc.

These are all important, because without them the message might not get through. But they are "secondary" because, without a clear message in the first place, even the most correct writing achieves nothing at all—like a pile of good bricks on the ground waiting to be formed into a house.

WHAT IS AN ESSAY?

The word "essay" comes from a French term that means a "try" or "attempt." Your "attempts" to explore a topic in essay form can be as short as one or two pages or as long as 20, 30 or even 50 pages. They can be a brief and spontaneous treatment of a subject you already know, like how you trained your dog or what happened when you broke the law, or they can be the product of weeks online or in the library researching a complex or specialized topic.

Since the form of an essay can vary so much, let's look separately at the two most common assignments: we will call them *short essays* and *research essays*. In this chapter we will explore "short essays," because it is these that are most often practised in writing courses, and because the strategies behind them are the main strategies of research papers as well.

Then at the end of this book, after examining the whole process of writing, we'll explore the more specialized tasks of research papers.

STARTING OUT: WHAT IS MY SUBJECT?

First of all, an essay has a subject. What will you write about? Teachers often answer that question by assigning a topic or choice of topics. Other times, you think up your own.

Many kinds of writing you may do later in life will have similarities to the essay. Your employer may demand written analyses of projects at work. As a family member, you might write a letter to explain or solve problems with a loved one. Or as a concerned citizen, you might write an "essay" of protest to your member of parliament, your mayor, or the editor of your newspaper. At crucial times in your life, you may even write out your private thoughts, as many people do, just to realize what you really think about your choices.

Whatever the subject and circumstances, the hardest part is to *begin*. If you need to choose from a list of topics, begin by comparing. Which topic do you already know something about? Which seems most important? Which do you *like*? Choose it, because you will do your best writing on topics that attract you. Some teachers of composition will ask you to produce your

YOU ARE HERE

DRAWING BY CHAS. ADDAMS. © 1974 THE NEW YORKER MAGAZINE, INC.

own topics. There are students who dread this, thinking they will have nothing to say; others love the challenge, because they can finally write what's on their mind.

In either case, choosing your own topic is an act that closely simulates your writing tasks in later life outside the classroom. But how is it done? Let's explore one powerful approach to this challenge of creating a topic.

PRIMING THE PUMP: FREEWRITING

Have you ever tried to get water from an old hand pump, but nothing came out? Have you ever stared at a blank screen with your hands on the keyboard, but nothing came out? In the case of the pump, hardly ever is the well dry. The problem lies simply in getting the flow started. Old-timers will pour a jar of water down the pump to seal the chamber; now their efforts will create a suction that pulls up that cold, clear water.

In the case of the blank screen, the well is not dry either. What needs to be done is a kind of mental priming, so that your efforts will pull up ideas from the depths of your mind.

One of the best priming exercises is **freewriting.** Put a piece of paper and a watch on the desk. Now for about five minutes, just write. Write *anything* that comes to mind, even if it seems like mental garbage. Get it down as fast as your fingers can move on the keyboard, or as fast as your pen can get words on paper. Then rush on to the next thought that arrives.

Do not stop the physical process of keyboarding or writing until the time is up. If the next thought does not come, keep repeating the last one till it does. At the beginning of it all, if not even the first thought will come, try this: Write "The" on the paper. Some word will then pop into your mind to follow "The," and another will follow it, until soon your first idea is out in the open.

Why write what may seem like garbage? Because researchers have found that thoughts tend to appear not in logical order but in sudden jumps of association. If we start with a few of these intuitive connections, we get the juices of thought flowing; we pump those raw materials of writing out into the open where our more logical thought processes can now work on them, shaping them into the logical arguments we wanted in the first place.

Here is an actual, unedited piece of freewriting. It took six minutes and 45 seconds, because the writer was on a roll with the emerging subject and didn't want to stop. It is also fairly long, because his keyboarding speed is fast.

Note his careless sentence structure: some passages run on and on with "ands," while others are cut off into partial sentences. Note also the careless spelling and typos, such as "foirget" for "forget" and "mosse" for "moose." There is also an error of fact: the "30 pound canoe pack" was really a "30 kilo canoe pack," as the writer realized later. Neither is this passage much of an argument, supporting a main point the way an essay is meant to do. It's more of a story, a narrative. This writer may still be searching for something to prove. **But in freewriting none of these things are errors, for the whole point is just to get thoughts out in the open, where now they can be shaped and developed.**

I'm always ready to try new things, so for the long weekend in August I thought a canoe trip was great. Ellen and I had never gone, but our friends Bob and Karen were experienced, and had a very good canoe. Unfortunately, the one we borrowed from another friend was about thirty years old, a heavy old fibreglkass thing, and little did we know we would hit that rock and the leak came in under our gear. Good thing Bob brought duct tape, real Canadian, eh?, and not only did we fix the leak but also taped together my paddle that broke on the same rock. Then the second day when high winds came up and the waves started to splash in a little at the bow, we got pushed off course down the wrong end of a channel and couldn't get back—so out came the map and we saw the only way to our nex5t lake was a portage of two kilometres. "The Portage from Hell" we finally called it. I'll never foirget the sight of Ellen up to her knees in mud, carrying the 30 pound canoe pack, or the sound of galloping hooves and then the huge cow mosse coming over the hill towards us on the path, and I was carrying the red canoe but she didn't see me till it was almost too late. And then those idiots at thew other end with a satellite locator, showing us this is exactly where we are. And not till we got back, the true symptoms of beaver fever because Bob's water filter broke and we were drinking lake water with iodine pills in it. But that last morning up at 6:15 because of the birds singing, and the mist totally covering the lake, and water still as glass, and we all dove in and felt we were swimming through the clouds—well, next year I'm going back.

This writer was lucky to start with a subject already in mind, so he didn't have to write a page of free association—jumping from one thought or image to another—before hitting on the idea of that canoe trip over the August long weekend.

Yet this early and spontaneous version of his thoughts is far from the argument he will produce by the end of his first draft or second draft. In fact, at this point it is hardly an argument at all, but more of an adventure story, a kind of narrative. But he does uncover ideas that could *become* an argument. For example, he seems preoccupied with the idea of new equipment vs. old equipment (Bob's new canoe vs. his own borrowed canoe that sprung a leak at the first rock it hit). Another idea is hardships—not only the leaky canoe and broken paddle, but the "Portage from Hell" where his companion Ellen sinks to her knees under the heavy pack, and where a moose almost runs them down. Another hardship is the beaver fever caused by drinking contaminated lake water. (You really don't want to hear the symptoms, so let's be glad he didn't go into them.) Despite these hardships, though, at the end he portrays the experience as beautiful, almost as paradise, on the morning the four friends "swim through the clouds."

So what will our writer focus on as he produces the first draft: How to do a canoe trip on the cheap? How a canoe trip is hard work, but pays off in the end? Will he even argue that his first taste of wilderness canoeing has converted him to a thrilling new sport? We don't know yet, and neither does he.

But one thing is sure: the six minutes and 45 seconds he spent racing away at the keyboard were highly productive: now he has a choice of ideas. **Keep this in mind when you write: it is surprising how often a piece of freewriting, like this one, uncovers the main point of the essay that will follow—how much it discovers even before the discovery draft begins.**

Think of your own experience in starting to write essays: Have you been afraid of the blank page? Has writer's block paralyzed you? Freewriting can move you past these common problems. After all, what do you have to lose—a few minutes of your time? By ignoring the old myth that writing is all planned in advance, you can take mental shortcuts that may save hours of time. The trick is to **think by writing.**

Even if a required topic leaves you cold, so that you feel you have nothing to say, you can avoid writer's block by freewriting. Launch into a few minutes of warmup by putting onto that blank screen or page *something, anything,* that relates to your topic. You will often be surprised at what comes out; you may sense that, even at this stage, *the writing has somehow begun.*

PRIMING THE PUMP: BRAINSTORMING

Brainstorming is like freewriting, with one main difference: it is not a piece of continuous writing but a **list of ideas put down in short form.**

Suppose the person whose freewriting we have just seen had done brainstorming instead. Thinking of that August canoe trip, he would jot down anything that came to mind, in any order. Even ideas that seemed irrelevant or silly could join the list. Some might seem random or illogical, but, as in freewriting, what is there to lose? Five minutes of time? And only he will see the list (except for us, looking over his shoulder right now).

A writer who brainstorms casts a net into the sea: when the catch is pulled in, it may include fish no one would want to eat. So what? They are thrown back and the good ones are kept.

As you look at the author's page of brainstorming, note the progression of thought. After one reference to going with experienced people, he devotes several lines to equipment: how he and Ellen took an old canoe and old paddles, which both gave them trouble, how even the experienced friend Bob suffered a broken water filter, and how Ellen sank in the mud under the weight of her pack. Is this a topic so far? Maybe so—because how does a student get money to buy good equipment that is lighter and stronger? At this point our author's message could be the need to borrow equipment or rent it or buy it used, or the need to substitute cheap equipment. (Why pay a hundred for a state-of-the-art self-inflating air mattress when a roll of foam from Canadian Tire costs a few dollars?)

But moving now to scary thoughts, our author mentions the wind and waves, and the threat of bears getting at the food—which means hanging the food pack from a tree at night. Even the quiet is "weird." Yet, on the other hand, the views from the canoe are "incredible," the quiet allows our author to finally hear the "sounds of nature," and nights at the campfire are a "blast." Clearly our author is trying to evaluate his new experience pro or con. So is this a topic too?

At the same time he is still thinking economics—because next he notes how the four friends had entered Crown land, rather than a provincial or national park, so there were no fees or permits. A fishing licence, though, does cost. And now he sums up the financial angle: canoeing is a "cheap holiday." (This really does look like the main point of an argument.) But when in the last line he turns again to the trip itself, saying that swimming in lakes is "glorious," especially the "last morning swimming in the mist," he has turned once from economics to experience.

So when he starts to write the actual essay, will he choose economics or experience as the overall point? Are there even further points that have not made it onto the list? We don't know yet. Neither does he. But what we do know is that in these few minutes of brainstorming, in short form, *the writing has already begun.*

PRIMING THE PUMP: A CLUSTER OUTLINE

A similar but more visual icebreaker is the cluster outline. (Many people think better visually, and you may be one of them.) As in brainstorming, write down the ideas in very short form as they come, but now connect them with lines in a diagram. On page 7 see how our author's thoughts about the canoe trip might have come out in this format. (See also how the content is a little different, because every try is different.)

Notice how this diagram sorts related ideas more easily into groups. The writer first circles the beginning thought of a "canoe trip" in the middle of the page. Then around it he jots down other words or ideas it brings to mind, such as "really different from city" or "cheap holiday" or "scary," and connects them with lines to the central words "canoe trip." Most of these new thoughts then lead to further thoughts connected again by lines and placed further out from the centre. The result, as our author looks over this cluster outline: three groups of related material. Now he has three leads for his main organizing point:

- the "scariness" of his first canoe trip
- how "different" the canoe trip was from life as usual in the city
- how "cheap" the holiday was

And in each case he even has a choice of subpoints to begin developing.

Wait a minute, he thinks already, the *scariness* was actually a part of how *different* the trip was from things back in the city. In fact, maybe the scariness got everyone ready for the highs of the trip, especially the last morning when the friends swam in the mist. Maybe those two groups in the outline are really one.

Or, he thinks, looking again at the words "cheap holiday," do I want to write on that more concrete subject? It would be easy, almost like a paper for Introduction to Business. But already he can feel his level of interest sag. He looks again at the experiential aspects of his wilderness trek. Sure enough, his excitement level is moving back up.

Right now it looks as though our writer has a subject that matters to him. It looks as though he will be motivated. As with freewriting and brainstorming, it looks as though *the writing has already begun.*

PRIMING THE PUMP: FIGHTING WRITER'S BLOCK WITH IMAGINATION

We have just looked at freewriting, brainstorming and the cluster outline. One of these should be enough, or at the most two, to help us move inside a subject. But sometimes the well-known literary disease of **writer's block** refuses to let us through. We all know the symptoms: sitting frozen in time, stealing glances at our watch, feeling the sweat on our face and the palms of our hands, and looking with rising emptiness at that object of fear in front of us—the blank page or computer screen.

CANOE TRIP

- good to go with experienced people
- equipment makes a difference
- old canoe, old paddle
- water filter broke
- heavy pack, Ellen sank in the mud
- good equipment expensive
- wind, waves scary. incredible views
- tie food pack up in tree, because of bears
- too quiet at first. Weird!
- but then noticed sounds of nature
- had a blast at the campfire
- Crown land. Don't have to buy permit. Fishing license costs money
- cheap holiday. Compare to Mexico or the Caribbean
- swimming in lakes glorious. Last morning swimming in the mist

It doesn't have to be this way. Don't let yourself be intimidated by *nothing*! If other approaches have not worked, **try a little craziness**. The following exercise operates on the reality that original thought is often irrational; that a strange link exists between madness and genius. Here's how it works:

1. First have in mind a possible subject or topic (from either the left-hand side of the exercise that follows, or your own topic).

2. Now run your eyes down the right-hand column of suggested perspectives, applying each in turn to your topic. Let your mind run wild. If what comes out is zany or ridiculous, is that a problem? If you are contemplating a traffic jam from the point of view of a virus, so what? After all, right now you are only getting ideas and finding motivation; no one says these early thoughts have to end up in your final draft.

3. Record your new ideas now, using any of the three prewriting techniques just discussed: freewriting, brainstorming or the cluster outline.

4. When you finish, see if this process has freed new insights, a new introduction, a first page, a way of seeing your topic, that *gets you writing*. There is a very good chance it has.

5. Using these new thoughts, write the first draft of your essay. Be fast. *Do it!*

6. Probably by the second or third page, the "craziness" you felt at the beginning will have resolved itself into your more usual factual and logical way of treating a topic. Let it happen: *this is what you were aiming for in the first place.*

7. When you reach the end of this first draft, let it lie. The next day, though, check out the weird parts you may have left at the beginning. If they go too far—if they make no sense at all—redo them now in the more logical mode you probably fell into on the second or third page. By now you are on your way to the final version.

These techniques are meant mainly for the short, informal essays often written in composition courses. While they may also have their place in kick-starting your response to a research essay topic, do keep it in mind that the highly factual and logical nature of research has its own distinctive requirements (see pages 213 to 244 at the end of this book).

THE THESIS STATEMENT

Once you have determined your topic and released some ideas through freewriting, brainstorming, or writing a cluster outline, you need to limit the scope and focus the purpose of the essay. Although the first version is a discovery draft, those discoveries take place within limits. If you kept wandering from one good thought to the next, you could write forever without reaching the heart of one chosen idea.

Instead, **always use that important device of organization, a THESIS STATEMENT. Usually one complete sentence (but if necessary two or three), and almost always near the beginning of the essay, a thesis statement will do two things very clearly:**

- **limit the scope of the argument**
- **focus the writer's purpose**

(*Note:* Some people think a title, such as "Canoeing in the Wilderness," is a thesis statement. It is not. A title is just a label, like the words "Tomato Soup" on a tin can. It is usually not even a sentence. You do need a title, but you need a thesis statement even more.)

Limiting the Scope, or "Less Is More"

Do you realize how short an essay is? A book may contain 100 000 words or more, a magazine article 2000 to 5000, but a classroom essay as few as 500 or even 250. So logic suggests *choosing either a small topic or a small aspect of a larger one.*

One student who didn't think of this decided to analyze communism, socialism and capitalism—certainly a worthy project—but he crammed these three major economic systems of the world into a grand total of two pages! Thinking of the thousands of entire books written on each of these systems, we could have predicted what came out: a collection of general statements everyone has already heard, with no analysis and not one example to bring the stuff alive. So what good did writing this essay do at all? How did it express the writer's knowledge, insights and point of view?

W O R K S H E E T

Using a Little Craziness to Overcome Writer's Block

Follow the directions just given, using this material to kick-start your imagination and motivation to write. The topics at the left are only examples to show how the exercise works: see how to pair one of them with each of the ideas at the right, to generate the "craziness" that gets you thinking. Now substitute your own topic(s), or the topic(s) assigned by your instructor. As number 3 above states, record your reactions to this material (on another page), using either freewriting, brainstorming or cluster outlines.

EXAMPLES OF TOPIC IDEAS	NEW PERSPECTIVES: IMAGINE YOUR TOPIC IN THESE WAYS:
the problem of traffic in the city	■ upside down
	■ in slow motion
	■ in black and white
	■ under a microscope
	■ a century ago or a century from now
	■ turned inside out
	■ with its parts disassembled
street people	■ as a computer game
	■ as a TV sitcom
	■ as science fiction
	■ in the time of the Neanderthals
	■ looking from outer space, or down from a mountaintop, or up from under the ocean
	■ in a country at war
	■ in the developing world
the new global economy	■ as music
	■ as a virus
	■ as a cartoon
	■ in summer, in winter, or at night
	■ as a crime
	■ as a sport
	■ as an earthquake, tornado, hurricane, blizzard or flood
stress	■ as a college or university course
	■ as a vehicle: motorcycle, car, truck or train
	■ from the point of view of an insect, bird, fish, cat or dog
	■ from the point of view of a disabled person in a wheelchair
	■ from the point of view of a baby or a very old person
	■ from the point of view of Adam or Eve, Wayne Gretzky, Bill Gates, Alanis Morissette, Homer or Marge or Bart Simpson, or a space
corporate downsizing	alien

Yet the author later confided to the teacher that he had real-life insights into one of these systems, for he had been a political prisoner in a country that practised it. Fascinated, the teacher made an immediate suggestion: if the writer had only *limited the scope* to a small part of the topic—say, his arrest or his trial or a day in his cell—he might have said far more about the system he had struggled against.

Think of writing as photography. Put aside the wide-angle lens that includes so much that everything is far away, and look through the telephoto lens that zooms you up close to a small part of the subject. Select the part most meaningful to you, the part most typical of the whole. Sharpen the focus. Then take the picture.

Focussing the Purpose

A thesis statement gives an opinion. It sets a direction for the main argument of the essay. It does not just state a fact, such as "Rumania was a communist country." The reader either knew that already or learns it while reading the sentence. In either case the idea is self-contained; it is over with once it is stated, and as a result has no impact. If there is no real point, then the essay will be "pointless."

By contrast, a strong thesis statement is usually a *generalization*—that is, an *opinion*. The French philosopher Voltaire, a man feared by his own government, said "To hold a pen is to be at war." He was exaggerating; his shopping list or diary or letters to his family may not have argued or fought. But his public essays certainly did: they were "attempts" to convince readers of the author's opinions—for example on different problems of society and how to address them.

Remembering his own time in prison, our politically minded essay writer who tried to cover all the major economic systems in two pages might have said something like this: "In Rumania, life in my prison cell was no worse than life in the streets." Now his essay could focus on the brutal guards, the dreary food, the sameness of the routine, perhaps even the rats and cockroaches—and through this "closeup," in the short space of an essay, create an impression of the country in general as it suffered from its economic system. In making the cell represent the country, this writer would be saying *more with less*.

Note also how a good thesis statement is arguable. Don't say "I feel that ..." or "I think that. ..." Instead, make a clear statement like the one about the prison cell. Here are more examples:

- Sales taxes victimize the poor.
- American television teaches violence.
- If major steps are not taken to fight global warming, humans are in serious danger.
- Wayne Gretzky was the greatest player in the history of hockey.
- Junk food is a serious threat to health.

Though each of these opinions is strong, it is also arguable. A person could just as well write from the opposite point of view—in favour of sales tax, American television, global warming, other hockey players, or junk food. The very fact that all options are open heightens the interest of both the writer and the reader. After all, if a thesis statement expresses a total motherhood issue that everyone has to agree with ("Murder is a serious crime"), then why bother developing it into an essay at all?

Thesis Statement: Where Does It Appear?

In most essays, especially long ones, the thesis statement is seldom the opening sentence of the introductory paragraph. First we read a little background so we can understand the statement when it occurs. Or first we read a paragraph or two designed to trap our attention: perhaps a funny or tragic story related to the topic, a pertinent quotation, or a frightening statistic. But toward the end of this introduction we normally do find the thesis statement, which alerts us to the scope and purpose of the argument to come.

In very short essays, say of two or three or four pages, the writer may feel like just launching out with a thesis statement as the first words. But such a beginning may seem abrupt, even in a very short paper. Rather than starting off so bluntly, why not begin with at least a sentence or two of preparation, to grab the reader's attention? Give a bit of background information, a funny or tragic incident, a pertinent quotation or statistic. Why not warm the reader up a bit, rather than starting off cold with the main point? (See pages 42–43 for more on how to write introductory paragraphs.)

W O R K S H E E T

Limiting the Scope

NAME _____

*For each of the general subjects below, supply five "**closeups**" that limit the scope to a size that might fit a short essay.*

Example:
   Computers
   a. *discussion groups on the Internet*
   b. *electronic banking*
   c. *video games*
   d. *buying a computer*
   e. *surviving in the school computer lab*

1. Music
   Example: *downloading music off the Internet*

   a.

   b.

   c.

   d.

   e.

2. Natural disasters
   Example: *the great ice storm of Quebec*

   a.

   b.

   c.

   d.

   e.

3. Poverty

    Example: *financial hardships of student life*

    a.

    b.

    c.

    d.

    e.

4. Professional sports

    Example: *the emergence of professional soccer in Canada*

    a.

    b.

    c.

    d.

    e.

5. Crime

    Example: *credit card fraud*

    a.

    b.

    c.

    d.

    e.

WORKSHEET

Making Thesis Statements

NAME _____

*Develop each of your "closeups" from the previous worksheet into a generalization (**an opinion**) meant to interest your reader and set a direction for your essay. Remember that a thesis statement is a **complete sentence**.*

Example (from the general subject of "Computers"):

a. Discussion groups on the Internet

For fanatics, Internet discussion groups are a substitute for real life.

b. Electronic banking

The main purpose of electronic banking is to reduce the number of bank employees.

c. Video games

The increasing violence of video games contributes to violence in the schools.

d. Buying a computer

The best way to select a computer is first to decide what software will be used, then what hardware is needed to run it.

e. Surviving in the school computer lab

Starting projects early is the key to survival in the computer lab.

1. a.

   b.

   c.

   d.

   e.

2. a.

   b.

   c.

   d.

   e.

3. a.

    b.

    c.

    d.

    e.

4. a.

    b.

    c.

    d.

    e.

5. a.

    b.

    c.

    d.

    e.

AUDIENCE: WHO IS MY READER?

An essential thing to do before starting the first draft is to *visualize your reader or readers.* Who are they? What approach will work with them?

After all, you adjust the way you talk to your listeners: Would you speak the same way and say the same things to a child and an old person? To a criminal and a judge? To your hockey coach and your member of parliament? Probably not. Neither would you write exactly the same things in the same way to these different people. To match your writing to your audience, ask three questions:

- *What is my reader's level?* An essay for your professor is one thing; a letter to your school newspaper is another; a postcard to your little brother or sister is still another. If your reader is very thoughtful, you may use demanding vocabulary and complex arguments. But if your audience is at an average or elementary level of reading and thinking, restrain your vocabulary and explain ideas plainly.

- *What does my reader know?* One look at the number of books in a library will convince us that we cannot learn everything. People specialize: not everyone can repair the faucet, write clear English, and also calculate the income tax. As you plan an essay or report, recognize the differences between people: try to estimate your own reader's knowledge of the subject. Is he or she experienced in some areas—and inexperienced in others?

Some writing courses encourage essays on a wide variety of subjects. You might write on globalization of the economy, on the Internet, on fibre optics or digital recording—with your English teacher as the audience. But watch out. If your own field is electronics, you might load your account of digital recording with terms this reader has never seen and may not find even in the dictionary. Have pity: If your reader is a nonspecialist, avoid most technical terms and define those you do use. Give background. Explain clearly. Use examples. Otherwise he or she will be lost. (For more on this, see "Jargon," page 91.)

On the other hand, the same approach to a literature paper on, say, a novel by Rohinton Mistry may cause problems. Your English teacher will not need explanation of terms she or he has used for 20 years, and may miss the challenge of a more complex argument. Therefore, estimate as well as you can the reader's command over your subject—and write accordingly.

- *What does my reader believe?* Are you likely to communicate by quoting Marx to a banker, the Bible to an atheist, or Henry Morgentaler to a right-to-life activist? Probably not. Be realistic: do not send a message that is sure to be rejected.

Of course you must tell the truth, but in terms acceptable to your audience. For example, build on assumptions that you and your reader can share. Do not preach to a capitalist that socialism is better—but you can certainly claim that capitalism is not perfect, giving examples such as the Great Depression, inflation, environmental pollution, corporate layoffs while stock prices rise, etc. At the end of it all, even the banker may recognize another point of view.

One serious problem in composition courses is deciding who is the *real* audience. Though it is usually the teacher (and sometimes classmates) who will actually read your papers, a course in writing is only practice for writing in the real world. Your *real* readers will be everyone you write for for the rest of your life. For this reason, it may be a good thing to discuss the matter in class, to make sure the teacher does not see your choice of audience in overly personal terms. Once everyone involved agrees who the audience is, you will have a clearer idea of how to proceed.

Who Are They ...?

Do not think of your readers in the abstract. Instead, *visualize* the person or persons who will read your essay. You may be writing alone at a desk, but in thought you are communicating face to face.

The next two worksheets explore this relationship but also pose another challenge. In writing for a teacher you have a known one-person audience, but in many other communication tasks you need to reach individuals with very different backgrounds, or even a variety of individuals within one group. Now you must think of them all: What arguments are universal enough to appeal to most people? What assumptions must be avoided because, although some people will agree, others will be alienated or even angry? And what level of vocabulary and style will communicate to your selected reader or readers?

Relating to Your Audience: In-Class Role Playing

Sometimes life is like a sitcom: stupid little things happen, and misunderstandings follow. Here are some typical examples. Break into small groups, with each group assigned one situation. Discuss your group's situation together. Then follow the directions for role playing in front of the class (decide who will play each character listed below the case described). As you get ready to perform, think hard about how you choose your way of talking and how you choose what to say—depending on what the situation is and who the other person is.

After you are done: *Among all the characters in your role-playing exercise, which did you identify as preferring to discuss at the highest level of thought and language (or, at least, higher than the other characters)? Now follow up your spoken comments to that person with a letter. Write a thesis statement, just as in an essay, that expresses your overall viewpoint on the event. Then support that idea strongly with reasons and examples.*

Be sure to use a level of language and thought that will communicate to your audience—the person receiving your letter.

1. Late on weekend nights, the neighbour in the next apartment cranks the sound system up and plays a kind of music that especially annoys you. You have asked the person politely several times to turn it down, with little effect, so lately your requests have taken the form of pounding on the wall. Finally, with the music booming at 2 a.m. the night before your midterm, you call the police. You hear voices in the hall, the music stops, but after the squad car has disappeared down the street, the music comes back louder than ever. So you call again. The neighbour must be looking out the window, because as soon as the squad car turns the corner, the music stops. This time the officer knocks at your door, with the neighbour standing behind smiling. Explain the situation to:

   - the angry police officer, who is accusing you of crank calls
   - the neighbour, who you run into the next day in the elevator
   - the apartment supervisor
   - your teacher, who calls you in for a conference about the 65 percent mark on your midterm

2. Your friend's printer has died, so she asks if she can use her floppy disk in your roommate's system (since you have no computer) to print out her essay due the next day. Your roommate is not around to ask, but you agree. Everything seems to go fine. But the next time your roommate boots up, "GOTCHA!!!" appears in big red letters on the screen, and you both realize a virus has struck. Explain the situation to:

   - your roommate
   - your friend who did the printing on your roommate's computer
   - your teacher, who is now counting your own essay late because you didn't have anything to print it with
   - your sister, a computer major, who has agreed to fix the problem

3. You and a friend are canoe camping at a provincial park over the long July weekend. The site is very large. When it is almost dark and your campfire is already burning, six people in three other canoes approach the shore. All the other campsites are taken, they say, and it is night and they are tired. Since your site is so big, can they camp there too, just for tonight? In the light of the fire, you see a large cooler in the nearest canoe, and a large portable sound system. Your permit for the site states that a maximum of three tents may be erected. Explain the situation to:

    ■ the late canoeists
    ■ the friend you are camping with, who was at the latrine back in the woods when the canoeists arrived
    ■ a park warden, who happens to stop by at that moment checking on the campsites

4. You have an identical twin. One day while you are walking down the street, someone you have never met approaches you and greets you with the name of your twin. Thinking you will play a joke, you say hi and start talking, as if you knew the person. But now the person takes out a twenty-dollar bill and hands it to you, saying "Thanks a lot for the loan." You take it, too embarrassed to admit you were faking your identity. The next week your twin tells you about a friend who falsely claims to have already repaid a loan of twenty dollars. Explain the situation to:

    ■ your twin
    ■ your grandfather, who is also in the kitchen hearing the conversation
    ■ the friend, when that weekend your twin introduces the two of you at a party

5. You are driving at night, having borrowed your parents' new car. "Be careful," your dad had said. At an advance turn signal the driver of the van behind you honks before you can hit the accelerator. Annoyed, you honk back. After you have turned the corner onto the next street, a little behind a bus that is in the right lane, the van rapidly speeds up and you realize the driver means to cut in front of you passing on the right. You speed up yourself, to avoid the insult, but the van roars into your lane, barely missing the bus, and creasing the fender of your parents' new car. Now a flashing red light shines in your mirror, and both your car and the van are soon at the side of the road, with an officer approaching. Explain the situation to:

    ■ the officer
    ■ the other driver, after the officer leaves
    ■ your father, later that night
    ■ the insurance company adjuster

W O R K S H E E T

Relating to Your Audience: In-Class Group Exploration

Form groups of three to five persons. From the left column, choose a topic and viewpoint that your group might want to argue in an essay. You know how readers are, though: they will agree or disagree with you, depending on how they already see things.

Now explore this challenge by examining the readers at the right: what attitudes, what assumptions, do you think each will probably hold about your chosen topic and point of view? While we do not want to stereotype, reality tells us that factors such as the following do powerfully influence people's views:

- *profession*
- *age*
- *level of income*
- *gender*
- *other life experiences*

Create at least one technique to help your argument work better on each potentially hostile member of your audience. (For example, bank executives might argue in favour of raising tuition costs, but do they realize their own children will have to pay too?) Finally, choose one member of your group to report your findings to the class.

against: genetically modified foods	a squeegee kid
against: child labour in the Third World	a union member
for: lowering the voting age	a member of the Liberal Party
against: social program cuts	a social worker
for: income tax cuts	a police officer
against: raising tuition fees	a high school principal
against: U.S. takeovers of Canadian companies	a bank executive
for: Quebec separation	a logger in British Columbia
for: reducing the national debt	a college or university student
against: mercy killing	a wealthy investor
for: spending more on a cure for AIDS	a retired widow
for: closing tax loopholes	a *National Post* subscriber
for: reducing violence on television	a single parent on welfare
for: photo radar	a very religious person
against: clearcutting of our forests	a grade five student
for: establishment of year-round school	a recent immigrant
	a feminist
	a subscriber to *Hot Rod* magazine
	a ballet dancer
	a native person
	a farmer
	a homeless person

THE DISCOVERY DRAFT

Now let's return to our writer who had never gone on a canoe trip before, who had almost no experience canoeing, but who accepted the invitation. He has done **freewriting** (pages 3–4), or **brainstorming** (pages 4–5) or a **cluster outline** (page 5), and perhaps a heuristic exercise (pages 5–8) to start ideas flowing. Now he is ready to give those ideas preliminary shape in a thesis statement. Here is one he might formulate:

> The canoe trip started out as one of the worst experiences of my life, but, to my amazement, it ended as one of the best.

Notice what a "closeup" this statement is. It is not about recreation in general, or outdoor life in general, or even about canoe trips in general—but about one particular canoe trip. Also, it zeroes in on one major aspect of that trip: how rewarding it was at the end, despite the fact that it seemed hard at the beginning. In other words, the thesis statement focusses on *one part of a potentially large subject:* how on one particular trip, one person was converted to a love of wilderness canoeing.

Note also how this thesis gives the topic a point of view, a *direction*. We already see what the writer thinks of canoe trips: he is an enthusiast. Now as we read the explanations and examples to come, we will be prepared to understand and appreciate that main idea.

But first our writer may be helped by one more planning step: an outline. We do all know people who plunge ahead with no outline at all. This may often work in a short essay, and sometimes even in a long one. But without at least some kind of plan, perhaps a few words to rough out the order of main points, a writer can end up like Stephen Leacock's famous horseman who "rode madly off in all directions."

Following the advice of researchers in composition, let's keep an outline short and *tentative*, because good new ideas will often strike *as we are writing* the first draft. If they do not fit the plan, we may even change the main point, despite what we have said in our thesis statement and outline. Remember that writing is discovery! You might recognize and promote this concept by calling your first version the "**discovery draft**."

Now here is our author's brief and tentative outline. Note that it includes the thesis statement:

My First Canoe Trip

I. Introduction
   A. background: friend Bob's past canoe trips
   B. Bob's invitation to go along
   C. thesis statement: <u>The canoe trip started as one of the worst experiences of my life, but, to my amazement, it ended as one of the best</u>.

II. Hardships
   A. poor equipment
   B. wind and waves
   C. the "Portage from Hell"

III. Rewards
   A. loons and other wildlife
   B. wild scenery while canoeing
   C. swimming "in the clouds"

IV. Conclusion: another canoe trip next year

With a tentative outline in front of you, you are ready for the discovery draft. Whether you use a computer or a pen, the tactics are similar. You keyboard or write rapidly, getting ideas out into the open without stopping the train of thought.

If the right word doesn't come, just leave a blank to fill in later. If your spell-check underlines a word, or if a sentence seems weird, don't stop to revise now: just leave it. If you are writing by hand you could underline places like this for now, and if you are keyboarding you could use some sort of a visual marker such as a row of ampersands (&&&&&&&&), so later you can locate and fix the problem. And don't even dream of perfecting your paragraphs now: some will be good on the first try, and the rest can be adjusted later—when your thoughts are safely out in front of you. The job right now is just to keep bringing the raw materials, your thoughts, out of your mind.

Finally, a special word for those writing by hand: be sure to double- or triple-space your discovery draft, so that later when you revise it, you will have room for more text. Cramming many words into a small space can be frustrating.

Now here is the author's discovery draft:

DISCOVERY DRAFT: My First Canoe Trip

1   My friend Bob had often talked about his canoe trips up north: he would come back bragging about how many hours he and his buddies paddled, and how big the waves were (and the mosquitoes!), and how much blood they lost to the black flies, and how there were so many bears hanging around that they had to hang their food from a tree at night so it wouldn't get eaten up. The worst part always seemed to be the "portages," which are times when you put a huge canoe on your back and carry it from one lake to the next, so you can do a long trip. I always thought these things Bob did up north were a little, well, excessive. Either that or he was making up stories, in the good old tradition of adventurers.

2   But then last summer he asked me if I'd like to try it. Like most Canadians I had paddled a canoe a couple of times here and there, but I was an almost total beginner. And since he was going to take Karen, we would need two canoes, so would Ellen want to come with me. (She was a total beginner too.) I asked her, thinking of how hard she would laugh, and was shocked when she said yes.

3   Now we were in big trouble. Little did I know that all Bob's stories were true. Little did I know how scarey our new experience was going to be, and how much hard work we were going to do. <u>The canoe trip started as one of the worst experiences of my life, but, to my amazement, it ended as one of the best.</u>

4   As we stood on the beach of the first lake (well, as we stood on the sharp rocks while waves pounded in from the distance and sprinkles fell from the grey sky), we looked at our sad array of equipment: a 30-year-old grey fibreglass canoe I had borrowed from my cousin, covered with scratches and gouges from old encounters with rocks, and weighing enough to be made of lead. Then our very old and bulky sleeping bags fastened in really high-tech garbage bags with twist ties. At least one thing was new: the padding, two rolls of foam bought for $5.95 each at Canadian Tire. Our life jackets (oh, pardon me, our personal flotation devices) borrowed

from my cousin looked like World War II surplus. Amd finally our paddles both had ominous cracks.

5   By contrast, Bob and Karen were tying their gleaming new gear into an ultra-lightweight kevlar and carbon fibre Langford canoe, sleek and fast, flame red, designed by computer. Their paddles were also light and sleek, of solid cherry, ad their high-tech freeze-dried food was all organized into its own plastic bags (at least the food they packed was to be used by all of us). As the rain picked up, Bob and Karen put on their Mountain Equipment Co-op Gore-Tex breathable and waterproof jackets and outdoor pants. Ellen and I pulled our $7.95 plastic ponchos over our heads.

6   Now there was no more waiting. Ellen got in the bow of our canoe, I took off my sneakers, rolled up my jeans, and pushed us out into Lake Galeiry. Despite the waves, we managed to move more or less straight for the first point down the lake, as I remembered my early experiences in paddling. But we fell seriously behind our friends. They kept waiting while we pulled hard to catch up.

7   Then, in the huge open part of the lake beyond the point, we felt the wind pick up seriously, and suddenly the grey waves were over two feet high pushing straight against our side, and the spray was splashing over the edge. I looked in panic at Bob. He and Karen were being pushed to our left, just as we were. Now the waves were whitecaps. There was no help for it: we turned left toward a long channel, to put the waves to our backs so they would not swamp our canoes.

8   Half an hour later, in a small sheltered cove, we checked the map. Trapped by the wind, we had only one way now to the next lake: instead of paddling the canoes, we had to carry them a kilometre and a half. A few minutes into the portage, Ellen gave a shout. I put down the canoe from my shoulders, and went to where she had sunk to her knees in mud, under the weight of the canoe pack and bags she was carrying. I pulled her out but she lost a boot. We recovered it, she put the slimy thing back on, and we carried on.

9   But now, marching up a steep hill behind Bob and Karen, we heard the galloping of hooves. We stopped. I lifted the end of the canoe I was carrying to see.

Over the hill came a huge moose without horns (a "cow" moose, Bob explained later) straight toward us. It stopped just in time, and skidded about two metres down the hill, before stopping and trying to stare us down. Time stood still. And then it was suddenly gone. The rest of the portage I hardly remember now: it was raining, and the weight of the old canoe was compressing my spine with every step. What seemed like hours later, we stumbled out onto the beach of Pen Lake and stood there like zombies.

10   Why am I here?, I thought. Why are we spending our August long weekend suffering instead of having fun. From the look she gave me, I knew Ellen was thinking the same thing. But when two guys stumbled with their gear out of the woods behind us and exclaimed "That was the Portage from Hell!," I felt a moment of-- well--what was the feeling exactly? And then when one raised his satellite locator to the sky, studied it, came over to us with his finger on the display and said "This is exactly where we are," I suddenly felt pity for him. Why are these idiots out here looking at their electronic equipment when the whole point is to be in the wilds living the life of the wilds?

11   A little shocked at my new insight, I didn't mind too much the work of the evening: setting up the tents and tarp in the rain, cooking supper on a little backpacking stove, later throwing a rope over a white pine branch and hauling the food up into the tree out of the reach of bears. We even got a fire going, with a few matches and some good birch bark. Then, at night, the wind died down and the frogs began to sing. Later, I don't know when, some loons flew overhead calling to each other with that eery, primitive, wild cry they have (Bob said the next morning that loons were living at the time of the dinosaurs. Were they crying the same call then?)

12   The next days is now almost a blur to me: sunshine now, bright blue water, high ridges of pine and spruce along the lakes, huge rock cliffs, ravens and hawks soaring above us as we paddled. My hands were sore but I didn't care. And at night, again, we heard the frogs and the wild loons. We also heard tiny mice scampering over our tent.

13   It was the next morning, though, the beginning of our last day, that totally changed my mind about canoeing in the North. Some loons woke us up early with their unearthly calls, and when I got out of the tent it was only 6:15. I looked out across Rock Lake, but saw nothing but white. The whole scene was covered by mist rising slowly in clouds from the warm water of August. I walked slowly like a hypnotized person to the huge rocks at water's edge. The water was still and smooth as glass. The next moment I was standing on a long rounded granite rock looking into the water, then I was suspended in the cool air, and then I was plunging beneath the glass into the water's warmth. The others must have heard my splash, because in a few minutes we were all floating along as if suspended in space, as if swimming through the clouds.

14   When in late afternoon we returned to the stony beach of the first day, our hands were blistered, our muscles sore, our bodies sunburned, our ears and necks itching from insect bites, our stomachs hungry for some serious food. But now I know one thing: next summer I am going back. Next summer I want to float again in the clouds.

REVISING THE DISCOVERY DRAFT

Now put yourself in the place of our writer. After the prewriting, he has taken the plunge into a "discovery draft." Writing it has given a certain satisfaction: he has been able to express an exciting new experience, including both the hardships and the highs, and has offered his perspective in more or less coherent form.

In the moments after writing the last word, and after reliving the whole experience, he may even consider the essay a masterpiece. He may have his family and friends read it, and consider them fools if they do not share his enthusiasm.

But a day later he has lost what we could call "the writer's high." As he looks over the draft more calmly, certain passages bother him. They don't seem as good as they did yesterday. Here is a "fact" that is wrong. And here is an idea that doesn't support the point.

But now another idea pops into his head. Why didn't he think of it yesterday? Our writer reaches again for the draft, and two hours later awakens from another "writer's high" to find the once-neat manuscript covered with messy revisions. He does feel lucky that none of his new ideas today destroyed his argument of yesterday (sometimes they do, which means seriously rewriting the whole thing and even changing the thesis statement). But he is truly surprised at how many more valuable details he remembered and added, and at how much more clearly he has now expressed the subject and his point of view on it.

Now let's see exactly what he did. On the next pages is his second draft, with all changes and additions underlined so you can see them at once. In the margins are some quick explanations of the changes as we go. Then right after the second draft, on pages 30–32, a fuller analysis tells why each change was made, as a practical demonstration of what you can do as you develop your own draft into the next draft.

Nowhere does word processing help the writer more than in the act of revising a draft.

Most experienced users key their discovery draft right into the machine (think of the time you used to waste writing all those words out first by hand!). Next it makes sense to fix the words highlighted by spell check (see page 198), then print out hard copy to edit, because most people see words better on paper. Be sure to double-space, leaving room for handwritten changes. Print in "draft" mode, which uses less ink or toner. If you are into recycling, print early drafts on the backs of used paper (first removing any staples).

After the first version cools off for a day, edit your hard copy as our author has edited his second draft, which follows. (Some people do all their editing on screen, printing nothing but the final version. This more direct way may work for you, but if not go back to paper.)

Whether you edit on paper and transfer handwritten changes to the screen or edit directly on screen, make sure you know all the commands that will speed your work: backspacing, deleting one letter, one word, a whole line, or all the rest of the page. Learn to move blocks of text, so that if you find, for example, that your key point is hidden in the middle of the paper, you can switch it to a more dramatic position at the end—without retyping.

While the draft is on screen, exploit the speed of your electronic thesaurus by using it on any word that is not exact enough or direct enough or strong enough or short enough. (See page 31.)

Finally, save each draft under a different file name (for example trip1, trip2, trip3, etc.), so you can go back to another version if you change your mind about what you revised or took out.

SECOND DRAFT: My First Canoe Trip

1

My friend Bob had often talked about his canoe trips up north: he would come back bragging about how many hours he and his <u>friends</u> paddled, how big the waves were, <u>how much blood they lost to the black flies and mosquitoes, and how they had to hang their food from a tree at night so the bears wouldn't eat it.</u> The worst part always seemed to be the "portages": <u>canoeists had to carry the boats and gear from one lake to the next, in order to progress on their trip route.</u> I always thought these things Bob did up north were a little, well, excessive. Either that or he was making up stories, in the good old tradition of adventurers.

2

But then last summer he asked me if I'd like to try it. Like most Canadians I had paddled a canoe a couple of times here and there, but I was an almost total beginner. And since he was going to take <u>his friend</u> Karen, we would need two canoes, so would Ellen want to come with m<u>e?</u> (She was a total beginner too.) I asked her, imagining how hard she would laugh, and was shocked when she said yes.

3

Now we were in big trouble. Little did I know that all Bob's stories were true. Little did I know how <u>scary</u> our new experience was going to be, and how much hard work we were going to do. ***The canoe trip started out as one of the worst experiences of my life, but, to my amazement, it ended as one of the best.***

4

As we stood on the beach of the first lake (well, as we stood on the sharp <u>little</u> rocks while waves pounded in from the distance and sprinkles fell from the grey sky), Ellen and I looked at our sad array of equipment: <u>my cousin's 30-year-old grey fibreglass canoe,</u> covered with scratches and gouges from encounters with rocks, and <u>in my imagination weighing about half as much as my car.</u> Then our very old and bulky sleeping bags fastened in really high-tech garbage bags with twist ties. At least <u>the padding was new</u>: two rolls of foam bought for $5.95 each at Canadian Tire. Our life jackets <u>borrowed from my cousin looked and smelled</u> like World War II surplus. And finally, our <u>well-used</u> paddles both had ominous cracks.

5

This whole paragraph exploits the powerful device of contrast: new gear vs. old gear.

By contrast, Bob and Karen were tying their gleaming new gear into an ultra-lightweight kevlar and carbon fibre Langford canoe, sleek and fast, flame red, designed by computer. Their paddles were also light and sleek, of solid cherry, and their high-tech freeze-dried food was all organized into its own plastic bags (at least the food they packed was to be used by all of us). As the rain picked up, Bob and Karen put on their Mountain Equipment Co-op Gore-Tex breathable and waterproof jackets and outdoor pants. Ellen and I pulled our $7.95 plastic ponchos over our heads.

6

Sentence 2 of draft 1 was a "comma splice," so the punctuation is now improved. The name of "Galeairy Lake" has also been fixed. A major reason for editing is to correct errors like these.

Now there was no more waiting. Ellen got in<u>to</u> the bow of our <u>canoe. I</u> took off my sneakers, rolled up my jeans, and pushed us out into <u>Galeairy Lake</u>. Despite the waves, we managed to move more or less straight for the first point down the lake, as I remembered my early experiences in paddling. But we fell seriously behind our friends. They kept waiting while we pulled hard to catch up.

7

Then, in the huge open part of the lake beyond the point, we felt the wind pick <u>up, and soon</u> the grey waves were over two feet high pushing straight against our side, <u>with spray</u> splashing over the edge. I looked in panic at Bob. He and Karen were being pushed to our left, just as we were. <u>By</u> now the waves were <u>becoming</u> whitecaps. There was no help for it: we turned left toward a long channel, to put the waves to our backs so they would not swamp our <u>boats</u>.

8

This key passage needed more detail to emphasize the hardships. Now readers have it: more on the waves pushing the boat, on the adrenaline, on the 30 kilos pushing Ellen into the mud.

<u>After half an hour of racing before the wind, working to keep the boats straight while big waves pushed them around from behind, we turned into a</u> sheltered cove <u>and</u> checked the map. <u>Our adrenaline returned to normal levels.</u> Trapped by the wind, <u>now</u> we had only one <u>way to</u> the next lake: instead of paddling the canoes, we had to carry them a kilometre and a half <u>on our shoulders</u>. A few minutes into the portage, Ellen gave a shout. I put <u>our</u> canoe <u>down and saw her</u> sunk to her knees in mud, under <u>thirty kilos of</u> canoe pack and bags she was carrying. I pulled her out but she lost a boot. We recovered it, she put the slimy thing back on, and we <u>continued</u>.

9

This low point of suffering needed more detail to make it stronger: the rain and mud, the insects, the numb shoulders, the compressed spine. After this, the writer has nowhere to go but up—toward the reward of his trip.

But now, marching up a steep hill behind Bob and Karen, we heard the galloping of hooves. We stopped. I tipped up the end of the canoe I was carrying to see. Over the hill came a huge moose without horns (a "cow" moose, Bob explained later) straight towards us on the path. It saw us just in time, skidding two metres toward us before stopping and trying to stare us down. Time stood still. And then it was suddenly gone. The rest of the portage I hardly remember now: rain was falling, I was slipping in the mud, I couldn't move my arms to swat the mosquitoes biting my neck, and the weight of the old canoe was numbing my shoulder muscles and compressing my spine further with every step. What seemed like hours later, we stumbled out onto the beach of Pen Lake, threw down our gear, and stood there like zombies.

10

This paragraph was strong in draft 1. It needed only a few adjustments, like the question mark added after the second question.

Why am I here?, I thought. Why are we spending our August long weekend suffering instead of having fun? From the look she gave me, I saw Ellen was thinking the same thing. But when two guys stumbled with their gear out of the woods behind us and exclaimed "That was the Portage from Hell!!!," I felt a moment of-- well--what was the feeling exactly? And then when one raised his satellite locator to the sky, studied it, came over to us with his finger on the display and said "This is exactly where we are," I suddenly felt pity for him. Why were these idiots out here, looking at their electronic equipment--when the whole point is to be in the wilds living the life of the wilds?

11

Now positive details (in both drafts) move the mood up. And draft 2 now tells how the birch bark was off a dead tree—so readers don't think these campers are vandals.

A little shocked at my new insight, I didn't mind too much the work of the evening: setting up the tents and tarp in the rain, cooking supper on a little back-packing stove, later throwing a rope over a white pine branch and hauling the food up into the tree out of the reach of bears. We even got a fire going, with a few matches and some good birch bark from a dead tree. Then at night the wind and rain died down and the frogs began to sing. Later, I don't know when, some loons flew overhead calling to each other with that eery, primitive, wild cry they have (Bob said the next morning that loons were living at the time of the dinosaurs. Were they crying the same call then?)

12

The author now remembers and adds the canoe leak, but keeps it low-key so readers stay tuned into the new highs of his trip. And the "mice" become "forest creatures" so readers are not turned off.

The next <u>day</u> is now almost a blur to me: sunshine now, bright blue water, high ridges of pine and spruce along the lakes, huge rock cliffs, ravens and hawks soaring above us as we paddled. My hands were sore but I didn't care. <u>When Ellen and I bashed a submerged rock, and water began to come in the old canoe, I didn't care either--because in a few minutes Bob patched the leak with a handy thing no canoeist is ever without: duct tape.</u> And at night, again, we heard the frogs, the wild loons, <u>and the tiny steps of forest creatures around our tent</u>.

13

As he begins the closing of his argument, the writer gives images of peace and sensual pleasure. Seeing how strong these were in draft 1, he changes almost nothing now.

It was the next morning, though, the beginning of our last day, that totally changed my mind about canoeing in the North. <u>Loons</u> woke us up early with their unearthly calls, and when I <u>stepped</u> out of the tent it was only 6:15. I looked out across Rock Lake, <u>and</u> saw nothing but white. The whole scene was covered by mist rising slowly in clouds from the warm water of August. I walked slowly like a hypnotized person to the huge rocks at water's edge. The water was still and smooth as glass. The next moment I was standing on a long rounded granite rock looking into the water, then I was suspended <u>in cool</u> air, and then I was plunging beneath the glass into the water's warmth. The others must have heard my splash, because in a few minutes we were all floating along as if suspended in space, as if swimming through the clouds.

14

This conclusion briefly summarizes the hardships (blisters, sore muscles, sunburn, insect bites and hunger), while bringing readers full circle to the "beach of the first day." It also moves readers into the future, a standard technique of closings, as the author realizes how much he has loved the canoe trip and wishes to "float again in the clouds."

When in late afternoon we returned to the stony beach of the first day, our hands were blistered, our muscles sore, our bodies sunburned, our ears and necks itching from insect bites, our stomachs hungry for some serious food. But now I know one thing: next summer I am going back. Next summer I want to float again in the clouds.

REVISIONS: HOW AND WHY

"Revision" literally means "seeing again." Our canoeist has "seen again" at several points in the writing process. The short outline was a "re-seeing" of the freewriting and other prewriting activities. The discovery draft was then a "re-seeing" of the thinking and planning that led up to it, and the second draft is a "re-seeing" of the discovery draft. For example, not every remark in the cluster outline ends up in the discovery draft. Though it is true the friends were canoeing on Crown land, where there are no fees, the economic aspect of their trip turned out to be far less important than the experiential aspect—so it falls back to make way for the real topic.

On the other hand, though the cluster outline makes only brief mention of the "Portage from Hell," the first draft expands on this ordeal, showing Ellen sinking into the mud under the weight of her packs, the near miss with the moose, the rain, and the weight of the old canoe on our author's back.

The "re-seeing" of this key event continues in the second draft: things get even worse, with our author slipping in the mud, helpless to fight insects because of the canoe he is carrying, and with more detail about the pressure on his spine. By the time our canoeist finishes, this passage and others like it have prepared us to see how great the rewards must have been to convince him to head north again next year for more.

Another kind of "re-seeing" also happens in the second draft. Parts of draft one (for example, the phrase "Bob and his buddies") bothered our author: they made him feel like someone telling stories in a pub. Granted, this is not a scholarly topic or a research essay, but still, he thinks, I have to tone things down so the account comes across as a major event in my life, leading to a major insight about who I am and what I like to do. So he crosses out "buddies" and substitutes "friends"—then makes a number of similar changes in tone throughout.

> Brief comments in the margin of the second draft draw your attention to many of these cases where our author "sees again"—as well as labelling standard structural features of the short essay. Now, let's see in more detail how and why our author has "seen again." (As you refer back to the drafts, note that paragraph numbers are the same in both versions.)

■ *Title:* When he looks again at his discovery draft, our author crosses out the title, "My First Canoe Trip," thinking it sounds too ordinary. With the Portage from Hell in mind, he substitutes "From Hell to Paradise." But that reminds him of a corny 1940s movie he has just seen on late-night TV. So he makes another try: "Floating in the Clouds." Now they'll wonder what I was smoking on this trip, he thinks. Besides, since the morning they "floated in the clouds" comes at the end of the piece, nobody will know what the title means till they have read the whole thing. So our author goes back to the original title, thinking he'll still change it if a better idea comes.

■ *Paragraph 1:* Compare the underlined revisions in the second draft to the original wording of the discovery draft. Bob's "buddies" are now his "friends," the bears are no longer "hanging around," and it is not "you" but "canoeists" who carry canoes on their backs. (Now our author won't sound overly informal, like someone telling stories in a pub.) Also the "black flies and mosquitoes" are now together where they belong, saving a few words in the process.

■ *Paragraph 2:* Our author now identifies Karen as Bob's "friend." Otherwise she is just another name. The introduction, he thinks, needs enough background information so the reader can follow. Then a few words later, he realizes the question has no question mark. Of course he adds it.

■ *Paragraph 3:* Our author still thinks the thesis statement does its job—limiting the scope and telling the purpose. And, fortunately, his discovery draft did not wander off in directions far from the ideas in the statement. (In his previous essay he had discovered his main point only after writing several pages, so then he had to change his mind and junk the thesis statement.) But he does see one little error: the spell check is telling him "scarey" is wrong, so he changes it to "scary."

■ *Paragraph 4:* Now revisions become more numerous. He adds "little" to rocks, so readers don't imagine he is launching the canoe over boulders. (I was there and they were not, he thinks, so I have to be exact.) He crosses out "a 30-year-old grey fibreglass canoe I had borrowed from my cousin" and saves five words by instead saying "my cousin's 30-year-old grey fibreglass canoe." Shorter is better, he thinks to himself, as long as the facts are still there.

And now he removes the silly image of a lead canoe from draft 1, and instead compares the weight of the boat to the weight of his car. Even the new version is a little too much, he thinks, but no better ideas come right now. I'll get back to it later, he concludes. Now he trims a couple of words from the sentence about the padding, and removes the joking comment about "personal flotation devices" (how much funny stuff should go in here, he asks himself, when I want to show the canoe trip as a significant moment in my life?). Finally, he remembers how badly the life jackets smelled, and says so in the new version (the five senses —smell, sight, hearing, taste and touch—can powerfully affect readers, he remembers).

■ *Paragraph 5:* No changes. All these concrete details really work, thinks our author. They show how good Bob and Karen's state-of-the-art equipment was, and how

---

The thesaurus has long been a major editing tool. If a word is too vague, too long, too elementary or too scholarly for your audience, or too cheerful or too angry for its context, a thesaurus lists alternatives. If the right word exists, you will spot it and use it.

All major word processing systems have an electronic thesaurus, not as complete as the book version of *Roget's*, but so fast that the essayist can afford to use it constantly.

Suppose that five or ten words per page of your discovery draft do not seem quite right. Whatever your software, you give the command that calls up the thesaurus. Then for each word from your draft that you wish to test out, the screen fills with alternatives. You did, of course, already know these other words, but the problem is that you just didn't think of them. Now with them all in front of you, it's easy to see if one is better than the word first used. If it is, choose it.

Once you get some practice, the electronic thesaurus is so fast that you will want to do much of your editing on screen.

See also page 198 on using the spell check.

---

ratty our own equipment was. Nothing like a *contrast*, he concludes. At least something went right in my first draft.

■ *Paragraph 6:* Here our author finds an error of punctuation: the comma between the words about Ellen getting into the canoe and the part beginning "I took off my sneakers ..." jams two complete sentences together. "Comma splice," thinks the writer. So he breaks them apart with a period. Then the name "Lake Galeiry" doesn't look quite right, and his spell check has certainly never heard of it. So he reaches under his bed to a stack of papers and takes out the canoe route map the friends had used, stained with water from the same lake. Seeing "Galeairy Lake" printed on the map, he makes the spelling correction.

■ *Paragraph 7:* Here he makes a few little changes in wording, for example using "with spray splashing over the edge" instead of the old phrase that had two words more.

■ *Paragraph 8:* Looking back at his first draft, our author is not satisfied. Canoeing before the wind and slogging through the "Portage from Hell" were key parts of his experience. Yet as he first expressed them the danger is not dangerous enough, the hardship is not hard enough—and, yes, the thrill is not thrilling enough. So now in his first sentence he speaks of "racing before the wind, working to keep the boats straight while big waves pushed them around from behind. ..." Then he tells of their adrenaline returning "to normal levels." A few other changes follow, especially the "thirty kilos" of the canoe pack that now makes Ellen sink in the mud. (Note that in his freewriting, on page 3, our author had said "thirty pounds." But now he realizes it was kilos, which more than doubles the weight! I wonder, he asks himself, what other dumb little mistakes I'm going to find.)

■ *Paragraph 9:* Here the canoeist has an even stronger feeling that the hardships were worse than he wrote. So now he makes things more exact and vivid. In particular, now he notes the rain, the "slipping" in the mud, the insects biting him undisturbed as his arms are busy carrying the canoe, the "numbing" of his shoulder muscles, etc. Then, after building up the hard work, he has the friends "throw down" their gear in relief when the portage ends at the next lake. Now, he reasons, my audience will really feel the contrast between the lows and highs of my trip.

■ *Paragraph 10:* Here is one part that came out right, he thinks. It's vivid and concise as is. No real changes to make.

■ *Paragraph 11:* This one is almost there, too, he thinks. He adds almost nothing except to make the rain, as well as the wind, die down at night.

■ *Paragraph 12:* First he sees a little careless error, so changes "the next days is almost a blur" to "the next day is almost a blur." More importantly, he now remembers an incident he had mentioned in his freewriting: that the old canoe had hit a rock and sprung a leak. So now he adds it, but, realizing that the high point of his whole experience is coming up in the next paragraph, minimizes the problem by showing Bob easily fixing the leak with duct tape. (In any case, he also reasons, details of how things are done interest the reader.)

Looking again at his last sentence of old paragraph 12, though, he thinks: Are readers going to dread the "mice scampering over our tent"? The mice really did, but will people be focussing on rodents rather than the idealism and fulfillment of my closing scene? So now he puts a better spin on things by substituting "the tiny steps of forest creatures around our tent." But now he asks himself, am I still telling the truth? He leaves it for now; there's a lot more to do today.

■ *Paragraphs 13 and 14:* Reading his two-paragraph conclusion over again, our writer is very happy. The passage brings it all back. He even starts reaching for his canoe map to plan next summer's trip, but then pulls his hand back and picks up the pen again. This part just came out right the first time, he thinks. Wish that would happen more often! The calm of the last morning, the dive into warm water, the companions joining him, all convey the thrill he finally experienced after all the sweat and pain. So in these two paragraphs he merely adjusts a word or two, for example "stepping" out of the tent instead of "getting" out. Why not show things as clearly as I can? he thinks.

The very last paragraph is totally unchanged. Somehow, in the act of writing, he had known the whole experience was being summed up in those words "float again in the clouds." Good technique, he concludes, to put the key phrase at the very end where it will endure in the mind of my reader.

FURTHER DRAFTS?

The essayist sits back from his writing desk after all these revisions, with a sense of having finished the job. However, that's the same feeling he had after draft 1— and look at all the improvements made since then. Maybe tonight more passages will be wrong, more "facts" will be untrue, or more new ideas or memories will prove too important to leave out.

Come to think of it, after adding the fact of the canoe hitting a rock and springing a leak, he had also remembered a tree near the latrine whose bark had been ripped and torn by the claws of a large animal. In fact, what could it be but a bear? He picks up his pen again, thinking to add this evidence of danger somewhere before the swim in the clouds.

And this thought leads him to another, that he would rather not have: though he had mentioned in his freewriting that Bob's high-tech water filter had broken, and they had ended up drinking lake water treated with iodine pills, he had conveniently forgot to include this in his draft. Well, maybe it wasn't forgetting ... maybe he just didn't even want to think about it, because while the friends were driving back home with the canoes tied onto the truck, their stomachs began to hurt and they made more rest stops than he wanted to remember. And when he got out in front of his place, he was almost too weak to walk. It was beaver fever, his doctor kindly explained, and prescribed a medicine so harsh that it almost did more damage to his stomach than to the parasite.

So, thinks our author, am I lying to my readers by leaving this out? Would they still believe I want to go back if I put it in? Or, in fact, would they be even more impressed by my motivation if I wanted to go back despite getting sick? But then he pauses and realizes a disturbing thought that had been growing on him: thinking of all these hardships, is it possible I may even not *want* to go back after all?

Too many questions! He concludes. Do I want to write this whole paper over? It's due tomorrow, and I have to study physics.

Now he gets up from his writing desk, puts on his jacket, and walks to the door. As he enters the park across the street and gazes up at the trees, he reflects on how complicated life is and how complicated writing is.

A S S I G N M E N T S

Process in Short Essays

The general subjects in the list below are far too broad to write on as topics. Choose any one of them, then focus it by applying the strategies of this chapter. Completing the following steps of the writing process, develop your subject into a good short essay:

1. Get in touch with your ideas by *freewriting* (pages 3–4), or *brainstorming* (pages 4–5) or making a *cluster outline* (page 5) of your general subject chosen below.

2. *Limit your scope* and *focus your purpose* in a *thesis statement* (pages 10–14).

3. *Visualize your reader* (pages 15–19). (You may be practising on your instructor, but who do you have in mind as the real readers in the outside world?)

4. Write a very short, tentative *outline* (page 20).

5. Write a *discovery draft* (pages 20–24). Be free, open and quick. Put off editing till later. Your instructor may collect this version and give written comments on it, or may have a short conference with you to discuss improvements, or may ask you to share reactions with a small group of classmates.

6. Write a *further draft or drafts* (pages 25–32), heightening your argument, giving more specifics, and now editing to improve your style and form.

If you are using this book in a class, writing clinic, or laboratory, your instructor may assign the above process of writing several times during the term (each time, of course, with a different general subject). Or you may be asked to write on other subjects, or invent your own.

   Now that you have studied this chapter, it is best to start right off with a first short essay, to enter the writing process, even though you haven't yet studied the editing skills discussed in later chapters. (If you waited till you had studied the whole book, how much time would be left for the actual writing?)

   Then in later assignments you can apply all the rest of the book studied so far, or you can jump ahead to chapters that you especially need (see the table of contents and index). *But the key strategy is to start writing now, and keep on writing.*

GENERAL SUBJECTS

1. aging	6. family life	11. leisure	16. success
2. business	7. the future	12. mass media	17. technology
3. the city	8. health	13. nature	18. travel
4. culture	9. housing	14. relationships	19. trends
5. education	10. language	15. science	20. work

Note: Be sure to retitle the subject you have chosen, to reflect the smaller focus you are giving it. For example, number 17, "technology," might become "Banking Machines as a Cause of Unemployment."

THREE MORE SHORT ESSAYS

By now you've probably studied most of this chapter so far, and discussed it in class. You may have tried out *freewriting, brainstorming* or a *cluster outline* to explore a good topic for your own short essay. You've probably thought about your *audience,* and what kind of argument may work with it. You've probably *focussed down* from a large subject area to a small piece of the subject, and have probably developed a *thesis statement* to reveal the point of view you will argue.

All this material leads into the sample short essay, "My First Canoe Trip." You've probably read it, and in class you've probably seen how its discovery draft is developed into its second draft. Before starting to write your own essays, though, you may want to see the three other sample essays that come next:

■ "The Internet: Productivity or Peril?"

■ "Dogs: Are They Worth It?"
■ "School and Cars: Do They Mix?"

While "My First Canoe Trip" is a little longer than some student essays—in order to show the details of how an essay is conceived and planned, then developed from one draft to another—these next three are in the 500-to-600-word range. Yet they demonstrate all the parts of the standard essay. The explanations are given through brief comments in the margin, next to the features explained.

You'll also see that these short essays develop a pattern found useful in many writing courses: the five-paragraph essay. Each one has a paragraph of introduction, three solid paragraphs of development, and a fifth paragraph of conclusion. In summary, whether you examine these three short essays at home or discuss them in class, they are very clear models for your own shorter essays.

The Internet: Productivity or Peril?

1

<u>Though the Internet is a powerful tool that can help individuals accomplish their personal and professional goals, it is also a source of addiction so compelling that it can wreck their lives both at work and at home.</u> Individuals do not realize how quickly they are falling into a new habit, how many hours they are spending on dubious activities at the computer, and what the consequences may be.

2

Excessive Internet use can waste the time of employees at the office, and can even cost them their jobs. One business person in a large Canadian city began joining chat rooms on his office computer. Nobody would notice what was on the screen, he thought. But soon his lack of productivity caught the attention of the boss, who reprimanded him in an office conference. Not long after, the employee's online activities took the form of correspondence with a new friend in a distant city. But the boss did not even have to carry out his intention of firing the worker, because one day the man bought a one-way ticket to that distant city and disappeared.

3

Another employee lost his job, not by leaving but by making a mistake at the computer. This math teacher, at a private school near another Canadian city, succumbed to the temptation to download pornography onto his office computer. One day as he was having an office conference with a student, he tried to bring the student's online essay up on the computer screen. Something went terribly wrong: instead of the essay, a pornographic image appeared. The student saw it, complained to the administration about sexual harassment, and shortly after the teacher was fired.

4

Computer addiction can wreck not only a person's career but also his or her relationships. In still another example, a young couple in a large Canadian city began married life with an elaborate wedding and reception. Things went well enough for them until the husband lost his job. Despite his employability, and the prospect that he would soon find other work, he retreated to the basement and the computer. He began to pass time on the Internet, and in a couple of months was spending hours and hours far into the night in front of the screen. The wife complained that she never saw him anymore. In another few weeks the young couple, married only three years, had separated. The wife took a lover. No one knows where the husband has gone.

5

In order to prevent objections, this closing does mention what the reader may be thinking, that the Internet does have a good side. But then, in a final image (the knife) it warns readers of the "destructive" side.

It is certainly true that the Internet is a major new tool for accomplishing people's goals, both professional and personal. The research capabilities of the World Wide Web, and the communication capabilities of e-mail, have transformed the working lives and the personal lives of many people today. Yet those people must also exercise caution. This tool is so powerful that, like a knife, it can serve purposes either constructive or destructive. It is up to each person to choose well.

Dogs: Are They Worth It?

1   <u>Although millions of people welcome dogs into their lives, this experience of pet ownership does not always have a happy ending.</u> Is the pleasure of a canine chasing sticks or wagging its tail in friendship really worth all the work, the expense, and even the danger? Many people have found it is not.

2   First, there is the work of training the puppy. It must be given a special place to sleep, must be taught gently what is allowed and what is not, must be house-trained, and must be given affection—almost like a human child. Then there are the walks. Not everyone who chooses a dog realizes how early the animal likes to be up and outside for its exercise. Instead of sleeping in till noon on weekends, the new pet owner may be roused out of bed when it is hardly light outside, and in many municipalities must even carry a little shovel and a bag to pick up after the animal. Then when the dog tears up the garden, or scratches the paint off a door, the work continues. Not everyone is ready for this.

3   If the amount of work is daunting, the cost of dog ownership can be staggering. First of all, many dogs are expensive to buy. Then comes registration. And soon come all the shots. Will the dog get rabies, or any one of many other diseases? Not if the owner pays enough money to the vet. Will the dog get heartworm and die? Not if the owner buys and administers the right medication. Will the male dog go after every female dog in sight? Will it swell the canine population of the neighbourhood, enraging the neighbours? Not if the owner pays for a neutering operation by the vet. Then there is the question of food: a large dog can eat its way through an immense supply, and many owners even feed costly delicacies such as steak. Then at holiday time, where does the dog stay while its owner is on the plane to Cancun? In the dog hotel, of course, again for a substantial price. Is the price of dog ownership right? Maybe not.

4   Of all aspects of dog ownership, though, the worst is the danger. The press carries stories on this theme every week. A dog bites the leg of a letter

The thesis statement (underlined) clearly labels the subject, and tells the author's viewpoint on it. Then the rest of the introduction develops that view in more detail. See how the terms "work," "expense" and "danger" label in advance the main points of the three supporting paragraphs that follow.

Here many short examples develop the topic of "work."

Another series of examples shows the "price" of dog ownership.

See how the final words of paragraphs 2 and 3 sum up each series of examples.

The most serious problem of all is put last, so paragraph 4 is a climax to the material against dogs.

carrier. A dog jumps over a fence and attacks a young child. When a student lets his arm fall over the edge of the bed, the German shepherd underneath snaps off a finger with his teeth. Sometimes these events take truly tragic proportions. Not long ago a medical doctor arrived to make a house call. The family pit bull—a variety of dog bred for its fighting temperament and menacing teeth—seized the physician's neck and killed this professional who had spent a decade training to save the lives of other humans.

5

Most good closings are short, like this one. Note how it reminds the reader one more time of the three main points against dog ownership.

Is dog ownership worth it? Some say yes, but many have found that the work, the cost, and even the danger are prices too high to pay.

School and Cars: Do They Mix?

The thesis state-
ment is underlined.
Note how it
depends on the
previous sentence
for part of its
meaning.

1

Many students view car ownership as a high priority, and will do almost anything to achieve the privilege of getting behind the wheel. <u>Little do they realize that, far from being an advantage, a car is one of the greatest disadvantages they could impose on themselves.</u> Soon these car-loving students will be working long hours at boring and menial jobs. They will spend their new money on car payments, maintenance, repairs and hefty insurance bills. And finally, at exam time, they will realize how much of their academic performance—and their potential future success—they have sacrificed in the quest to own two tonnes of steel.

See how the rest of
this introduction
labels in advance
the three main sup-
porting points of
the argument: the
work, money and
academic sacrifice
caused by student
ownership of cars.

2

Few really good jobs are open to students. The person is often considered too young for a real salary, and the fact of also going to school puts the person into the marginal category of part-time help. All too often the result means working at jobs such as washing dishes in restaurants, doing late-night security shifts, waiting tables, or renting the latest videos to customers at the corner store. The pay may be low, or even minimum-wage, with few or no benefits. The status is also low. To make matters worse, the boss often hounds part-time student workers to increase their hours, at whatever expense to their own studies and personal time.

In this first
supporting para-
graph, several
quick examples
show how
undesirable the
work can be.

3

Once the hard-earned money does start to come in, it goes right back out again. Students who opt for the ideal gleaming new car will have crushing payments to meet every month. On the other hand, those who buy an old car on the cheap will soon be paying hefty repair bills. Not everyone realizes that a brake job or a set of tires or a new exhaust system can cost $500, a new computer chip to control the engine can cost $1500, and a new transmission can cost $2000 or more. Even routine maintenance, such as oil changes, a new air filter or a new set of spark plugs, can be costly. Gas and oil are not cheap, either. Probably worst of all is the insurance, especially for young male drivers. It can set the student worker back $2000, or with a bad accident record, even $5000 a year. That's a lot of dishes to wash.

In this second
supporting para-
graph, even
more concrete
examples—some
with actual dollar
figures—show how
high the cost can
be.

4

Finally, the real casualty of all this work and expense is the student's own progress in school. Study after study shows that on the average, the more hours of employment a student works, the poorer his or her academic performance is. How can a person who has tended bar till long past midnight understand the 8 a.m. history lecture or answer questions from the teacher? How can the late-shift dishwasher get all the reading done? And, after driving home from work in a new car, what level of writing is the sleepy security guard going to reach while churning out a term paper in half the time?

5

Our society does severely tempt students to own cars. The proof is in the swelling number of autos in school parking lots across the country. But if those student car owners had thought longer about the sacrifices they were going to make in low-level work, in high-level expenses, and in sinking grades, they might have thought again. In fact, they might have thought about whether their friends who walk or take transit to school are going to get to their real destination faster: a good career, and with it all the rewards, including really good cars.

PART TWO

Paragraphs

𝒥magine a book, or even a magazine article, without white space. You, the reader, are staring at a solid mass of grey print, with no breaks, no breathing spots, no room to give encouragement or show where one part ends and the next begins. You begin to sweat. It is hard to breathe. You have thoughts of climbers labouring up the cliffs of Mount Everest. Does anyone think you will actually read the thing? What is missing, obviously, is the user-friendly device of *paragraphing*.

Everyone knows what paragraphs are: units of thought several sentences long, set off from each other by an indented first line (the first word begins several spaces in from the margin). And most people have some natural feeling for how to paragraph: without even thinking about it, they pause at the end of a passage. They close off that part, mentally take a breath, then indent the next line to signal a plunge into the next phase of the topic.

The first chapter, "Process in Short Essays," suggests this approach for discovery drafts. If you concentrate on too many things at once—thinking about paragraphing while trying to fill up that monitor screen or blank page—you might not have enough attention left to generate your argument. But once your thoughts are safely out in the open, you can look over what you've done and tinker with it. As you examine the spontaneous paragraphing in your discovery draft, see whether it is user-friendly. Have you fallen into one of these traps?

1. *Ignoring paragraphs totally.* Some inexperienced writers will crank out a whole paper with no paragraph breaks at all. In effect, their one "paragraph" might be five pages long. After their breathless first draft they must now go back to find the natural breaks in their thought—and signal them by indenting. If they do not, the reader is standing at the foot of Mount Everest.

2. *Making paragraphs too short and too numerous.* This weakness is far more common. A whole essay of mini-paragraphs only one or two sentences long may at first appear reasonable, especially if you are not computing; after all, if your handwriting is large and you are double-spacing, even a tiny paragraph can *look* big. Besides, paragraphs as short as one sentence or even one word sometimes do serve to give special emphasis. But a series of mini-paragraphs will almost always identify an essay that is seriously underdeveloped—that lacks enough examples to be interesting or even clear.

   People who fall into this trap may be thinking of newspaper style. A good news article, though, is not underdeveloped; it is simply indented after every sentence or two because of the newspaper's single-column format. An eight-sentence paragraph in a single column would look so long that it could scare off readers (especially of newspapers that devote themselves to UFOs, axe murders, and sightings of Elvis). But in the full-page format of your own word-processed essay, as in the full-page format of a printed book, a longer paragraph looks fine. Where you need eight sentences to round out a good point, anything less is too little. *Remember:* **The average well-developed paragraph is about five to eight sentences long.**

3. *Using "block" form in an essay.* In block form there are no indentations at the beginning of paragraphs, but

instead there is an extra line of blank space between each paragraph. This format is very popular and perfectly clear—but is normally reserved for documents such as business letters and reports. It is seldom used in the essay, and may in fact be seen by your teacher as an error. So do indent each paragraph. And, once you have done so, avoid extra spaces between paragraphs. (Look again at our sample short essays in Part One, pages 35–40, to see this format in use.) One caution: When you do use block form in other classes, for a business letter or report, do always remember the extra space between paragraphs; without either indentation or extra spaces, the reader may not know where one paragraph ends and the next begins.

KINDS OF PARAGRAPHS

The way many teachers and textbooks used to explain paragraphing, you would have thought these chunks of writing were cars rolling off the assembly line. The head designer had found the right formula, the workers made sure each nut and bolt was in place, and then someone at quality control checked to make sure each unit was alike. The only problem with this logical view is that it did not correspond to real life.

Picture the students of an English class: after making sure each paragraph of their essay had a beginning, a middle, and an end, all in exactly five sentences, the students would go home, pick up some magazine, and see paragraphs missing most or all of these features. So why were published writers getting away with things that English teachers said were wrong? It was because *there are many kinds of paragraphs that serve many different purposes*—a fact that we see much more clearly today. Now we'll look at each of these major kinds of paragraph:

- the introductory paragraph
- the "main" paragraph
- the paragraph of narration
- the "bridge" paragraph
- the closing paragraph

The Introductory Paragraph

Let's begin with this, since it begins the essay. A short paper might have only one paragraph of introduction, while a longer one might have two or more.

Therefore an introductory paragraph may do its work all alone or with other paragraphs. Whatever the case, an introduction has two main functions: to *interest* and to *prepare* the reader.

Rather than putting your potential reader to sleep with a flat statement of intent, tease your reader's curiosity. Note the difference in effect between these potential introductions to the same paper:

A. This essay will be about governmental spending cutbacks and the ways in which they affect the lives of students. It will attempt to show some of the difficulties the average postsecondary student has when expenses go up in response to these cutbacks. Finally, it will endeavour to suggest solutions to this growing problem in today's society.

B. One community college student, Paul, used to think he could have it all. With a summer job and part-time work on weekends he could pay tuition, buy textbooks, go to clubs, and even keep driving the car he had in high school. What Paul did not foresee, though, was the cuts to education that the provincial government would soon make in its attempt to fight the public debt. When tuition fees rose out of sight, when parking fees tripled and lab fees skyrocketed, Paul got his dose of the new reality. "It was bad enough when I couldn't keep up the payments on my car," he said over a meal of poutine at the school cafeteria. "I began working so many hours that my grades went down, but I lost the car anyway. Now if things get much worse I'll lose my computer, too. Did I tell you," he added with a grim smile, "that I'm a computer major?"

Across Canada thousands of students, like Paul, are now tightening their belts, doing with less, and even dropping out of school. In a time of severe governmental cutbacks, what can these potential workers and leaders of society do to keep their future on track?

How do these two potential introductions compare? Let's face it, version A is a bore. It does announce its subject, but in a clumsy and official manner. By contrast, version B seduces the readers with a story (and who doesn't like stories?). It *shows* an actual example of the problem, the plight of one student who represents the many. It even "shows" what he is eating: an unhealthy but cheap meal of poutine—french fries with cheese curd and gravy. Now, having attracted our concern for Paul, this introduction moves into its short second paragraph with the user-friendly device of a question, which will then lead to the main point of the paper: the approach these victims of educational cutbacks can take to keep their future alive.

Note that version A has only three sentences, a sign that this introduction may be underdeveloped. Instead of "showing" us anything at all, it drones along with generalizations and stuffy phrases such as "This essay will be about ..."; "It will attempt to show ..."; and "it will endeavour to suggest. ..." By contrast, version B is well enough developed that it actually has two paragraphs, "showing" Paul to the readers, as well as generalizing on the subject. Its energy level is higher too: it attracts our interest with dynamic and concrete phrases such as "rose out of sight," "skyrocketed" and "got his dose of the new reality."

The first introduction tries for a *thesis statement* as a base for the argument that will follow, but merely gives a vague idea that solutions will be offered. In contrast, B moves toward its point more surely: in times like these, when citizens cannot depend much on their governments, what can students, themselves, do to ensure their future? Now readers are prepared for a thesis statement, coming next, which will begin to answer the question. (Of course, placement of the thesis statement depends on length of the whole essay. In very short essays, the thesis statement does often come in the first paragraph, but ideally still with a bit of introduction and preparation.)

On page 8 we have already seen how the thesis statement introduces, focusses and then guides the essay. Now let's examine more closely the other function of an introduction: to *interest* the reader. Try these widespread techniques in your introductory paragraphs:

◼ **Fill in some background information.** If your topic is unusual or difficult, help your audience relate to it by sketching in the context: give a bit of historical, social or technical background.

◼ **Tell an anecdote.** Everyone likes a story. As in the account of Paul and his financial troubles, tell a short incident—unusual, perhaps funny or tragic—that leads to your topic. This favourite technique of public speakers works equally well on paper.

◼ **Give a quotation.** Use the index of *Colombo's Canadian Quotations* or *Bartlett's Familiar Quotations* to find a good opening. (See the online version of Bartlett at <http://www.columbia.edu/acis/bartleby/bartlett>.) Whether your subject is war, sex, taxes or sport, find out what Shakespeare or Albert Einstein or Margaret Atwood said about it. Then lead from this to your own thesis.

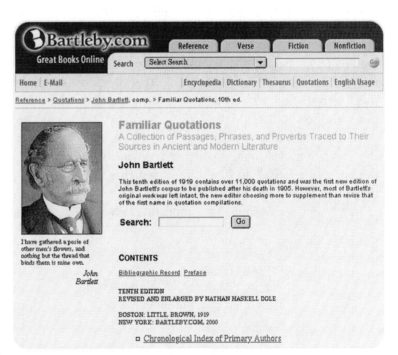

COURTESY OF STEVEN VAN LEEUWEN, www.bartelby.com.

◼ **Give statistics** to introduce your topic. Use the newspapers or consult such collections as the *World Almanac and Book of Facts* or the *Canadian Almanac and Directory*. The statistics with most impact are those that alarm or even scare the reader.

◼ **Make an unusual or puzzling statement that draws readers into your topic.** Do not exaggerate or falsify, but do search for an unusual angle that will tease your reader's curiosity.

The "Main" Paragraph

Between the introduction and conclusion of an essay comes the main part, the "body," which is made up mostly of what we could call "main" paragraphs. **Here is where the "main" work of illustrating, explaining, arguing and convincing takes place.** Since they do similar work, "main" paragraphs tend to be alike in at least two ways:

1. Almost all have a "topic sentence" that announces the point to be developed in the paragraph.
2. Everything else in the paragraph develops that point.

Let's look more closely at these two features.

The Topic Sentence

Researchers in the field of composition have debunked the old idea that *every* paragraph must have a *topic sentence.* In fact, on the average, fewer than half of all paragraphs in published writing have one, because many paragraphs have other specific uses: introducing, narrating, bridging major sections, and concluding.

But almost all of the workhorse paragraphs that do the illustrating, explaining, arguing and convincing in the body of an essay do have a topic sentence and develop it throughout their other sentences. In this sense a "main" paragraph is like a miniature essay:

■ The topic sentence (like a thesis statement) sets out the point of the paragraph.
■ Every single thing in all the rest of the paragraph (like all the content of an essay) in some way develops that topic sentence.

Let's see how Annie Dillard uses this pattern in a paragraph from her book *Pilgrim at Tinker Creek:*

Parasitic two-winged insects, such as flies and mosquitoes, abound. It is these that cause hippos to live in the mud and frenzied caribou to trample their young. Twenty thousand head of domestic livestock died in Europe from a host of black flies that swarmed from the banks of the Danube in 1923. Some parasitic flies live in the stomachs of horses, zebras, and elephants; others live in the nostrils and eyes of frogs. Some feed on earthworms, snails, and slugs; others attack and successfully pierce mosquitoes already engorged on stolen blood. Still others live on such delicate fare as the brains of ants, the blood of nestling songbirds, or the fluid in the wings of lacewings and butterflies.

After reading this paragraph, can you reasonably doubt that "parasitic two-winged insects, such as flies and mosquitoes, abound"? Every sentence, by use of example, tries to deepen your understanding of the main point and your belief in its validity. Not one given fact is irrelevant to the topic sentence.

How does a topic sentence work? It normally does these three things:

■ A topic sentence limits the scope of its paragraph.
■ A topic sentence makes a generalization.
■ A topic sentence usually occurs at or near the beginning of its paragraph.

Now let's look more closely at these points:

■ **A topic sentence *limits the scope* of its paragraph.** It cuts off a chunk of thought that is neither too large nor too small for treatment in the several sentences of a paragraph. Some subjects are so minuscule or so obvious that to state them in one sentence is enough. A statement such as "I have brown eyes" is hardly worth building a paragraph around, for it is self-evident once it is said.

The opposite case is by far the more common problem: a statement that is too large in scope for development in the small space of a paragraph. Pity the person who begins a paragraph with the words "Many countries are interesting to visit." How many countries does this writer hope to cram into five or eight sentences, and in what ways are they all "interesting"? In fact, what does "interesting" mean? One reader may expect an account of historical and cultural sites, another an account of bars and nightclubs, and another an account of the characters this traveller met while hitchhiking.

The fact that entire books are written about one country sheds some light on this writer's problem: the topic is far too broad. Let's narrow it down drastically to "Spaniards are the friendliest people I have ever met" or "Camping on the beach in Mexico was the most dangerous thing I have ever done" or "It is easy to get lost in the Paris subway." Now a few good examples will bring these topic sentences alive.

■ **A topic sentence, like a thesis statement, often makes a *generalization*.** You could simply state a fact, such as "Fifty thousand Canadian lakes have died from acid rain," but if you can also give this information a direction (present it as an *opinion*), it will make for a stronger paragraph: "The fifty thousand Canadian lakes that have died from acid rain are proof that our industrial society is in trouble."

Of course the way you cast your topic sentence depends on the flow of your argument: what you wrote in paragraphs that came before and what you will write in those that come after. For example, you may often need a paragraph of pure fact to develop a preceding part of the argument. But where possible, begin a "main" paragraph with an idea worth supporting, not just a fact alone.

■ **A topic sentence usually occurs *at or near the beginning of its paragraph*.** Thus the reader sees what is coming and is better prepared to deal with it. Annie Dillard's passage about insects is a typical example of this most common of all paragraph forms. It is easy to understand, because a kind of summary in advance tells readers what to look for as they pass through the sentences that follow.

If you don't feel like playing it safe, though, in special cases this order can be reversed. By putting the details first, and waiting till the end to make the point, you can introduce a suspense that greatly increases the drama of the argument. This approach requires some polish, though. It is best reserved for an occasional special effect.

Unity in "Main" Paragraphs

When a topic sentence is used in a paragraph, it should dominate. **A paragraph is unified when every single sentence in some way supports the main idea in the topic sentence.** Where does the following paragraph go wrong?

> Three memorable rides have cured me forever of my desire to hitchhike. The first was a speedy trip

in an Alfa-Romeo that met its fate on a cliffside road in Spain. We sideswiped a long truck, were whirled right around and came to rest with one wheel over the cliff. I looked down at the Bay of Biscay as the driver cried over his twisted car. The next was a ride with a wild young Kentuckian who had the most decrepit Chevy I've ever seen. Every time he swerved to make a pedestrian jump into the ditch, my door swung open and I grabbed for the seat to stay aboard. One of the best rides I've ever had, though, was with a family going to Montreal. They let me drive their new Camry and even bought me lunch at the rest stop. All in all, I've found hitchhiking to be exciting—too exciting for me.

It doesn't take long to see how this writer has given two examples that strongly support the topic sentence, but a third that contradicts it. The result is a weak argument: we're not sure what this person does think of hitchhiking. Let's replace that third example with one that does support the point. Here's the revised paragraph (with the new part in italics):

> Three memorable rides have cured me forever of my desire to hitchhike. The first was a speedy trip in an Alfa-Romeo that met its fate on a cliffside road in Spain. We sideswiped a long truck, were whirled right around and came to rest with one wheel over the cliff. I looked down at the Bay of Biscay as the driver cried over his twisted car. The next was a ride with a wild young Kentuckian who had the most decrepit Chevy I've ever seen. Every time he swerved to make a pedestrian jump into the ditch, my door swung open and I grabbed for the seat to stay aboard. *The third ride was an early morning trip on glare ice. My driver seemed to think his Honda Si-6 coupe could go twice as fast as anything else on the road. It did: we soon passed all the traffic while sliding backwards, on our way to the shoulder where we snapped off two guard posts and sank into the ditch.* All in all, I've found hitchhiking to be exciting—too exciting for me.

Coherence in "Main" Paragraphs

A house of bricks without mortar would collapse of its own weight. So would a paragraph of ideas without transitions. You've just seen how important unity is to paragraphs: how each part supports the main idea. But that unity should also be signalled by words or expressions that make ideas and examples connect. "Main" paragraphs, especially, need these signals to organize their longer content of explanation, detail and example.

Look once more at our revised paragraph about hitchhiking. The author gives three examples to show why he or she has stopped thumbing rides. How are these three wild car trips held together? By *transition signals,* shown in boldface below:

> Three memorable rides have cured me forever of my desire to hitchhike. **The first** was a speedy trip in an Alfa-Romeo that met its fate on a cliffside road in Spain. We sideswiped a long truck, were whirled right around and came to rest with one wheel over the cliff. I looked down at the Bay of Biscay as the driver cried over his twisted car. **The next** was a ride with a wild young Kentuckian who had the most decrepit Chevy I've ever seen. Every time he swerved to make a pedestrian jump into the ditch, my door swung open and I grabbed for the seat to stay aboard. **The third ride** was an early morning trip on glare ice. My driver seemed to think his Honda Si-6 coupe could go twice as fast as anything else on the road. It did: we soon passed all the traffic while sliding backwards, on our way to the shoulder where we snapped off two guard posts and sank into the ditch. **All in all**, I've found hitchhiking to be exciting—too exciting for me.

What could be easier than inserting expressions like "the first," "the next," and "the third" between parts?

And what could make more sense than adding an expression like "all in all" or "therefore" or "in conclusion" before the closing? Yet many writers of essays routinely neglect to link ideas together. Their houses of bricks are ready to collapse. You can do better.

Here are some of the most useful transitions. Study them, and use more of them as you edit future papers.

A. Time signals: **first, second, third, next, last, finally, after, as long as, at last, before, during, later, often, sometimes, soon, when, while, yet.**

B. Logic signals: **also, although, and, anyway, as, because, besides, by contrast, even though, however, if, in addition, in conclusion, in fact, instead, likewise, nevertheless, similarly, since, so that, still, therefore, unless, whether.** (Choosing the most exact signal for each case is one of the very best ways to help readers understand and appreciate your argument.)

C. Pronouns: **it, he, she, that, them, these, they, this, those, which.** When used accurately, pronouns have a unifying effect because they refer to something else in the paragraph. (If your pronouns need brushing up, see pages 149–158.)

Finally, look ahead to the section on "Bridge Paragraphs" (pages 63–64). These are transitions on a larger scale, cementing together whole paragraphs and sections of essays as the argument of your essay develops.

WORKSHEET

The "Main" Paragraph

NAME _____

*Good topic sentences often give an opinion. See how each one below does. Support that opinion with at least four examples. (If you disagree with the opinion given, change it and then support your own.) In either case, as you fill out **a** through **d**, avoid any material that does not support its topic sentence.*

1. E-mail is bringing back, in new form, the lost art of letter writing.

    a.

    b.

    c.

    d.

2. Going back to school is one of the hardest things a person over 25 can do.

    a.

    b.

    c.

    d.

3. The main cause of road rage is the hectic pace of our daily lives.

    a.

    b.

    c.

    d.

4. Sports are excellent training for life.

    a.

    b.

    c.

    d.

5. Credit cards are the single biggest threat to the average person's budget.

   a.

   b.

   c.

   d.

Think of a good topic sentence to unite each of the following groups of material. Write it in the blank.

1. _____

   _____

   a. Online discussion groups can be addictive, consuming hours of a person's time every day.

   b. It is tempting to surf the Web for hours at a time.

   c. Many online investors check their stocks several times a day, when they are supposed to be working.

   d. Some people check their e-mail as much as 10 times a day.

2. _____

   _____

   a. The average new car loses over half its value in four years.

   b. Many older cars cost over $2000 a year in maintenance.

   c. Parking in Canada's big cities can cost $20 a day.

   d. Many car owners fill up the tank twice a week.

   e. Car insurance can cost as much as $5000 a year.

3. _____

   _____

   a. French fries contain large amounts of oil and salt.

   b. Most milkshakes contain artificial colour and flavour, as well as large amounts of sugar.

   c. Hamburgers are made of fatty beef and served on buns made of white flour.

   d. Soft drinks are basically water, sugar, and artificial flavours and dyes.

4. _____

   _____

   a. Clearcutting, in such places as Vancouver Island, turns old-growth forest into wastelands of stumps and dead branches.

   b. Heavy rains in British Columbia wash away the soil from clearcut hills and mountains, polluting trout and salmon streams.

   c. Many species of wildlife have become endangered because of clearcutting in British Columbia.

   d. The dried brush left after clearcutting is a major fire hazard.

5. _____

_____

    a. With long hours of use, some types of contact lenses can irritate or even damage the eye.

    b. If a piece of grit gets under a contact lens, the eye can hurt so much that the person sees stars.

    c. Contact lenses are often lost on the bathroom floor or even down the lavatory drain.

    d. Many sleepy drivers have rubbed their eyes, which accidentally pushes their contact lens off the cornea, so that suddenly all is a blur.

W O R K S H E E T

Topic Sentences

NAME _____

Underline the statement you think would make the best topic sentence of a paragraph. Remember that a point of view or opinion is preferable; a statement of pure fact may not be enough.

1. a. It used to start snowing in November, but the last few years we haven't seen snow till December or even January.
   b. My parents' snowblower has not been out of the garage for two years.
   c. Evidence all around shows that global warming is for real.

2. a. Our hospitals are in serious trouble, and so are we.
   b. The average waiting time for a cancer operation is now two and a half months.
   c. Last week a woman suffering from a heart attack lay for three hours in the hospital corridor and died before the staff had time to treat her.

3. a. Some people lose their shirts on the stock market.
   b. My uncle made $80,000 in one year on Internet stocks.
   c. Only by diversifying into several economic sectors can the average investor reduce the risk of playing the stock market.

4. a. Ice cream is a popular food.
   b. I often eat ice cream as a snack.
   c. Ice cream contains more chemical additives than almost any other food we eat.

5. a. Our competitive instincts are at their peak during rush hour on the subway.
   b. Some people push others aside so they can be first into the subway car.
   c. Many feet are trampled during the rush in and out of subway car doors.

6. a. My mother likes a drink or two on a Saturday night.
   b. Alcohol is a major cause of heart disease.
   c. Wine is popular around the world.

7. a. Many people do crazy things these days.
   b. Skydiving has been popular for a number of years.
   c. Skydiving is one of the most dangerous sports ever invented.

8. a. Some novels are a bore.
   b. The more concise a novel is, the more interesting it tends to be.
   c. *Wuthering Heights* is the first novel we studied in Introduction to Literature.

9. a. After a day's work I can eat a medium triple-cheese pizza all by myself.
   b. Many people don't like anchovies on their pizza.
   c. With carbohydrates, protein and even vegetables, pizza is one of the most nutritious foods around.

10. a. Twice this month we have seen a fox in our back yard.

   b. Many wild animals, having lost their fear of humans, are now entering our towns and cities.

   c. Driving home late one night I saw a coyote lope across Queen Street, and then turn to look at me with its yellow-green eyes shining in the headlights.

11. a. Medical drugs can be just as dangerous as street drugs.

   b. I often take two aspirins when I'm getting a cold.

   c. Drugs sometimes have a negative effect on the human body.

12. a. Twice in 18 months I had to replace the floppy drive of my computer.

   b. The CD-ROM drive failed in my sister's computer.

   c. The computer, even today, is not as reliable as we think.

13. a. Last August in Algonquin Park, I counted 14 canoes at one portage.

   b. The best canoe campsites of Algonquin Park are used so much that the soil is eroding and trees are being cut for firewood.

   c. Canoeing is now so popular that Algonquin Park is suffering from overuse.

14. a. French fries are often served dripping in oil.

   b. Hamburgers are filled with fat.

   c. Eating fast food is one of the surest ways to gain weight.

15. a. Scuba diving can be a safe sport if you know what you are doing.

   b. A scuba diver I know almost drowned when he caught his foot on some old wire at the bottom of a river.

   c. The word "scuba" stands for "self-contained underwater breathing apparatus."

16. a. My sister spends hours a day on the Internet.

   b. The "information highway" is growing every year.

   c. Most of what I read on the Internet discussion groups is garbage.

17. a. With regular exercise, most people can stay fit and active in old age.

   b. I have a second cousin who ran the New York Marathon at age 73.

   c. My grandfather played doubles tennis until age 85.

18. a. The bicycle is the most energy-efficient form of transportation ever invented.

   b. Someone stole my mountain bike by cutting the chain.

   c. My cousin rides her bicycle all year round except January and February.

19. a. A terrible windstorm recently flattened millions of trees in central France.

   b. Our climate is changing for the worse.

   c. Last year heavy rains caused disastrous flooding and mud slides in South America.

20. a. State-of-the-art skis can cost $600 a pair.

   b. Downhill skiing is one of the most expensive sports around.

   c. Ski clothes can easily cost over $500.

W O R K S H E E T

Unity in "Main" Paragraphs

NAME _____

Revise the following paragraphs to achieve unity of purpose. First underline the topic sentence. Then delete or revise any material that does not support it. If the paragraph does not reflect the topic sentence at all, revise the topic sentence.

1. Sports utility vehicles (SUVs) are the coolest product ever to hit the automotive world. With truck-like styling, and optional off-road features such as four-wheel drive, SUVs combine the ruggedness and frontier feeling of the light truck with all the comforts of the luxury car: big engine, air conditioning, sun roof, leather seats, and automatic everything. No one even minds the huge profit margin for auto companies, resulting in a price ten or fifteen thousand dollars more than for an equivalent car. And the fact that during collisions SUVs roll four times more frequently than cars, often throwing their occupants out the windows to their deaths, means little to the many SUV fans clamouring to buy these classy vehicles.

2. Now that the age of "extreme sports" has dawned, the old and boring act of hiking has been transformed into the new exciting sport of trail running. No longer does the hiker trudge slowly for 10 or 20 kilometres, interrupting progress to have lunch, listen to the birds singing, admire a waterfall or the view from a cliff. Now, extreme hikers throw their boots back in the closet, lace up their cross-trainers, and run at least 50 kilometres, jumping over rocks and fallen logs, never stopping except when a companion falls and breaks a leg, or becomes sick from dehydration, or suffers a heart attack from exhaustion at age 20. At the end of the day, the trail runner can take pride, in our age of competition, from having survived and arrived first.

3. Many English teachers dress poorly. They wear blue jeans, corduroy jackets and sandals, as if they were still living in the 1960s. Or they wear ragged pants and old baggy sweaters, as if they plan to dig in the garden after class. Or they wear shockingly mismatched colours—blue pants, brown jacket and purple tie—as if they were colour-blind. However, I once had a math teacher who looked even worse: he wore a blue and red plaid jacket, green bow tie, and grey and white pinstriped trousers.

4. My favourite job was delivering pizza last summer. The restaurant I worked for made excellent pizza with homemade sausage and generous amounts of cheese. Every night I got a free pizza for supper, plus a soft drink. When five or eight pizzas were ready in their boxes, I would roar around town in my old Pontiac, waving at my friends on the street and collecting big tips from the customers. I also collected ten or twelve traffic tickets, because although I usually drove at twice the speed limit, the boss called me "Speedy" because he thought I was so slow. And one night the clutch went out, costing me $425 in repairs. The boss lent me his van in the meantime, but charged an exorbitant rate for mileage. He was the worst skinflint I have ever seen.

5. Having to share a bedroom with my brother taught me how to get along with others. We each had to respect the other person's half of the room, for example by not throwing our dirty clothes on each other's bed. We had to take turns cleaning and sweeping. We had to discuss what colour to paint the walls and which posters to put up. Most important of all, we had to be quiet when the other person was trying to study or sleep. As a result of this trying experience, I have learned that it is hard to get along with others. I'm glad that I have left home, because now all the fighting is over.

6. Only by using computers can today's students keep up with the workload. Laborious recopying of drafts is now a thing of the past. School notes can be quickly keyed in, then printed off for study. And online searches of the Web provide fast research. Of course software glitches, virus attacks and sudden hard drive crashes can lead to days or even weeks of down time. As well, many students need to work long hours at menial jobs to afford their computers. Then there is the temptation to "chat" and "surf" endlessly when they should be studying. In fact, the best way for students to save time is to shun the computer altogether.

7. Driving to work is greatly preferable to taking the bus or subway. First of all, being enclosed by the car affords a privacy impossible to achieve in public transit. Secondly, no matter how long your car is stuck in a traffic jam, you can relax by turning on the radio and having a cigarette. Need we mention the fact that no transit connections, involving lineups in the heat or cold, need to be made by the motorist? And finally, although it is true that driving costs about five times as much as taking the transit, some people can deduct this cost as a business expense.

8. Jogging is an excellent means to physical fitness. Heavy persons should avoid it, though, to prevent a heart attack caused by the sudden overload of violent action. Women are advised to avoid jogging, too, because in some cases the movement can cause the uterus to loosen—a potentially serious medical problem. Bone spurs in the foot, tearing of the Achilles' tendon, and deterioration of the knee joint are other common hazards of jogging. Some joggers have even been killed by traffic, because people with jobs often run at night when visibility is poor. But all in all, jogging has become one of our most popular forms of exercise.

9. The book as we know it will soon be obsolete. No longer will we have to turn from one page to the next, or insert a bookmark at the end of a chapter when we stop for lunch. Soon we will be downloading the latest Stephen King novel off the Web into our computer, and then, with new software, downloading from the computer to our electronic "book." Once we have charged up the batteries and mastered the commands for scrolling and for progressing from one "page" to the next, and once we have learned how to hold this heavy object comfortably for long periods of time, we can sit in the subway on the way to work, thrilling to the plot of our novel. In the next few years the eye strain caused by hours of reading a flickering screen will probably be reduced, too, by even newer technology. Never again will we have to use our library card to borrow the obsolescent item made of paper, but will merely buy the software, buy the electronic device (before long it will be affordable to most of us), and send our credit card number over the Internet to buy the digital text for our next read.

10. The cell phone has radically improved our lives. No longer do we have to be out of touch, out of reach of those who need to communicate with us. It used to be that employees would waste their time while at home with their families, or on the road travelling from one activity to another. They would take coffee breaks, read a newspaper, eat, or even find a place to sleep, rather than producing for their employers. Now, however, the boss can ring them up in the car, at the restaurant, at the movie theatre, at home at the dinner table, in bed, any time of day or night. The former "unreachables," as one cell phone ad put it, can now take satisfaction in being more productive members of the employment team.

Coherence in "Main" Paragraphs, Level 1

N A M E _____

In the following long paragraph, circle or highlight all the transitions that build coherence by linking examples and ideas.

Raves have become an obsession among many people of student age. What began as a small movement of urbanites in Canada's biggest cities has spread until now all over the country as many as 20 000 people at one event dance hypnotically to music not only all night but even into the next day. At first parents thought raves were innocent, because normally no alcohol is allowed. What is becoming more and more apparent, though, is the quantity of drugs consumed and even sold right on the dance floor. A person 15 years old or even younger will take one or more pills of Ecstasy, a drug known since the 1930s but only now used recreationally. This "hit," according to those who use it, will deepen the appeal of the music, deepen the feelings of friendship and "family" the dancers have for each other, and prolong their ability to stay moving on the dance floor. But at what cost? The homemade drug varies in quality and strength, so users never know what dose they are taking, or even whether the pill is something else such as Valium. Worse, some users take as many as three or four tablets, as did one young raver in the Maritimes, who collapsed and died right on the dance floor. Because of tragedies like this, society is at last waking up to the hazards of the rave, and, as a result, stricter regulation is coming.

WORKSHEET

Coherence in "Main" Paragraphs, Level 2

NAME _____

The following paragraph is slow-moving and hard to read, because it is missing almost all the transitions between its examples and ideas. Read it through. Then, looking at this list of transitions below, write each one in the blank at the best place. Although each expression has a place, it is all right to use a term more than once as long as each makes sense where you put it.

Hint: The listed words that are capitalized begin sentences in the exercise.

Soon	Finally	sometimes	constantly
since	in fact	that	From now on
When	After	still	A long time ago
at last	and		

Good planning is the key to a good holiday. Little did my sister and I know, when we decided to spend three weeks cycling in New Zealand, _____ the friends planning our trip did not know what they were doing. _____ they had driven, not cycled, through these mountains. _____ we arrived with our touring bikes, everything seemed good. The cyclists were all excited. The sun was shining. _____, it was shining too hard: _____ the ozone layer of that southern latitude has almost disappeared, we had to cover ourselves with sunscreen _____ to avoid skin cancer. _____ we learned what it was to bike up a steep mountain, in first gear all the way. Semis roared past, _____ the wind _____ pushed us into the ditch. A panel truck got too close and hit two bikers. One is _____ in hospital with a broken leg. _____ a day of such extreme effort, the camping was too much work. _____ several people quit and rented a car for the rest of the holiday. My sister and I were glad to get home _____. We were happy to be alive. _____ we will be very careful planning holidays.

WORKSHEET

Coherence in "Main" Paragraphs, Level 2

NAME _____

The following paragraph is choppy and hard to follow, because it is missing links between parts. Write the links in wherever needed, choosing the most logical one for each place. Also use transitions here and there to improve style by combining overly short sentences. (Refer to page 46 to review some common transitions.)

The scariest experience of my life so far was exploring a cave. Two friends and I put on our oldest clothes, loaded new batteries into our flashlights, and drove to a high limestone cliff two hours north of the city. At its base was a small black opening hidden behind some bushes. We entered. It was very dark. We turned on the flashlights. We walked through mud. We splashed through water. I was freezing. My shirt tore on a sharp rock. I felt blood under the rip. We entered a large room. The ceiling was high. In the middle was a big flat rock, like a table. Or was it like an altar? Images of cave dwellers making human sacrifices went through my head. We sat there and ate our sandwiches. Pushing further into the cliff, we felt the walls narrow and the ceiling grow lower. We were crawling through the passage on hands and knees. I thought of the tiny closet my kindergarten teacher had locked me in after I got into a fight. My light flickered. Appalled, we suddenly turned back. My light went dead. As we passed the altar, the second flashlight failed. Only as the third and last flashlight was growing dim did we see a faint glimmer ahead. Shivering, scraped raw by rocks, covered in slime, our clothes in rags, we crawled out the entrance as early humans must have done. A fiery sun was setting in a mass of red clouds. I can understand people who have claustrophobia.

Coherence in "Main" Paragraphs, Level 3

NAME _____

Choose one of the following potential topic sentences. Freewrite on it for about five minutes, then look over what you have produced. (If necessary, review freewriting on pages 3–4.) If the freewriting is good, now use the best of it to produce a well-developed paragraph. (If it is not good, try another.) When you have finished writing the paragraph, circle or highlight every transition used. (If necessary, review the list of transitions on page 46.)

1. E-mail has changed my communication habits.

2. As the song says, "Breaking up is hard to do."

3. Television is addictive.

4. The bicycle is an effective means of transportation in the city.

5. Lovers should also be friends.

The Paragraph of Narration

Since people love stories, *narration* is a natural and attractive way to communicate. In our "Introductory Paragraph" section (pages 42–43), we saw how the anecdote about Paul's financial problems could lead into an analysis of cutbacks to postsecondary education, and to the effects on students. Narrative can also serve other parts of an essay: the *body* and the *closing*.

Often several paragraphs of narration will occur in a row, to tell a story illustrating a point. In such a case it is clear that individual paragraphs will not have the common "main" paragraph structure of topic sentence and development, but will merely tell a chunk of the story in time order. Furthermore, if people in the story are speaking, we indent each time the speaker changes, to help the reader know who says what. Such a paragraph can be tiny or large, but in either case will be different from the "main paragraph"—because its function is different.

Now let's look at a series of narrative paragraphs that might appear in our essay about cutbacks to education:

> The new cutbacks take a toll not only in student finances but also time. Paul now spends an hour and a half taking two buses, the subway and another bus to school from his parents' home outside the city. "If I still had my car," he said in the corridor between classes, "I'd be there in half an hour. Or if I could afford my own room, I'd be there in ten minutes."
>
> Looking at his watch, he added, "By the time I got here this morning all the computers were taken in the lab, so now I have to spend noon hour working on spreadsheets instead of eating lunch. It'll save $3.98 anyway."
>
> "Hey Paul," said a friend passing by, "Coming to the party tonight?"
>
> "No, I'm working."
>
> "Thought you just worked weekends."
>
> "Well, that was last year."

Note how short these narrative paragraphs are, and how none but the first contains anything resembling a topic sentence. Also note that although these paragraphs are not standardized and do not argue a point in logical fashion, their overall effect is to provide a strong example that illustrates the main point of the essay: student hardships in a time of cutbacks to education.

*Note: **In academic writing such as research papers, narration is rarely used.*** In personal, less formal writing, though, you may use paragraphs of narration now and then when they work well to support your ideas. Remember, though, that a composition made up entirely of narrative will not be an essay at all; it might be fiction, news, history or autobiography.

The "Bridge" Paragraph

Bridges help to unify geographical regions: they permit us to cross from one part to another. They do the same for an essay, easing us from one main section to another. In short papers a "bridge" may be just a

word or two of transition: "then" or "first" or "next" or "finally" or "in conclusion." Longer essays use not only these, but also longer "bridge paragraphs" that move us from one main section to another. Let's examine one:

> Despite his economic problems this year, Paul is one of the lucky ones. His parents give him free room and board, and he has part-time jobs that more or less pay his bills. But what about the less lucky students? How about those whose parents cannot help them because they themselves may have been laid off and lost their homes? How about those who cannot find part-time or summer jobs? How about single parents who do not have time to raise their own children, work to support them, and also go to school?

The opening reference to Paul recalls earlier parts of the essay that focus on his individual example. The next sentence then sets up a contrast between Paul, whose troubles are at least still manageable, and those who have even more serious problems. Finally, the series of questions moves us forward, setting the stage for the next section about the students hardest hit by cutbacks.

Perhaps a later bridge paragraph will link this next section to a concluding part, which will fulfill the promise of the introduction: showing ways in which Paul and the other students can try to overcome the problems posed by cutbacks. Like our "bridge" above, it will probably be short, and will look in two directions—backward at what has just been said, and forward at what is coming next.

Bridge paragraphs, then, differ from "main" paragraphs. Their opening may resemble a topic sentence, as in our example. But unlike "main" paragraphs, bridge paragraphs do not develop such a statement throughout, for part of the way through comes the shift that moves us on to the next topic. Paragraphs are certainly not all alike. As in architecture, form follows function.

The Closing Paragraph

Like an introductory paragraph, a closing paragraph is specialized because of its location. You have probably seen how productions as different as a speech, a sermon, a play or a film close on a high point, or climax. From symphonies to rock and roll, music ends literally on a "high note," while TV police dramas close with the excitement of a tire-screeching car chase or a shootout. (This approach is not new; have you ever counted the bodies lying onstage in the last scene of *Hamlet*?)

Most essays follow this pattern of ending in excitement. What could be worse than a closing paragraph that trails off into minor details? Suppose that our essay on student cutbacks ended like this:

> In conclusion, the cutbacks to education that have been implemented by provincial governments have placed undue burdens on postsecondary students. Only through real motivation and a good plan of action can these victims of government policy stay in school and finish their education. Things will probably get better, though, in the future. Ten years from now, when they are mowing grass at their houses in the suburbs, these people will probably have forgot all about their former financial troubles, not to mention the other minor problems that students have from day to day.

This paragraph ignores a major principle: the ending occupies the most prominent position in an essay. Its potential either for impact or for boredom is even greater than that of the introduction. If our closing paragraph or paragraphs do not leave the reader convinced or inspired, we have wrecked the rest of the essay as well, no matter how good it was. Let's look now at an alternative model:

> In conclusion, today's students can no longer rely on their governments to help them through school. As legislators continue their fascination with the "bottom line," the state of the deficit will seem more important than the future of the citizens. At a time when lawmakers are turning their backs on postsecondary students, the victims must heighten their motivation and carefully construct a plan of action that enables them to stay in school. Only in this self-reliant way can they achieve the education that their parents' generation took for granted. If they fail in this task, then the students of today will become the unemployed of tomorrow.

See how instead of trailing off, this closing paragraph rises to its peak of significance in the last words. As it does so, it also moves upward in time from the present to the future. Both these movements merge in the final ominous phrase, "the unemployed of tomorrow," which impresses upon readers the importance of the whole essay.

Though closing paragraphs come in many kinds, most good ones follow the upward pattern of our example, like the grand finale of a symphony. Often the best closings end deliberately on a key word. (In fact, keep this technique in mind for all paragraphs: play around with the last sentence until you can place the most important word at the very end, where it will do the most good.)

Here are the most widespread techniques used for the closing paragraph or paragraphs of an essay:

■ *Refer back to the thesis statement*, to give a sense of completion. But do not just repeat the thesis.

■ *Ask a question* that either makes your reader think or that has an answer obvious from the content of your essay. Either method will encourage involvement, through your reader's participation in the closing.

■ *Use a quotation* that seals your argument with the opinion of an authority, or that puts your view in more vivid or memorable terms than you could devise yourself. As with introductory quotations, consult the index of *Colombo's Canadian Quotations* or *Bartlett's Familiar Quotations* (see the excellent online version of the latter at <http://www.columbia.edu/acis/bartleby/bartlett>).

■ *Use transition signals.* In combination with other closing techniques, use expressions such as "finally," "last," "in summary" or "in conclusion" to prepare the reader for your final words.

■ *Reveal the significance* of your argument, as in our sample closing, which points to unemployment as the long-term result of cutbacks. Showing the importance of your point will help to involve the reader personally.

■ *Provide a summary*, but only at the closing of essays so long or complex that your reader may have forgot key points. Avoid boring repetition; keep any summary short.

■ *Draw a conclusion.* A "conclusion" is not just an ending ("the place where you got tired of thinking," as one piece of e-mail humour puts it). Rather, it is a diagnosis or verdict on the subject of your essay: taxes should be raised or lowered, mercy killing outlawed or permitted, nuclear weapons maintained or scrapped, the voting age raised or lowered. As you close your essay, increase its power by making any important judgement—or "conclusion"—that is rooted clearly in the logic of your argument.

■ *Make a prediction.* What could be more appropriate than closing a discussion of a subject's past or present with a look at its probable future? (Remember the financially burdened students of today who may become the unemployed of tomorrow.) This approach is a good way to "reveal the significance."

LENGTH OF PARAGRAPHS

Since there are different kinds of paragraphs, with different jobs to do, they will of course have different lengths. Specialized paragraphs that introduce, narrate, bridge or close an essay can be as short as one sentence, for special effect, or can be several sentences long. Most tend to be short, though, in the range of two to five sentences, because major explanations tend to occur in the "body."

"Main" paragraphs of the body can also vary in length—from one sentence, for special effect, to as many as ten or more sentences in a complex explanation. Keep this natural range in mind:

■ Vary the lengths of "main" paragraphs so your style is not flat or boring.
■ Aim for an up-and-down effect like that of waves in the ocean.

On the average, "main" paragraphs are substantial: from about five to eight sentences. Of course sentences, too, vary in length, and this in turn affects the length of paragraphs. A tense passage of ten short sentences may result in a fairly small paragraph, while a single very long and involved sentence may create its own long paragraph. (If you have read Victorian novels, you have seen more than a few of these.)

Whatever the lengths of their sentences, if your "main" paragraphs are too short, you cripple your impact as a writer. We have already discussed this common flaw of "making paragraphs too short and too numerous" (page 41).

Find an essay you have written in the past and count the number of sentences in each paragraph. You could be surprised to find that most of your paragraphs are only two or three sentences long, especially if you wrote by hand, which makes everything look longer than it is. Using the graph that follows, compare your numbers to the number of sentences in the paragraphs from the revised draft of our sample short essay "My First Canoe Trip" (pages 26–29).

Though variety is achieved by paragraphs as short as three sentences, the overall average for "My First Canoe Trip" is a healthy 5.4 sentences per paragraph, and one paragraph has 9.

Are your own paragraphs big enough? Do they have the depth of detail that allows for clear thought? Do they sparkle with examples, with images, with facts? Or are they "thin"? Do they just limp along half-developed, only half doing their job? Your own sentence count should help you decide. If they are "thin," you should take very seriously the exercise on page 67: "Improving 'Thin' Paragraphs." Do it, review it, remember it, and in your own essays apply it.

Finally, remember that we save these concerns mostly for the editing process. Do try to generate details as you write your discovery draft, but at that early stage avoid the tactical error of stopping to rework a paragraph: by the time you get it right, the next ten things you were going to say may have slipped from your mind. It is later, in the second or even third draft, that we practise carefully the art of paragraphing.

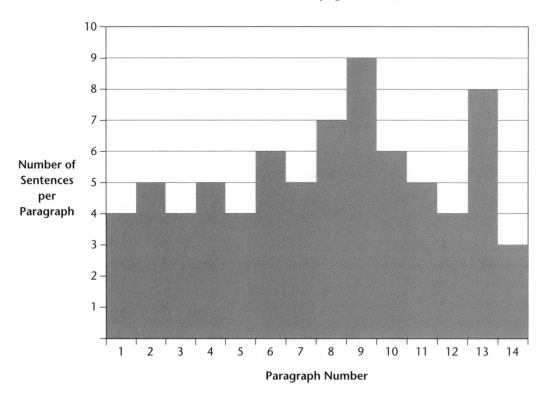

**Paragraph Lengths
in the Short Essay "My First Canoe Trip"
(second draft, pages 26–29)**

Number of Sentences per Paragraph

Paragraph Number

Improving "Thin" Paragraphs

N A M E _____

*The most frequent weakness of paragraphs is "**thinness.**" Add details to develop the following examples into vivid and convincing paragraphs. Write your new versions on a separate page, adding words, phrases or whole sentences of example, image or fact. Remember to follow, all the way through, the direction set by the topic sentence. If you disagree with the point of view in the topic sentence, change it before you revise what follows.*

1. Major highways have become war zones. Many motorists show aggressive behaviour of various kinds. There is a higher volume of traffic, going at higher speeds. Worst of all for the car driver are the many trucks.

2. Postal service in Canada leaves something to be desired. Items are often late. Other times mail has been damaged in processing. Stamp prices are high, and for what?

3. Never before has music been so closely identified with the lives of its fans. People who dress in certain fashions and adopt a particular behaviour tend to favour one kind of music, or even a specific band. This music then becomes an expression of their lifestyle.

4. Having brothers or sisters is not easy. You have to tolerate each other's behaviour, and you must learn to share. But this effort is worthwhile, because it prepares you for your own family life in the future.

5. Voice mail is one of the more annoying aspects of modern life. The caller may spend large amounts of time in a vain effort to contact a person or organization. Tasteless music is forced upon the victim while he or she waits. Sometimes the attempt to communicate is even terminated automatically.

6. Pets are expensive. Dogs, for example, require certain shots. They need food. They must be cared for somehow while the owners are away. And as dogs grow older and suffer health problems, veterinarians' bills may include bigger and bigger items.

7. School cafeteria food leaves something to be desired. It is heavy in starches, grease and sugar. It tends to be overcooked. Finally, it is often expensive.

8. American television drama has a heavy influence on our own. Many Canadians think CBC series are boring, and would rather turn to American sitcoms or police shows. Thus Canadian producers are tempted to win viewers by imitating the format and style of the American product.

9. Junk mail is getting out of hand. Numerous items arrive most days. Many of these beg for money. Some even use high-pressure sales techniques.

10. The Internet has taken over many people's social lives. They spend a great deal of time on it daily, communicating electronically with others on the Net. As a result, their contact with "R.L."—real life—has diminished.

PART THREE

Editing: The Rest of the Process

Now that we have done the "big" things, we turn to the "little" things. Now that we have zeroed in on our topic, our thesis and our audience, now that we have unleashed our ideas in a draft or two, we move on to the finer points of editing.

This phase covers a lot of ground. Each "little" thing contributes, for good or for bad, to the total effect of an essay. Now we tinker with words, replacing a weak one with a strong one, a vague one with a concrete one. We fix weird sentences. We change punctuation. We reach for the dictionary. And at the very end we give our good copy the final quality control of proofreading.

Frankly, the process doesn't always follow this plan. We did a bit of word-tinkering and happened to see a few errors even in the discovery draft. We didn't make an issue of it then, because we didn't want to lose our train of thought. But we took a moment here and there to change a comma to a period or replace "there" with "their."

And now that we're set to do all these things in the editing stage, the reverse may happen: a new idea may come rushing out of our mind—just the thing to round off a point that we thought we had already finished. So we may interrupt the "little" things we are doing and for a while move back to the "big" things.

But apart from these exceptions, we now turn our attention to editing—to the material in the following sections of this chapter. Different teachers will use the editing chapter in different ways. Some will select the parts they view as most important, to discuss and to practise in class with exercises. Others will choose sections and exercises as needed, according to what they see in essays from the class. Still others will assign a section only to individuals who need that particular skill. Whatever the approach of your teacher, though, keep four things in mind:

1. Not everyone needs everything in this chapter. If your punctuation is already good, turn your attention to other things, such as economy.

2. Almost everyone does need certain parts of this chapter that cover chronic problems. The two most often needed tend to be "Editing for Pronoun Reference" and "Editing for Agreement."

3. Whatever material your teacher assigns, and in whatever order, remember that you can also use this chapter as a reference. If you feel unsure about commas, look them up. If your teacher has written "cliché" beside your favourite expression, find that section and study it. If your last paper was wordy, study "Editing for Economy." To find things, use the table of contents, the index, or simply the "Editing Guide" on the inside back cover.

   If you wish to do exercises on your own, note the answers given at the back of the book.

4. Above all, do not study all the editing sections *before* you write. If we tried to master the "little" before the "big," we'd never get to the first line of our first essay. Start writing, keep writing, and apply each new skill as you learn it.

EDITING FOR ECONOMY

One day you go shopping for shoes. The first store has a nice pair for $50. The second store has the identical shoes for $100, and a third has them for $150. *Need we ask which store gets your business?* Yet even though most students would spend the fewest possible dollars, when they use words they may spend like millionaires.

"Talk is cheap," the old saying tells us. Well, sometimes. People can yak for hours in the cafeteria, not caring if others forget every word they say. But using words to pass the time is one thing; using them to make a point is another.

In essay writing, "talk" is not cheap at all. If we "spend" too much, our message suffocates under a mass of words. The reader yawns. The teacher reaches for the red pen. But if we spend words carefully like dollars, making each one contribute to the overall point, the power of our message grows and grows. What we say is easily read, quickly grasped, strongly felt.

Economy is central to other aspects of writing as well. For example, revising an early draft to make it more direct and concise automatically improves grammar, for streamlining our language gives errors fewer places to occur. Since time will be saved in other stages of revision, give this matter a high priority: edit for economy *before* you edit for the aspects of grammar discussed later in this chapter.

The two worst enemies of economical writing are *wordiness* and *repetition*.

Wordiness

Make every word count. Get rid of those that do not.

A. **Move swiftly to the main point of an essay** rather than padding the introduction. Avoid wordy beginnings like this one from an actual student essay:

> Well, the question I am going to write about raises a lot of problems, and can easily be debated with many people taking either side.

Any question worth writing an essay about "can easily be debated," and in a debate people usually take "either side." The author has wasted words telling us what we already know, but has failed to tell us the most important thing: the topic. (See pages 42–43 for more discussion of introductions.)

B. **Stay on topic.** Give your reader all the explanation needed to understand your point, but do not waste time with information that does not explain it:

> Running promotes health. Excess weight that might someday cause a heart attack is burned off. After a few years, the heart becomes so strong that it may beat as few as 40 times per minute. Muscles become strong and flexible, so that the runner may cope more easily with the tasks of everyday life. *And running is an inexpensive sport, costing only four or five cents per kilometre for shoes.*

Saving money has little to do with health. Even if the last sentence interests the reader, here it wastes time. Let's remove it, then, and save it for a future paragraph that does discuss the cost of running.

C. **Be plain rather than fancy.** Avoid trying to make your writing seem more important than it is:

> With a college education one looks forward to gaining sufficient knowledge whereby one can assist in the development of society. This education can assist in enlightening the masses of society or even in the utilization of knowledge gained to establish an institution to further scatter abroad information.

(This author would make a fine speech writer for a politician who must talk for hours while promising nothing.)

> The students who rioted were exterminated from school.

(This writer, pushing her vocabulary too hard, has had her subjects murdered instead of expelled.)

> The smells were sweet to his nasal palate.

(In other words, something smelled good to him. This writer should avoid decorating the message, and instead just deliver it.)

One of the surest ways to weaken your writing is to deliberately choose big words. Some people go all through the first draft of an essay replacing small or plain words with long or fancy ones dug up from the thesaurus. "Think" becomes "ponder" or "cogitate"; "read" becomes "peruse"; "chew" becomes "masticate." In trying to seem bigger and better than it is, such writing is flabby, dishonest, and even ridiculous. Do use a big word when it is most appropriate, but in general choose the smallest one that exactly fits your meaning.

(For related material, see "Jargon," page 91.)

A True Story: A Painter Turns to Writing

Emily Carr (1871–1945, born in Victoria, British Columbia) was one of Canada's most gifted and original painters. But when ill health made her turn from painting expeditions to writing, she suddenly became one of our most gifted and original writers too. How? As she wrote in her book *Growing Pains*, "I did not know book rules. I made two for myself. They were about the same as the principles I use in painting; get to the point as directly as you can; never use a big word if a little one will do."

D. Manipulate sentence structure to avoid wordiness.
One student wrote this:

> The flavour of coffee tastes delicious to me. (8 words)

Did we not know coffee has a flavour? Let's omit the first three words, then, by using "coffee" rather than "flavour" as a subject:

> Coffee tastes delicious to me. (5 words)

So far, so good, but we could further concentrate the statement by using "I" as a subject:

> I love coffee. (3 words)

Another student wrote this sincere but wasteful message:

> The purpose of my composition is to give an explanation of why I do not drink strong beverages. The reason why I do not indulge in strong drink is based on my religious convictions. (34 words)

Note how the second sentence restates much of the first. Let's combine them:

> This composition will explain how my religious convictions prevent me from indulging in strong drink. (15 words)

So far we have fewer than half the original words, but the sentence is still inflated. Why mention "this composition" if we already realize this is the author's own composition? Why mention "convictions" if they can be assumed from the idea of religion? And why use "indulging in strong drink" instead of the single word "drinking," which in this context clearly refers to alcohol? Let's try a new sentence, "spending" as little as possible:

> My religion keeps me from drinking. (6 words)

E. Normally avoid the passive voice, which is wordy and weak; use the active voice, which is concise and strong.

PASSIVE

> The contest was won by me. (6 words)

ACTIVE

> I won the contest. (4 words)

PASSIVE

> The crash was witnessed by five people. (7 words)

ACTIVE

> Five people witnessed the crash. (5 words)

Repetition

Saying something more than once is by far the most common way of wasting words. To improve your efficiency and your style, avoid repetition of fact and of vocabulary.

A. Avoid stating a fact more than once.

> Computer viruses are a danger *and a hazard* to our future.

How much difference is there between a "danger" and a "hazard"? If not much, then in this statement one of them is a waste.

B. Avoid stating a fact easily assumed from another fact already given.

A sign in a jewellery store said, "Ears pierced *while you wait*." Are those last three words really needed? How could the ears be pierced if we did not wait? Here's another example of wasteful language, from a student essay:

The chair was green *in colour.*

Did the author think we do not know green is a colour? Or did she just neglect to edit? Let's help her by chopping out the last two words. Here is another example:

Knowledge is crucial to the survival of the *investor's investment.*

Did this writer think we do not know investors invest? Are we going in circles? Then let's chop out the word "investor's."

Radio and TV personalities use repetitious language so often that certain expressions will pop into your mind as you write. *Avoid these self-repeaters and any like them:*

absolutely perfect
at this point in time
completely surrounded

"It was Saturday night. The clock on my office wall showed the time to be eleven-forty-five. There are times when a private eye does not necessarily feel like being a private eye. This was one of those times. The elevator door down the hall clanked open with a clank familiar to anyone on the fourth floor who had had an office on the fourth floor as long as I had had an office on the fourth floor. Footsteps came down the darkened hall and stopped outside my door. They were the footsteps of a woman. . . ."

consensus of opinion
contributing factor
crisis situation
deeply profound
an emergency situation
end result
equally as good
final conclusion
free gift
future generations to come
in actual fact
many different kinds
mutual agreement
mutual cooperation
my personal opinion
no other alternative
repeat again
return back
solid fact
sufficient enough reason
truly remarkable

C. **Avoid trying to strengthen a word that is already strong. Intensifiers such as "very," "highly" and "extremely" add nothing to words such as these:**

crucial	miserable
definite	obese
fascinating	perfect
horrible	tragic
impossible	unique
intriguing	wonderful

One person wrote this:

Training a cat to do tricks is *very* impossible.

How can something be more impossible than "impossible"? Let's remove "very" and remember that it's one of the most overused words in our language.

D. If you **avoid repeating words, especially long ones,** your message will be more efficient and your style will be more pleasing.
A sign in a church parking lot proclaimed this:

Parking *permitted by permission* only. (5 words)

Naturally, "permission" implies that something is "permitted." Let's omit the word:

Parking by *permission* only. (4 words)

The student who wrote this one may have been desperate to meet a required essay length:

The author's imagination is very imaginative. (6 words)

Not only is the sentence wasteful, but it irritates the reader, who is being led in circles. An obvious revision is to remove one of the repetitious words:

The author is very *imaginative.* (5 words)

The word "imaginative," though, is strong enough that we can also omit "very":

The author is *imaginative.* (4 words)

Better still, we could use "imagination" as the subject of a sentence that gets on to the next point:

The author's *imagination* is evident in the fresh imagery of the poem.

Finally, we must recognize that not all repetition is bad. Would the following passage be as effective if the main word occurred only once?

We drive *American* cars, read *American* books, listen to *American* music and go to *American* movies. If our habits do not change, we may someday even become *American.*

This repetition of "American" is deliberate, not accidental. Far from wasting words, it strengthens and emphasizes the message. Feel free to use repetition this way as a device of style—as long as you realize what you are doing.

E. **Repetition even of sound can irritate, and in such cases should be avoided.** Read drafts aloud to detect clunkers like this:

Population *density* of great *intensity* creates social chaos.

Let's revise to avoid the accidental rhyme:

High population *density* creates social chaos.

Many people find it easier to cut waste from the computer screen than from the page. Learn how your system deletes text. Simple commands will instantly remove a letter, a word, a whole line, or a page. Other commands will bring these back in case you realize you made a mistake.

Once such moves are automatic, words shift constantly, moving into gaps left by vanishing waste. Passages shrink in size as they expand in power.

Your system no doubt has a thesaurus (see page 31). Use it. This tool is so fast that you can afford to check all the flabby words of your discovery draft and replace them with short and strong ones, and ones that more sharply convey your meaning.

If you suspect you are repeating a certain word too often, try your system's "search" function to find each occurrence quickly and then see whether it could be changed (see page 140). Reserve this technique for long papers, where it may save you time.

Count words electronically. Most word-processing software allows you to do so quickly, either through the speller or through a separate menu. Consult your manual for the commands. Count often, to track your gains in economy.

Is a passage hopeless? Move it down the screen with your Enter key, put the cursor in the empty space, and do a quick new version not looking at the old one. If it comes out shorter and better, delete the original.

In summary, word processing frees you up to do the experimenting which is at the heart not only of economy, but of our whole "process" approach to writing.

DIAGNOSTIC

Economy

NAME _____

Put an "X" beside each passage that clearly contains wordiness or undesirable repetition.

1. Crying happens in both sexes, men and women. _____

2. In terms of the climate of Somalia, it is very hot and dry. _____

3. Society considers pit bulls to be killers because a few of these dogs have killed or fatally injured someone or another animal. _____

4. What can I say about culture in Vancouver? Well, first it is a multicultural culture. _____

5. Today in industrialized nations, 80 percent of the people live in urban areas, while 20 percent live in rural areas. _____

6. I closed my eyes to relive the incredible experience again. _____

7. The front of the building faces north while the back faces south. _____

8. Choosing a life partner is not easy. _____

9. In today's society having a computer is very crucial. _____

10. The best job I have ever had was at the London Public Library. It was the best job because it was interesting. There were a number of facts that made the job interesting. One of the major facts that made the job interesting was the people who worked at the library. _____

11. It was New Year's Eve night. _____

12. The average wattage of a car sound system ranges between 100 and 300 watts. _____

13. Last year I had many different teachers. One of my favourite teachers was the calculus teacher. _____

14. Even though the novel *Erewhon* came under some criticism, the overall opinion was that of a positive one. _____

15. I must admit that I have only one addiction in life. That addiction is television. _____

16. My full-time job was two hours away. _____

17. It is very stressful for students to juggle school and work at the same time. _____

18. My grandmother once broke her leg. As a result, she limps quite a bit when she is walking. _____

19. The piston is connected to a connecting rod, which in turn is connected to the crankshaft. The crankshaft is connected to a large metal disk called the flywheel. _____

20. Relationships are brief and short-lived. _____

21. After ten minutes in the cold, I could hardly feel the existence of my limbs. _____

22. We find that some teachers are negligent of criteria essential to the students' comprehension of a subject. _____

23. My cousin Jason is 15 years old. He feels that in order for him to look and feel good, he must have the latest clothes. _____

24. It is hard to get a job. _____

25. In the opinion of my dad, he says that the quality of luxury cars is what sets them apart from economy cars. _____

26. Swimmers who vary their pace will get very exhausted. _____

27. With a tax increase, it can create a black market or an underground economy. _____

28. Why do teenagers marry? There are many reasons why teenagers marry. _____

29. Many companies pollute by releasing harmful levels of pollutants into the environment. _____

30. Taking a trip to Mexico would be the trip of a lifetime for us. _____

31. Walking is the safest exercise. _____

32. I'm sure that France, Japan or Spain have beautiful languages, but the fact is I simply do not converse in any of these languages. _____

33. Smoking is a major risk in women's pregnancies. _____

34. Winter is very unique. _____

35. To be able to communicate in more than one language does nothing more than add to one's relative competitive advantage when dealing with other people. _____

36. A family is something you will always have forever. _____

37. The difference between a room with plants in it and one with no plants is extremely obvious. _____

38. The only seasons Indonesia has are the wet season and the dry season. _____

39. Politicians know that if they want to be reelected, they must lower taxes. _____

40. There is a Chinese saying that says, "A family that has an elderly person has a treasure." _____

W O R K S H E E T

Economy, Level 1

NAME _____

To chop waste from your draft, examine each word. Does one repeat another? Does one even imply the meaning of another? If so, cross one of them out. Practise this strategy on the following expressions that were found in actual student essays.

1. ~~truly~~ astounded

2. in the future ahead

3. ~~products~~ produced by industries

4. the final result

5. good advantages

6. emotional feelings

7. cheap in cost

8. ~~very~~ fascinating

9. ~~a true~~ fact

10. at that moment in time

11. ~~very~~ unique

12. share together

13. 8 a.m. in the morning

14. in the coming future

15. our surrounding environment

16. ~~very~~ crucial

17. fatal deaths

18. self-confidence in myself

19. and etc.

20. ~~$~~150 dollars

21. ~~quite~~ obvious

22. ~~very~~ fascinating

23. ~~extremely~~ miserable

24. ~~positive~~ self-esteem

25. reappear again

26. wet moisture

27. ~~very~~ obvious

28. 600 hundred students

29. ~~positively~~ sure

30. ~~so~~ crucial

31. rectangular ~~in shape~~

32. a light green colour

33. ~~highly~~ impossible

34. in the month of June

35. in the year 1998

36. light brown in colour

37. rather unique

38. no other alternative

39. competitive competition

40. in my own personal opinion

WORKSHEET

Economy, Level 2

NAME _____

Heighten the economy and style of these passages by crossing out wordiness and repetition, or where necessary by revising more fully in the space provided. If no revision is needed, write "Concise" in the space.

Example: England offered me fascinating scenery ~~to see~~.

1. Every day he usually got up at 4 a.m. in the morning.
    _____

2. I have noticed a change in my mental attitude.
    _____

3. My room is square in shape.
    _____

4. From a worldwide perspective, Canada has been rated as one of the top countries in the world in which to live.
    _____
    _____

5. In my opinion, I think Canada should increase its level of immigration, because the increase of immigration will boost up Canada's economy.
    _____
    _____

6. Gravelbourg, Saskatchewan, is a French community of 1800 hundred persons.
    _____

7. Many teenagers' lives have been snuffed out by fatal car accidents.
    _____

8. The Phoenix is quite an amazing club.
    _____

9. With a word processor you can delete any paragraph you don't like and write another.
    _____
    _____

10. I could, at this point, carry on and stretch this paper to maybe 10 pages, but I'm sure you could easily recognize the padding.
    _____
    _____

11. It was interesting to hear the British accent when people spoke.
    _____

12. Another useful item is the grape crusher, which crushes the grapes.

_____

13. In today's society, people just don't like to write. They'd rather do things orally, or by talking.

_____

_____

14. My boss was very obese.

_____

15. Nicotine gum contains nicotine, which will help smokers to avoid a sudden drop of nicotine in their blood when they quit smoking.

_____

_____

16. One disadvantage of the assembly line is that the worker on the line is dehumanized and not treated as a living person. Manufacturers and business executives are turning blue-collar workers into things.

_____

_____

_____

17. The oil machines have openings which, when opened, allow the oil to flow into a filtering machine, which filters the oil.

_____

_____

18. There are different credit cards for every type of purchase. Some examples of credit cards are major credit cards, store credit cards and even gasoline credit cards.

_____

_____

19. There should be no hesitation to use chemical food additives in our food, since they provide safety, freshness and many other protections to our food which we as consumers should have.

_____

_____

_____

20. The subway must be the worst way to travel around town. Several times I've been literally pulled out of a subway car. On one occasion when I was pulled out of the subway car, at Yonge and Bloor, the man who pulled me out of the subway car ripped my shirt. When the doors began to close, I retaliated and gave him a punch in the face.

_____

_____

_____

_____

WORKSHEET

Economy, Level 3

NAME _____

Heighten the economy and style of these passages by crossing out wordiness and repetition, or where necessary by revising more fully in the space provided.

1. Last year I began volunteering at the Rexdale Women's Centre. At the centre, I personally dealt with ladies who spoke Punjabi and some of them understood only Punjabi. I had a lot of problems because I didn't speak fluent Punjabi. When I was being interviewed for the position, the interviewer specifically stated that she wanted to hire someone who was fluent in Punjabi.

_____

_____

_____

_____

_____

_____

_____

2. The heavy lifting was fine with me, but what I really hated was the dirt on the clutches. It was unbelievable to see so much dirt on the clutches. I was always working with the dirt, having only a laboratory coat protecting me from the dirt. My pants were black all the time from working with the dirt.

_____

_____

_____

_____

_____

_____

_____

3. For my English assignment, I am supposed to describe the best or worst job I have ever had. The topic of the essay has made me think. What is a best or worst job? What has been my best or worst job? I have pondered on the topic for a while, and have come to the conclusion that there is no best or worst job. Any job can be either enjoyed or hated, because all jobs possess both good and bad points. In other words, a job is what you make it.

_____

_____

_____
_____
_____
_____
_____
_____

4. When a fluorescent light is first turned on, the light seems to slowly float through the room. The light from a fluorescent bulb travels at the same speed as the light from an incandescent bulb, but it does not seem to be as responsive. The light from a fluorescent tube is produced by the emission of radiation from the tube. The light that is produced seems to be a pale, dull-blue light. There is very little heat generated from the tube, but a slight humming can be heard from within the tube. The life of a fluorescent tube is much longer than that of an incandescent bulb. The average bulb would last six to twelve months, but most tubes last three to five years.

_____
_____
_____
_____
_____
_____
_____

5. We all know healthy food is essential to our health. Dietitians and nutritionists always talk about the importance of healthy food. Yet most of the people in North America don't always eat healthy food. Instead they eat junk food. Many fast-food businesses spend lots of money on advertising junk food through television or newspapers. In other words, junk food is popular, well promoted and widespread. Every day, large numbers of food stores or restaurants sell greasy hamburgers, hot dogs, and french fries. As a result, many people who eat junk food suffer short-term and long-term health problems.

_____
_____
_____
_____
_____
_____
_____

EDITING OUT LANGUAGE ABUSE

Good writing is honest. Just as people have many reasons to speak, people have many reasons to write. Some want to reveal facts, while others want to cover them up. Some want to make an issue clear, while others want to cloud it over. Most writers do want to convince us of something, which is a normal human desire. But while some argue fairly, through appeals to our reason, others bypass this process to twist the truth and even to attack our emotions. These language abusers actually hope we will *not* think.

Such attempts to avoid logical communication, to avoid real thought, may seem almost normal in our world of advertising campaigns, corporate hype and political propaganda. Our exposure to this abuse has been immense. Yet as you will see in the examples that follow, dishonesty of different kinds can produce not only self-serving and antisocial writing, but sometimes lazy, weak and boring writing as well.

As you study the clichés, euphemisms, bias words and jargon that follow, you will note how categories overlap: euphemisms and bias words tend to be clichés, and jargon tends to be euphemism. The reason for this may be the very fact that, in different ways, they can all be dishonest. Even when these creep into your essays by accident, as they often do, they can harm your argument by misleading the reader. *Edit them out of your writing.*

Clichés

A large part of writing honestly is being original. We all know that handing in another's essay as our own is a serious offence, and that someone who copies another person's book for publication will end up in court like any other thief. Yet many of us cheerfully repeat other people's expressions every time we write. These worn-out sayings are termed *clichés*, after the French word for a printing plate that makes many copies of one original.

Every time we write "sadder but wiser," "few and far between," "a sight for sore eyes" and "hit the nail on the head," we are lazily avoiding the work of being original. Like parrots, we are letting our language slip into preestablished channels, a process that discourages real thought and therefore bores the reader.

It must have taken real imagination for the first person to say for the first time, "I've got butterflies in my stomach." The first listener was probably dazzled by this new image that so clearly described nervousness. But today, when we hear those words for the thousandth time, we don't even think about butterflies. We may not think about anything at all, because repetition has deadened us.

Other clichés describe situations that no longer exist. A sailor once had to "learn the ropes," but do we? If not, why do we write it to describe our job driving a taxi or programming computers? People still say "Hold your horses," though for a hundred years we have driven cars. The bubonic plague once killed off a third of Europe; with today's antibiotics we no longer fear the disease, yet we still avoid things "like the plague."

When we no longer "see" what a cliché means, we will unknowingly stick it into ridiculous situations. One student wrote, "Right off the bat, nine seconds into the hockey game, a goal was scored by the guest team." We might be so numbed by the cliché that we do not "see" its image. But if we do, we might wonder what a bat is doing in a hockey game. This example, like the others above, shows the harm that clichés

"You're right. It *was* a herd of elephants up here."

COURTESY OF BEN WICKS.

can do: *they keep us from thinking.* For that reason, ***avoid them all.***

Are clichés automatic? See for yourself. How many of the following expressions can you complete without even thinking about them?

1. *birds of a* _____

2. *blind as a* _____

3. *by hook or by* _____

4. *cool as a* _____

5. *a diamond in the* _____

6. *hook, line and* _____

7. *in the nick of* _____

8. *last but not* _____

9. *make a mountain out of a* _____

10. *raining cats and* _____

WORKSHEET

Clichés

NAME _____

Here are some notorious old clichés found in student writing. First circle or highlight each cliché, then substitute a fresher word or expression to fit the meaning. When you see a passage free of clichés, write "Correct" in the space.

enthusiastic

Example: The first day at work I was ~~bright-eyed and bushy-tailed.~~

1. I grabbed the front of the toboggan, holding on for dear life.

   _____

   _____

2. There was never a dull moment at work. I was on my toes day in and day out.

   _____

   _____

3. The next year I played defence on the soccer team.

   _____

4. When June rolled around, Standard Tube hired me and I was ready to put my shoulder to the wheel.

   _____

   _____

5. The government tried to battle inflation, but the unemployment crisis was bursting at its seams like a swollen dam.

   _____

   _____

   _____

6. Calculus was the last straw. I was bored stiff.

   _____

   _____

7. Two of my bosom buddies and I found a neat little apartment overlooking English Bay. I was on cloud nine.

   _____

   _____

8. In this day and age, family members need to touch base each and every day.

   _____

   _____

9.   Rush hour in Montreal is not my cup of tea. The buses and subway cars are jammed like sardines.

10.   My new interest in fitness is mind-boggling, because in the past I avoided exercise like the plague.

11.   The hustle and bustle of the city takes its toll, and the individual can only grin and bear it.

12.   My three weeks in the woods made me realize that life is not a bowl of cherries.

13.   I passed my ordeal with flying colours. It was a breeze.

14.   The bottom line is that parents should be on their toes whenever their children are glued to the tube for hours on end.

15.   Marsha's schools, clothes and even friends were chosen by her parents.

16.   Our country is going down the tubes. The feds are pulling the wool over our eyes, and the public is on the short end of the stick.

17.   Most stores decided to bite the bullet and open on Sunday.

18. A great book shows the whole world and its problems in a nutshell.

_____

_____

19. I was spending money left, right and centre for my entertainment.

_____

_____

20. With spring just around the corner, I'm thinking about a summer job.

_____

_____

21. Going to the cafeteria and paying an arm and a leg for two Dad's oatmeal cookies really gets my goat.

_____

_____

_____

22. At age three I was ready, willing and able to take on the trials and tribulations of nursery school.

_____

_____

_____

23. It's in my blood to get up and go.

_____

_____

24. I get sick and tired of working the bugs out of the system each and every time.

_____

_____

25. Canada is really and truly at a standstill. It's time to get the lead out, and jump-start the economy.

_____

_____

_____

26. If the big cheeses get away with murder on their tax returns, why should the rest of us toe the line?

_____

_____

_____

27. It was just my luck to have roommates who smoked like chimneys.

   _____

   _____

28. Many pets are spoiled rotten.

   _____

   _____

29. Each and every night I burn the midnight oil.

   _____

   _____

30. Canada has become a mere clone of the United States. It's about time for Canadians to stand on their own two feet and start making waves.

   _____

   _____

   _____

Euphemisms

Every Day, in Every Way, We Are Getting Better and Better

When we use one word instead of another, we choose not only meanings but also feelings. Why do we call one person "slim" but another "skinny"? Is it because we like the "slim" one better? The philosopher Bertrand Russell poked fun at our habit of selecting terms to promote our attitudes, when he said **"I am firm; you are stubborn; he is pigheaded."**

Some people view language as an objective system, a kind of Morse Code of words that reveals truth clearly and fairly. But of course language is as human as we are, reflecting all our own feelings and prejudices. The experienced writer knows that the same "facts" can be made to sound good or bad, cheerful or gloomy, plain or fancy, approving or condemning, all depending on what words they are dressed in.

Consider the terms people choose to describe their professional roles. Since we all want to feel worthwhile, a janitor is now a maintenance engineer, a garbage worker is a sanitary engineer, and a barber is a hair stylist. An undertaker, who at the time of Shakespeare was called a "grave digger," later rose in status to become a "mortician" (rhymes with "physician"), and in our own time, as a "funeral director," has risen even further to become an executive. **Terms like these, which make things seem better than they were, are called** *euphemisms.*

Lawnmowing—or Vegetation Management?

Companies naturally hope consumers will feel good about their products and services. Again, euphemisms do the job. When hamburger becomes "Salisbury steak," when lawn mowing becomes "vegetation management," when dangerous pesticides are now only "crop protection materials," when ink is "writing fluid" and pens are "writing instruments," when glasses are "eyewear," when used cars are only "pre-owned" and when hairdressing becomes "hair sculpture"—we spend and companies profit.

Like people, organizations want to be popular, so they choose carefully the words that describe their actions. In our time of cutbacks and layoffs, companies no longer fire people or give them the boot or throw them in the street; now companies only "dehire" us, "uninstall" us, or do us the honour of "selecting us out." In fact, some employers no longer even perform these kindnesses themselves, but hire a "career transition company" to supply "outplacement consultants" who will properly "downsize" and "rationalize" the "human resources" that are "redundant," so that "nonretention" can take place. If the employer is feeling particularly generous, we might even receive a "termination gratuity" as we go out the door.

How to Get Rich While Losing Money

If none of this enhances the company's "productivity" and it is still losing money, we will read in the business section that the company is achieving "negative economic growth" or even earning "negative profits." And of course the government will never raise the company's taxes, but will only require more "revenue enhancement measures."

Speaking of governments, in our polite new times their armies never "attack" or "kill," but only "control," "manage" or even "pacify" (literally "make peaceful") the enemy. And for some time now countries making war have not indulged in propaganda or lies, but only in "disinformation."

For years this desire of individuals and organizations to improve their image through euphemisms has grown. In our time, though, a new and controversial twist has appeared. We all know that words naming groups of people can be loaded, and that reasonable persons have never used the insulting terms for those of other races, cultures or gender. But now word choice has become a political struggle. Groups that have felt marginalized, shut out of economic or social or political power, are now using and demanding language that is *"politically correct."*

The New World of PC, and We Don't Mean Personal Computers

Our language is changing, as a whole new code of "PC" (politically correct) terms has emerged. People who were once "disabled" are now "differently abled." The formerly "deaf" are now "hearing-impaired" and the formerly "blind" are now "visually impaired." While "moron," "imbecile" and "idiot" were once standard ratings of intelligence found in psychology textbooks, people with low academic skills are now "developmentally challenged." And people who were once rape or incest "victims" are now rape or incest "survivors." Those once "dying of" AIDS are now persons "living with" AIDS.

In our cosmopolitan nation, even names of racial and cultural groups are changing. For example, those once called "Indians," then later called "native peoples," are now increasingly called "first nations peoples"—to remind others that they owned this country first.

Persons of good will have always called people what they have wanted to be called. After all, those terms are meant to convey kindness and respect, in a society in which everyone belongs to a minority.

Lately, though, some people have grown uneasy about the whole trend, sensing extremism and even totalitarianism in language. Jokes circulate about formerly "bald" people now being "folically challenged" (follicles being the cells that used to hold the hairs onto their head). And the idea of saying "herstory" for "history" or "animal companion" for "pet" now reminds some people of George Orwell's nightmare novel *1984*, in which a police state literally rewrites the dictionary so that words like "liberty" and "democracy," which once made rebellion thinkable, are now forgotten. Some who object to the new "political correctness" in our own society accuse its proponents of using censorship to tyrannize over others.

Your Choice ...

So who is right? No one can tell you. As an essayist, you can feel good about writing some euphemisms out of kindness to others. Your grandparents may not be "old" but merely "senior citizens." However, there may come a time when you sense you are not writing the truth but stretching it to the breaking point. When that happens, *you must make your own decision—one that is at the same time linguistic and political.*

W O R K S H E E T

Euphemisms

N A M E _____

All the following terms are euphemisms. Circle those you would feel comfortable using in an essay, and in the space explain why. Cross out those you would not use in an essay, and in the space explain why. (Of course there is no set of "correct" answers; this exercise is meant to encourage your own awareness and free choice.)

1. informal housing (for "slums" or "shacks")

2. animal companion (for "pet")

3. between jobs (for "unemployed")

4. big (for "fat")

5. sex worker (for "prostitute")

6. correction (for a "drop" in the stock market)

7. developing nations (for "poor" nations)

8. expectorate (for "spit")

9. eye fashions (for "glasses")

10. account manager (for "stockbroker")

11. golden agers (for "old people")

12.   hearing-impaired (for "deaf")

13.   decruitment (for "being fired")

14.   low-income neighbourhood (for "slum")

15.   negative assets (for "debt")

16.   pass away (for "die")

17.   perspire (for "sweat")

18.   selected out (for "fired")

19.   senior citizens (for "old people")

20.   visually impaired (for "blind")

21.   hearing instrument (for "hearing aid")

22.   starter home (for "small house")

23.   terminate (for "fire" or for "kill")

24.   upscale (for "expensive")

25.   sleeping together (for "having sex")

W O R K S H E E T

Euphemisms and Their Opposite: Words Biased Pro or Con

NAME _____

If euphemisms distort truth by making things look better than they are, negative bias words distort truth by making things look worse than they are. In this exercise practise identifying both extremes, so you can more easily detect and avoid bias in your own writing.

   Here are 20 words that can be used for "underweight." Write each in the column where you think it belongs. Use the dictionary if necessary.

bony, cadaverous, fleshless, gaunt, lanky, lean, raw-boned, scrawny, skeletal, skinny, slender, slight, slim, spare, spindly, svelte, thin, underfed, undernourished, underweight

VERY NEGATIVE	NEGATIVE	NEUTRAL	POSITIVE	VERY POSITIVE

Here are 20 words that can be used for "overweight." Write each in the column where you think it belongs. Again, use the dictionary if necessary.

beefy, big, bulky, burly, chubby, elephantine, fat, fleshy, heavy-set, obese, overweight, paunchy, plump, pudgy, stocky, stout, thick-set, tubby, well-fed, well-padded

VERY NEGATIVE	NEGATIVE	NEUTRAL	POSITIVE	VERY POSITIVE

Jargon

Our society adores technology. Now that we humans have walked on the moon, explored the ocean floor, cooked our meal in five minutes with electronic rays, and walked around with our telephone in our pocket, we find ourselves speaking and writing like the scientists and technicians we admire.

Even in nonscientific areas like the arts, many of us borrow technical or showy words to dress up the message. Those who prefer the direct approach describe such talk as "bafflegab," "technobabble" or "gobbledygook." Its more common name is *jargon.*

Tech Talk ...

Of course technical words have their place. Computer engineers could hardly discuss their work without referring to "megabytes," "motherboards," "macros" and "merge codes." But now the rest of us cannot hold a meeting without "interfacing" through "input" and "output," without "accessing" data within our "parameters," and without "feedback" on how all this will "impact" our "outcomes." A visitor from Mars, hearing us talk, might think that humans, themselves, were machines.

At its extreme, jargon takes on the impenetrable and ugly quality of this example which the linguist Mario Pei found at "a great university":

> The functional methodology shall be based on an inter-disciplinary process model, which employs a lateral feed-back syndrome across a sanction-constituency interface, coupled with a circular-spiral recapitulatory function for variable-flux accommodation and policy modification.*

Do you know what the passage means? Maybe you weren't supposed to. One Toronto executive admits to writing short and plain reports when he has something to say, but long and fancy ones when he does not. On those occasions he seeks not only technical terms but any other intimidating and unclear language, such as "cognizant" for "aware," "impact negatively upon" for "harm," and "in the foreseeable future" for "soon."

The Case of the Yellow Bees

Other times jargon is simply unclear. One journalist interviewing an executive from Nortel Networks kept wondering what the "yellow bees" were that the man kept mentioning. He finally asked. The executive roared with laughter, and explained how he was not talking about "yellow bees" but "LOBs"—which means "lines of business."

FTBOMH :) (From the Bottom of My Heart)

To be honest, though, such expressions do have their place. Like slang terms, they can define an in-group and make its users feel they belong. For example, chat groups on the Web have

*Mario Pei, *Double Speak in America* (New York: Hawthorn Books, Inc., 1973). © 1973 Hawthorn.

developed an elaborate vocabulary of jargon that abbreviates phrases into initials. Some examples:

A/S/L	=	age/sex/location
C&G	=	chuckle and grin
CU	=	see you
FTBOMH	=	from the bottom of my heart
HT	=	hi there
JK	=	just kidding
MTF	=	more to follow
RL	=	real life
TOY	=	thinking of you
YBS	=	you'll be sorry
WTG	=	way to go

For these and many other examples, check the *Chatter's Jargon Dictionary* at <**http://www.steve grossman.com/jarpge.htm**>. Of course, to use in-group terms like these, you have to be communicating with others in the group. So although some jargon may be fun or even meaningful, it is not going to work on your grandmother or your cousin in Italy.

Other jargon can be no fun at all, and in fact has a sinister purpose: it is designed to make a subject appear so important or difficult that the average person will leave it to the experts. In this way institutions such as business and government can hide their true objectives, and professionals such as lawyers and tax accountants can force us to buy their services because, on our own, we cannot understand official documents.

All in the Nuclear Family ...

Some jargon has invaded even our personal lives, as terms from fields such as sociology spread into everyday conversation. We no longer go on dates with girlfriends or boyfriends, but with a "significant other." We no longer have mothers and fathers, but "caregivers," and no longer have sisters and brothers, but "siblings." Then when we, ourselves, join with our significant other to form a "nuclear family," we will no longer raise children but attempt a thing called "parenting," which, if well done, involves a great deal of "dialoguing." At the end of it all, we no longer aim for happiness but for a thing called "self-actualization." We might well ask, now that everyday life has got technologized like everything else, whether it is better than it was.

Say No to Jargon

Self-important language or clunky terminology like these examples may be creeping into our speech, but as essay writers we can reject it. When we actually *need* technical words, let's use them (making sure to define any term the audience may not know). But in non-technical applications, jargon leads to wordiness, clichés and euphemisms. It is often confusing and even dishonest. *Avoid it.*

(See page 15 for the related topic of *audience*, and see page 65 for another related topic, *economy*.)

W O R K S H E E T

Jargon

NAME _____

Here is some widespread jargon. Translate each example into plain, honest English, using the dictionary or thesaurus where necessary.

Example: ~~due to the fact that~~   *because*

1. to access   _____

2. on the back burner   _____

3. significant other   _____

4. the bottom line   _____

5. decision-making process   _____

6. dialoguing   _____

7. discussant   _____

8. feedback   _____

9. guesstimate   _____

10. sibling   _____

11. to impact on   _____

12. input, output   _____

13. all systems go   _____

14. to interface   _____

15. time frame   _____

16. low profile, high profile   _____

17. maximize, finalize, utilize   _____

18. a must   _____

19. parameters   _____

20. parenting   _____

21. at this point in time   _____

22. the principal thrust   _____

23. profitwise (and most other "-wise" words)   _____

24. shortfall   _____

25. outcomes   _____

EDITING FOR APPROPRIATE LANGUAGE

As we we'll see in the next section, "Editing for Complete Sentences," people tend to write as they speak. If you grew up hearing people say "can't hardly" or "real good," you probably say these expressions yourself—and if you say them, you may also write them.

The problem is not that "can't hardly" or "real good" are not as clear as the "Queen's English," but just that they are not found in the work of experienced writers. Since we don't see these expressions in carefully produced books, magazines and newspapers (except in dialogue to represent people talking), they seem inappropriate for important writing tasks.

Though such expressions will always work in conversation with people who are used to hearing them, we also need to **write in language appropriate for our readers.** This means that in essays, reports and business letters, we use the same "standard" English that other writers use.

Appropriate language in writing also means avoiding the slang that seems so natural when you speak. Napoleon's invasion of Russia may have been a failure, but in your history essay he did not make a "boo-boo," get "put down" or get "trashed."

Though no linguist would call standard English "better" than nonstandard, everyone knows how important a tool it is for success of the individual in society. The main thing is to be practical. Look over the material that follows, to be sure that when you write you are using the standard and appropriate language that gives people the right signals.

Better yet for the long term, cultivate the reading habit, to avoid the trap of writing the way you speak. The more "standard English" you run through your head in the form of other peoples' writing, the more easily and surely you produce your own. (See page 212 for suggested reading matter.)

Finally, as with other editing, revise for appropriate language *after* you have the content of your essay safely down on paper.

Standard and Nonstandard English

"Standard" English is what you usually read in a book or magazine, and what well-read persons normally say in conversation. Though "nonstandard" expressions such as "hadn't ought" or "I seen" may be accepted or even expected by many people in conversation, depending on their background, almost all readers—and above all, teachers—view such usages in an essay, report or formal letter simply as errors.

Common sense tells us that, although nonstandard English may be as appropriate in some situations as standard English is in others, if we wish our academic writing to succeed, we need to use the standard code of expressions that readers expect. In the list that follows, identify any nonstandard expressions you use in writing, and instead use the "standard" equivalents.

NONSTANDARD	STANDARD
ain't	is not, am not, etc.
alot	a lot
anyways, anywheres, somewheres	anyway, anywhere, somewhere
can't hardly	can hardly
could of, might of, must of, should of, would of	could have, might have, must have, should have, would have
different than	different from
disinterested (meaning "not interested")	uninterested ("disinterested" means fair or impartial)
enormity (meaning "hugeness")	enormousness (an "enormity" is a terrible wrongdoing)
enthused	enthusiastic
hadn't ought	should not, ought not
in regards to	in regard to
irregardless	regardless
_____ is when	_____ is
a long ways	a long way
most all	most, almost all
the reason is because	the reason is that
real good	very good
I seen, they seen	I saw, they saw
this here	this
try and	try to
where you are at	where you are
youse	you, all of you

Slang and Colloquialisms

When's the last time you *went postal*? Was it when you were fired by a *chainsaw consultant*, so you had to leave your desk in the *cube farm*? Slang, with its colourful expressions, is fun. So are the somewhat less racy words and expressions called **colloquialisms**— that is, very conversational language. These ways of speaking make us feel like part of the group, giving the sensation of being with it and being cool. Slang and colloquialisms may even be stronger than other language, because they are so concise and vivid. So why do teachers say not to use them in your essays? Are they just stopping your fun? Well, see how much fun it is to read this:

> Well, I was so stiff I nearly turkeyed off from the line, but I decided to wait. I pulled out from the line at 4 a.m. and hailed a limber on the road. Fritz landed a daisycutter and the transport driver done his block and took his hook. He absolutely dropped his bundle, and, to make matters worse, I had started off with a duck's breakfast, but I saw a cook-house and decided to give it a pop for a binder.*

Having trouble? Going postal? The problem may be the fact that you are not from New Zealand, and that you did not fight in World War I—because this passage is filled with the slang of New Zealanders who did fight that war. Living now and in Canada, how could you know these terms? You've just seen three problems with slang: it is often restricted to a certain time, restricted to a certain place, and restricted to a certain group.

Your own slang will be equally remote to people of a different age, geographical area or group. The conclusion is obvious: avoid most slang when writing for the general reader. This means, for example, in essays.

*A. E. Strong of Auckland, New Zealand, quoted by Eric Partridge, *Slang To-day and Yesterday*, 4th ed. (London: Routledge and Kegan Paul Ltd., 1970), p. 287.

Let's Buy a Really Bad Car ...

Another problem is that slang words are slippery. For example what, exactly, does "bad" mean these days, as in a "bad" car? Would you want to avoid this one or buy it? Would your grandfather want to avoid it or buy it?

Other slang terms, such as "goon" and "pig," are so loaded that they convey a bias unworthy of serious

"**Don't make any erratic movements, Miss Halloway. . . . Not only is the truculent nature of this species amply documented, but, as you can discern for yourself, the little suckers can really jump.**"

writing, which should be fair and objective. What is just as bad, many slang terms are clichés that replace original thought by rushing automatically to mind. It was fun to hear "couch potato" the first 500 times, but now it's getting a little old.

If Hubby Doesn't Toe the Line ...

Colloquial language is not quite as vivid as slang, and not as restrictive, but is still too chatty for essays, reports and business letters. It is the breezy language of conversation, of sports reporting, of disk jockeys and of the lovelorn columns ("If hubby doesn't toe the line for a sweetie like you, he's the dumbest jerk around"). You hardly want to sound like this, or like someone telling jokes in a bar, when you are analyzing a novel by Michael Ondaatje or assessing the future of Canada without Quebec. Instead, *choose language appropriate to the situation.*

Finally, putting quotation marks around slang and colloquial expressions does not so much tame them for serious writing as merely call attention to them. Avoid examples like this:

> I believe that our police force is not just a "dinky" one.

A few of the slang and colloquial terms that follow have stayed current for many years; others are long out of date but still used by people who wear haircuts from the 1950s; still others will become dated by the time you see them here. So think of these lists as only a demonstration of what extremely informal language is like, so you can detect other examples when you write them. The division between slang and colloquialisms is, of course, not exact, because even dictionaries disagree as to the status of expressions.

SLANG	COLLOQUIALISMS
bad (amazing)	blab
booze can	brainer
cheesy	chill out
mouse potato	cool
ego trip	cop
geek	to eyeball
dough (money)	hangup
head honcho	heavy
humongous	hick
nerd	kind of, sort of
pig (police officer)	loser
psyched	nitty gritty
rad	not!
to rip off	OK or okay
stoked	pal
to trash	slob
turkey (person)	snow job
wasted	street smart
wicked (amazing)	surf the Web
wimp	wheels (car)
wired	thug
Xer	veg out

W O R K S H E E T

Slang and Colloquialisms

N A M E _____

Cross out the slang and colloquial language in the passages that follow, and replace it with more objective terms appropriate to an essay, report or business letter. If a passage is already free of slang or colloquialisms, write "Appropriate" after it.

bother

Example: Mosquitoes, ants and black flies really b~~ug~~ me.

1. In English class there's this one guy that has a mouth like a hippo, but he's an okay person.

2. When a computer makes a boo-boo it's usually a biggie.

3. People were eating up the grunge trend, big time. That goes to show that as long as a popular musician sports something new, people will die for it. Whether it be good-looking or ugly doesn't matter. It is the new trend on the block and that is all that matters. If you're not down with the latest trend, you're simply not hip.

4. Yesterday in history we yakked for a whole hour about Hitler and his hangups.

5. Pressure drives students bananas.

6. Stopping at the traffic light, I noticed a black-and-white pig machine beside me.

7. I used to get tons of jobs babysitting around the neighbourhood.

8. I am a diehard Leaf fan, even when my team is smoked to the tune of 10–1.

9. To verify your account, you must go to the computer lab at W73 in Kerr Hall. There a computer dude will make sure you actually have an account and that it functions properly.

10. Max Beerbohm is not a serious writer.

11. Some people think gambling is an alright thing to do, but it turns me right off.

12. Saccharin, which was the most widely used artificial sweetener, was shot to pieces after a study showed toxicity in rats.

13. I'm really into the outdoors.

14. When I was in grade school, having the most friends and belonging to the coolest group was where I was at.

15. Mr. Ebert is a really cool old man to talk to if you're into stuff like war stories.

16. Sending a document by express mail costs at least twenty bucks. Sending it by snail mail is cheaper.

17. At a party, I feel separated from other people because they begin to feel "high" while I am still "straight."

18. Don't gripe and beef, just get with it.

19. In a game between Toronto and Philadelphia a few years ago, a Leaf player was sent to the penalty box for fighting. The fans at Philadelphia went "nuts." They tried to get at the Leaf player while he was in the "cooler." They threw beer cans, shoes and eggs at him. They even tried to break the protective glass around the "cooler" so they could get hold of the poor Leaf player. Finally the cops were called to escort the helpless guy to his dressing room and safety from the mild-mannered hockey fans.

20. For students new to the e-mail scene, there are a couple of things to follow so you can surf the Net.

21. Usually when one of my friends calls to shoot the breeze, I'm up to my eyeballs in homework.

22. Nuclear plants scare the hell out of me.

23. Almost anyone can get married.

24. Well, I took care of the first guy that hassled me, but the other two I couldn't handle.

25. Many people who play electronic games don't know what's going on. How many times have you watched people playing a game shout "All right!" when really they got blown away?

26. By 7 a.m. I was busting my butt down the dirty rows of the tobacco field.

27. My grandma is just shy of 70, but every morning she treks on out to work.

28. To change your image, you must trash part of your existing wardrobe.

29. Had Darcy not hurt Elizabeth's pride, they could have got it on a lot sooner, but then Jane Austen wouldn't have had anything to write about.

30. My brother-in-law, who lives in Montreal, must get up at five to make it to work by seven-thirty. That poor fellow! What does he do for the two hours it takes him to commute to work? He sits on his bum, on the subway or bus.

EDITING FOR COMPLETE SENTENCES

Sometimes people talk like this:

"Hi. How's goin'?"

"Good. You?"

"*Killer* math test. What a week!"

"Yeah. Goin' out tonight?"

"No, gotta work."

"Too bad."

"What *you* doing?"

"Don't know yet. No money. Hey, got some?"

"A little."

"Lend me ten?"

"Uh. ..."

Seeing a conversation like this on the page, we recognize its fragmentary nature: many words are *left out*. But is there any doubt that our two speakers understand each other?

Their words are only one part—maybe the smallest part—of their real communication. As any actor learning a script will know, those words are heightened by ups and downs of the voice, by posture, gesture and other body language, and by facial expressions so obvious that a small child could "read" them. And if either person does fail to catch something, a quick "What?" will clear things up. The reason, of course, is that *the speakers are in the same place.*

When they go home to write their essay for English or history or economics, though, they will enter a totally different situation. If they write as they speak, they may produce "sentences" like these found in student essays:

A love affair that was doomed.

New highways leading to smaller cities.

Although his children encouraged him to retire.

Medicine and law, two rewarding fields.

The reader of these partial statements will hear no voice, see no gesture, ask no question. All he or she will have are these symbols on the page—and in their incomplete form these symbols are not enough to make the message clear.

No wonder, then, that readers expect complete sentences. This tradition is so strong—at least in serious

explanatory writing such as essays, reports and formal letters—that an incomplete sentence (or ***sentence fragment***) is usually perceived as a serious error. Here and there we may accept a *fragment* that is deliberately placed for emphasis. But probably the most important step in editing errors out of a manuscript is to revise all accidental fragments into complete sentences.

A word about technical terms: Although overuse of technical terms can be an abuse of language, some terms really are needed. Just as computer users need to say "gigabyte" or "docking station" or "floppy disk" or "active matrix display" to talk about their subject, we will need a few terms to talk about ours. You probably know the main ones already. Learn the rest as you study this section, because you'll need them in later sections.

Words are only part—maybe the smallest part—of communication face to face.

PHOTO REPRINTED WITH PERMISSION OF SUZANNE CONRAD.

The essential parts of a complete sentence are one SUBJECT and one VERB. The subject is what the sentence is about, and the verb tells us what the subject does or is.

SUBJECT	VERB
Cars	pollute.
Snow	fell.
Roger	sleeps.
Jane	studies.
They	danced.
We	won.
Honesty	pays.
Time	flies.

The Subject

The SUBJECT is a noun or pronoun. A NOUN is a person, place or thing, while a PRONOUN is a word such as "she" or "they" which substitutes for the noun. A sentence with a pronoun as the subject can be "complete" even if we don't know what the pronoun refers to:

They danced.

Of course if nearby sentences don't show us what is going on by revealing who "they" are, then another problem occurs: faulty pronoun reference (see pages 149 to 150).

Some subjects, such as "honesty" and "time" in our examples, do not have a physical form. Yet these abstract nouns are "things," because they do exist and we can state what they do:

Honesty pays.

Time flies.

The Verb

The VERB is usually described as an action word, such as "danced" and "flies" in our list of examples. But even in our other sentence "Roger sleeps," where there is no obvious action, the verb still tells what the subject *does*. Other verbs, such as "is," "am" and "are," tell not what the subject *does* but what it *is*:

Canada *is* the second-largest country in the world.

I *am* a Nova Scotian.

Women and men *are* equal in law.

In statements like these, words of explanation are added to the verb. The verb plus all the words that complete its meaning are together called the *predicate*. We could enlarge our definition of the sentence, then, by saying that **a complete sentence has a subject and a predicate.** Yet that predicate means nothing without its key part, the verb:

Canada the second-largest country in the world.

I a Nova Scotian.

Women and men equal in law.

Some verbs are made of more than one word. Instead of saying "We *won*," we could say "We *have won*." Or we could substitute any of the following and many more:

had won	may win
had been winning	might win
were winning	might have won
could win	might be winning
could have won	might have been winning
did win	would win
have been winning	shall win
are winning	will win
do win	will have won
can win	will have been winning

Each of these, like a one-word verb, can be called a complete verb, and in the sentence each functions like a one-word verb.

Directions and commands are exceptions to the normal sentence pattern, since often they have only a verb. The unwritten subject is "understood":

Stop! (*You* stop!)

Begin. (*You* begin.)

Drive carefully. (*You* drive carefully.)

W O R K S H E E T

Completing Sentences

NAME _____

Try this short exercise, designed to show how natural and easy it is to provide the noun and verb. In this first part, add a NOUN or PRONOUN to form a subject and thus complete the sentence. Circle the verb.

1. A hungry _____ ate my lunch.

2. A large _____ ran down our street.

3. My _____ always chases cars.

4. Seven _____ escaped from the penitentiary.

5. _____ are really expensive.

6. An old _____ slept on the park bench.

7. _____ hopes to be the next prime minister.

8. A _____ attacked the swimmer.

9. _____ is the best film I have ever seen.

10. A large _____ climbed the tree.

In this second part, add a VERB to complete the sentence. Circle the subject.

1. My car _____ when it is out of gas.

2. The team always _____ before the game.

3. Seven witnesses _____ the accident.

4. Money _____ the root of all evil.

5. My uncle and aunt _____ their money in Las Vegas.

6. The rain _____ in torrents.

7. After the film we _____ at a restaurant.

8. The riot police _____ the demonstrators.

9. The guitar _____ my favourite musical instrument.

10. After the game the fans _____ the referee.

Variations on the Sentence

Reverse Sentence Order

The subject usually comes before the verb, a pattern that helps us identify both. Do not be confused, though, by the occasional sentence that puts the verb before the subject:

> V S
> At last *came spring.*

> V   S
> In the car *were* five *gangsters.*

Remember that the *subject* is what the sentence is about, while the *verb* tells what the subject does or is. Just think of the sentence in normal word order, to make sure it has both a subject and a verb:

> S V
> *Spring came* at last.

> S   V
> Five *gangsters were* in the car.

Compound Subjects and Verbs

A sentence may have two or more subjects:

> S   S
> *Summer* and *fall* are Quebec's best seasons.

A sentence may also have two or more verbs:

> V   V
> Spring *comes* late and *is* short.

A sentence may have two or more subjects and two or more verbs:

> S   S V   V
> *May* and *June are* beautiful but *go* too fast.

Do not make fragments by separating the parts of a compound subject or verb:

> SENTENCE   FRAGMENT
>
> May and June are beautiful. But go too fast.

Longer Sentences

To discuss sentences longer than our example so far, we need more concepts:

A. A PHRASE is a word group that does not contain both a subject and a complete verb. Alone, it is a fragment:

> waiting for spring
>
> night and day
>
> after the robbery

To make sense, these must be added to a complete sentence:

>   S   V
> Waiting for spring, *Jane studied* night and day.

>   S   V
> *The gangsters escaped* after the robbery.

These phrases now do a job, giving more detail to explain the core sentence.

B. A CLAUSE is a word group that has both a complete verb and its subject:

- An *independent clause* can stand alone as a sentence:

  > Spring arrived.
  >
  > Jane studied.
  >
  > The gangsters escaped.

- A *dependent clause* cannot stand alone as a sentence. By itself it is a *fragment*:

  > though spring arrived
  >
  > while Jane studied
  >
  > when gangsters escape

  (See pages 107–109 for a fuller explanation of dependent clauses.)

C. Longer sentences, then, can be made of several combinations:

- A *compound sentence* has two or more independent clauses, usually joined by words such as "and" or "but":

S   V   S   V
Spring arrived and *summer followed.*

S   V   S   V
Jane studied but *Roger slept.*

S   V   S   V
The police came but *the gangsters escaped.*

- A *complex sentence* has at least one independent clause and at least one dependent clause:

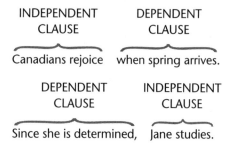

INDEPENDENT   DEPENDENT
CLAUSE   CLAUSE

Canadians rejoice   when spring arrives.

DEPENDENT   INDEPENDENT
CLAUSE   CLAUSE

Since she is determined, Jane studies.

- A *compound-complex* sentence has two or more independent clauses and at least one dependent clause:

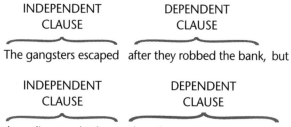

INDEPENDENT   DEPENDENT
CLAUSE   CLAUSE

The gangsters escaped after they robbed the bank, but

INDEPENDENT   DEPENDENT
CLAUSE   CLAUSE

the police caught them when they were at the next bank.

In any combination of clauses, *phrases* such as "at noon" or "in the car" may be added to help explain the clauses.

> In summary, it is mainly these patterns that give sentences length and variety, and that enable them to explain things in depth. Remember, though, that any combination of word groups, to be a complete sentence, must have at least one independent clause. As we said at the beginning, it will have *a subject and a verb.*

Causes of Sentence Fragments

Now that we have examined the basic parts of the sentence, let's look at the most common ways in which those parts are omitted or are prevented from doing their work.

A. Fragments can lack a subject or verb, or both, because of plain old *carelessness:*

> Am a Blue Jays fan. (no subject)
>
> I a Blue Jays fan. (no verb)

Such errors are usually caused by hurry or by fatigue, and can be caught more easily later as you edit. If you make fragments this way, be especially careful in your editing and proofreading. When you are checking, *don't let your eyes glide along the lines. Make them stop at every word,* because when you read fast your mind will supply words that your eyes do not see. *Try isolating sentences from each other by checking the final sentence first, then the second-to-last, and so on from back to front. And try reading aloud, so your ears can help your eyes.*

The correction for careless fragments, then, is of course to supply the missing word(s):

> S V
> *I am* a Blue Jays fan.

B. Fragments can occur *when writing is confused with speech.* As we saw in the little dialogue that opens this section, fragments may be fine in speech but are troublesome errors in writing. If you listen too much to that inner voice in your head, you will end up writing as you speak. The result will be fragments like these:

> Maybe.
>
> One more point.
>
> No way.

Do not rely on speech, then, as your model for writing. Instead, take other peoples' writing as your model. This means turning the TV off and reaching often for a newspaper, magazine or book. (See page 212 for a suggested list of good books.)

C. Other fragments result from a deeper cause: *unfamiliarity* with sentence structure. Most people with this problem have not read enough to have control of their own writing. Again, the solution is reading. Over the long term, one of the best investments you can make in your future is to read regularly—an hour or two a day outside of studies. However, if you are only now beginning the reading habit, then the short-term solution is to study and apply the points that follow.

Fragments: More Causes and Solutions

Participles, Gerunds and Infinitives

Some words *look* like verbs but are not. Used as verbs, they produce fragments. **A PRESENT PARTICIPLE is a verb form ending in -*ing*:**

Roger *sleeping.*

This fragment does not state anything clearly because it lacks a real verb. (Though "sleeping" is a kind of verb, note how it does not tell us when the action occurs. In English, all complete verbs specify a *tense*— that is, a time period—whether past, present or future.) Now let's try some verbs that do this:

Roger *is* sleeping.
Roger *was* sleeping.
Roger *has been* sleeping.
Roger *could have been* sleeping.

Do not confuse present participles with gerunds. A **GERUND looks like a present participle but is used as a noun.** It can be the subject of a sentence:

    S   V
Sleeping is Roger's hobby.

An INFINITIVE is the word "to" plus a verb:

Roger *to sleep.*

This confusing little statement is a fragment, because the subject, Roger, lacks a real verb. Let's try some:

Roger *wants* to sleep.

Roger *has* to sleep.
Roger *decided* to sleep.

Now the infinitive *to sleep* is part of a complete verb (*wants to sleep*) that completes its sentence.

Fragments caused by infinitives occur most often in lists like this one:

This essay has three purposes. To describe the computer in its earliest forms. To explain the functions of a modern computer. And to show how mass production has lowered the price of this extraordinary machine.

Let's punctuate the list as one sentence so that the subject and verb, *essay has,* make all that follows complete:

This *essay has* three purposes: to describe the computer in its earliest forms, to explain the functions of a modern computer, and to show how mass production has lowered the price of this extraordinary machine.

Note that although an infinitive cannot be a complete verb, it can be the subject of a sentence:

  S   V
To sleep is Roger's wish.

Relative Pronouns

Relative pronouns (*who, whose, whom, which, that*) can be a problem. As the name suggests, a **RELATIVE PRONOUN** *relates* word groups to each other:

INDEPENDENT CLAUSE	DEPENDENT CLAUSE
Some people drive too fast,	*which* causes accidents.

Make sure, then, that you do not break the *relationship* by putting a period before the relative pronoun:

INDEPENDENT CLAUSE	FRAGMENT
Some people drive too much.	*Which* causes accidents.

The resulting fragment is corrected, of course, by removing the period and restoring the comma. Like this one, most fragments involving a relative pronoun are corrected by being joined to the previous sentence.

Sometimes, though, a relative pronoun does not belong in its sentence at all:

FRAGMENT

Surprisingly, with education becoming so popular *that* a university degree is no longer enough to guarantee a job.

Getting a good night's sleep is the best way to avoid errors like this. If you discover such a fragment, remove the relative pronoun:

SENTENCE

Surprisingly, with education becoming so popular, a university

S   V

degree is no longer enough to guarantee a job.

Subordinators

Certain words can change a sentence to a fragment. **Put before a subject and verb, these words will SUBORDINATE, or make less important, what follows. We can therefore call these words** *subordinators*. They produce the *dependent clauses* which, as we said on page 105, cannot stand alone as sentences. There are several kinds of subordinators:

■ *Words of time relationship: as, after, as long as, before, till, until, when, whenever, while*

■ *Words of logical relationship: although, as if, as though, because, even though, except that, if, in order that, since, so that, though, unless, whereas, whether, why*

■ *The words "where" and "wherever"*

The examples in the following table show how these words can instantly subordinate sentences into fragments.

SENTENCE	FRAGMENT
The sun rose.	*While* the sun rose
We ate breakfast.	*As* we ate breakfast
We packed the canoe.	*After* we packed the canoe
We pushed off from shore.	*When* we pushed off from shore
The river was high.	*Even though* the river was high
We entered the rapids.	*When* we entered the rapids
The canoe hit a rock.	*Where* the canoe hit a rock
The canoe tipped over.	*So that* the canoe tipped over
We swam.	*After* we swam
We could grab a log.	*Until* we could grab a log
It was fastened to the shore.	*Because* it was fastened to the shore
We dried out.	*As* we dried out
We discussed next summer's mountain-climbing trip.	*While* we discussed next summer's mountain-climbing trip

The sentences on the left make sense, because they are self-contained. The fragments on the right do not make sense, though, because their subordinators tell us to expect more. (Read the fragments aloud to feel their lack of meaning.) What should we do, then, to correct the fragments? Let's look at two alternatives:

■ *Remove the subordinator.* This simple method gives us what we began with, the complete sentences on the left. Our fragments are now corrected. But have you noticed how short these sentences are, and how choppy they would sound together? Read them aloud: the story will make you think of your grade one reader.

Removing a subordinator, then, can correct a fragment here and there, but usually there is a better way:

■ *Combine fragments with sentences.* You've no doubt noticed how some of the examples belong together logically: one explains another or follows another in time. Subordinators are *signals* that point out these relationships. As you proofread a paper, realize that *a fragment beginning with a subordinator will almost always belong to either the sentence before or the one after it.* Join the two, in most cases just by changing a period to a comma and the following capital to a small letter. This gives us a *complex sentence*, whose pattern we discussed on page 106: an independent clause with a dependent clause. Let's try the pattern, taking a sentence and a dependent clause (fragment) from our list:

| | DEPENDENT |
| S V | CLAUSE |

The sun rose   *as* we ate breakfast.

| | DEPENDENT |
| S V | CLAUSE |

We ate breakfast   *as* the sun rose.

| DEPENDENT | |
| CLAUSE | S V |

As the sun rose,   we ate breakfast.

| DEPENDENT | |
| CLAUSE | S V |

As we ate breakfast,   the sun rose.

Finally, here is a point that confuses some people: are these last two examples fragments because the subordinator comes before everything else? They sound complete. And they are, because a subordinator affects only the words to which its meaning applies:

SUBORDINATED   S V

As the sun rose,   we ate breakfast.

SUBORDINATED   S V

As we ate breakfast,   the sun rose.

Note that the subordination usually ends at a comma, after which a subject and verb complete the sentence.

> Since we can usually correct a fragment by joining it to a neighbouring sentence, *we could describe most fragments as punctuation errors: periods in the wrong places.* Don't take this idea to extremes, though, by simply avoiding periods for fear of making fragments. (The next section will show the bad effects of using *too few* periods.)

Now let's look at a new version of the whole list:

> We ate breakfast *while* the sun rose. *After* we packed the canoe, we pushed off from shore. The river was high. *When* we entered the rapids, the canoe hit a rock and tipped over. We swam *until* we could grab a log fastened to the shore. *As* we dried out, we discussed next summer's mountain-climbing trip.

The story is now correct and reasonably clear. It might do for a diary or postcard, but we can hardly call it a work of art. To become a developed piece of writing it needs all the expansion, focus and purpose discussed in the opening chapters of this book. And if it is to please us with its style, it will then need the kind of extensive editing discussed in the rest of this chapter.

"Correctness" alone is certainly not enough. Our readers do require it, but if the larger purposes of writing are not met, no degree of correctness will convey our message. Getting rid of errors is essential, but is only one part of the writing process.

DIAGNOSTIC

Complete Sentences

NAME _____

Write "F" in the blank beside each passage that contains a fragment. In sentences already complete, underline the subject and circle the verb. After your answers have been checked, your instructor may ask you to correct the fragments.

1. Although the climate in Japan is calm and beautiful. _____

2. I was among strangers. Strangers who all knew where they were going except me. _____

3. For example, blood cancer. _____

4. A study shows that children under five watch an average of 23.5 hours of TV a week. _____

5. When bringing groceries from a car into a house is a very easy task. _____

6. Who are the homeless? They are people just like you and me. All with similar needs and desires. _____

7. Murder is everywhere. The latest victim being a transit attendant burned to death by some teenagers. _____

8. Spider webs on the ceiling, ripped wallpaper, dirty ashtrays and old carpets that spew dust when a person steps on them. _____

9. All my roommates give me a hard time about the amount of television I watch. The big joke around our place is that I am the human TV guide. A title I am not proud of. _____

10. Ignoring my injured leg, I continued to practise. _____

11. Moving out on my own enabled me to be free. Free from being a prisoner in my parents' house. _____

12. By owning a computer gives you an edge in the world. _____

13. Although I cannot imagine my life without my family. _____

14. I used to work for the Toronto Board of Education during summer school as a teacher assistant. Because I speak Chinese, which made my job easier and better. _____

15. Running up the escalator to save those extra seconds, so I could catch the next train. _____

16. AIDS is essentially a disease of the immune system. Because it destroys the very mechanisms that we rely on for protection. _____

17. The basic sports fan who sits in front of the television set, with eyes glued to the tube, moving only when necessary to grab a can of beer.   _____

18. I knew that at some moment I would have to confront my doctor about the swelling and the pain in the lower left side of my back.   _____

19. There was also the night life for those over 21. Which I can always look forward to experiencing, since I was only 15 during my visit to the city.   _____

20. By not depending on a man for my financial welfare meant that I had to decide how I was going to look after myself.   _____

21. Ever since I can remember I have had a sweet tooth. From fruit-flavoured gum drops, to milk chocolate candy bars. I loved it all!   _____

22. Winter is a time when the trees are bare and people wear heavy coats to keep warm.   _____

23. A telephone call takes only about five minutes. Whereas it may take weeks for somebody who's busy to get around to writing back.   _____

24. I am convinced that the majority of teachers are like prophets. For example my English teacher, who taught me to love the language when I was in grade three.   _____

25. After changing into work clothes, which consist of long johns, two pairs of work socks, a heavy sweater, overalls, a safety belt, a hard hat and safety shoes.   _____

26. Educating new drivers is more important than fining them, because after an accident everything is too late.   _____

27. To avoid robbery, it is wise not to wear too many valuables such as jewellery. Especially when you are in New York City.   _____

28. Petroleum refineries produce two major things that we need to survive. Fuel and plastics.   _____

29. Shaking nervously as he smokes his cigarette at the gaming table. Waiting for the roulette wheel to stop on his number, because he had put all the money he had on that number.   _____

30. Crowds of people everywhere in the streets, in the subway and restaurants. The frenzy of people rushing around racing to get to their destination.   _____

31. If teenagers don't have strong guidance from their parents, they will follow their peers to seek life on the streets: a life full of excitement and danger.   _____

32. The feeling you get when you find that one little restaurant or store with the perfect atmosphere, food and service. The one you just happened to stumble across by accident. It feels like your own little treasure, a place that nobody else knows about.   _____

33. As I focus the picture in my mind, imagining myself behind a huge office desk, at the helm of a huge company, slouched into a lazyboy office chair, looking out the window from the 51st floor of my newly acquired company office tower.   _____

34. Different types of computers such as laptops (the ability to type at any location at any time), mainframe (used by large companies and organizations in which many people need access to the company's files), and the supercomputer (used to solve complex mathematical problems and to analyze seismic data for oil companies). _____

35. On holiday mornings in Jamaica some families go shopping while others cook an elaborate breakfast. For instance, ackee and salt cod or calaloo with salt fish, fried dumplings, fried plantains and cocoa. _____

W O R K S H E E T

Complete Sentences, Level 1

NAME _____

Underline the complete sentences. Correct all the fragments, adding or changing words or punctuation where necessary.

I saw garbage

Example: ~~Garbage~~ in the streets.

1.   The family all around the table.

2.   To work my way to the top.

3.   My mother, a 51-year-old woman who looks 35.

4.   There are three major types of students. The perfectionists, the naturalists and the procrastinators.

5.   People pushing each other to get by.

6.   I heard screams of fear as the roller coaster unleashed its power.

7.   Tourism being the number one employer in Canada and the world.

8.   When people are drunk they do things that normally they would not. For instance, race cars.

9.   In the rain forest many species of mammals, reptiles, insects, birds and fish.

10.   By reducing the amount of time watching television.

11.   Looking out my window, up at the bright twinkling stars.

12.   Because the stores open on Sunday.

13. "Beautiful British Columbia," according to the licence plates.

14. Women or men who are qualified to work at a certain job.

15. Deep black smoke poured from the house across the street.

16. My father, a professional worrier.

17. On a bright winter's day, warmth and sunshine coming through our windows.

18. Since many physicians have concluded that high-fibre foods can protect people against many diseases such as cancer and cardiovascular disease.

19. Cars speed down the street, with horns honking and people yelling out their windows.

20. Vancouver is experiencing an employment crisis. Which leaves many people on the streets. Lining up at food banks.

21. Two years ago I found out I was going to attend university at Ryerson. In Toronto. A big city. I am from Peterborough. A smaller city that is surrounded by farming country.

22. Sports fans, a group of people screaming and yelling when a goal is scored or a penalty is called.

23. I moved out on my own because I wanted to be independent. For example, cook my own food, wash my own clothes and pay my own bills.

24. If you peeped in Carol's bedroom you would be shocked. Clothes everywhere, shoes, books, papers everywhere, an unmade bed, a terrible sight.

25. Vietnam is a country that has all kinds of fresh fruit. For example bananas, coconuts, mangos, oranges and pineapples.

WORKSHEET

Complete Sentences, Level 2

NAME _____

Underline all the complete sentences. Correct all the fragments, adding or changing words or punctuation where necessary.

1. Warning: after spending hours of surfing the information highway in cyberspace. You may have a huge appetite for food.

2. On April 27, 2000, seemed to start like any other day.

3. When I think of Montreal, I always picture St-Denis Street. Especially between Ste-Catherine and Ontario. That was my favourite place. A very French district of Montreal. Where you can smell the odour of strong coffee and the famous Gitanes cigarettes.

4. Ah, cruising down the Don Valley Parkway in a silver 2000 Honda Civic Special Edition coupe.

5. One objective of the course is to solve three-dimensional problems through descriptive geometry. Finding the true size of a plane, piercing points of two triangles or the distance between a point and a plane in space.

6. The pushing and shoving of people trying to get on the subway, packing one another into a boxcar like a herd of cattle going into the city.

7. For people who have never been in an abusive situation, it is not a pleasant experience to scream in silence. A silence so deafening, so all-consuming, that the victims continue to be battered because they are certain their cries for help will never be heard.

8. Oh yes, the plate of cookies and glass of milk that the children leave out for Santa Claus when he comes on Christmas Eve to bring goodies to fill the stockings and give the presents that he's read about in the letters.

9. Hearing the sound of jet fighter engines in the sky, looking up and seeing the fighters diving to bombard you. A few seconds later when the smoke and dust settle down, nothing but blood and dead bodies everywhere.

10. I cannot speak of Toronto without mentioning Yonge Street. The longest street in the world. Much action goes on there at night. Especially between Bloor and College. Squeegee kids, prostitutes, drunks, people shopping, others working. A very typical scene on Yonge Street.

11. When the doctors finished with my back, they took me to the x-ray department. There they threw me on the table like a sack of potatoes.

12. Horror movies have spine-chilling gruesome scenes involving extraterrestrial beings. Movies such as *Aliens*, starring Sigourney Weaver, and *Nightmare on Elm Street*, starring Robert Englund.

13. People all around splashing in the water, tanning their bodies on the beach, and couples walking hand in hand along the shore.

14. The ways in which computers have helped us are unlimited. From providing luxuries in communication like voice mail, e-mail, etc., to luxuries in typing like spell check, the thesaurus, grammar check, etc.

15. When I moved to Brooklyn, the first thing I noticed was the rudeness of the people. Individuals would shove their way through crowds without even one "excuse me." People pushing their way onto the subway with no respect for one another.

16. After a while I realized that teenagers here in Canada express their emotions freely. Not like in the culture I grew up with, where emotion is suppressed.

17. Every kind of person was downtown that night: punkers with pink and green Mohawk haircuts, leather fanatics, and men singing songs about dreams that would never come true.

18. As I walked down the street peering in the windows at electronic equipment and fashionable clothing, thinking how nice everything looked, wishing I could have it all.

19. There was a rush of people through the streets. Each one on the way to somewhere or anywhere. Some in business suits and others in everyday clothes. It is fun to imagine the destination of each person.

20. The entertainment section of the Internet features many art galleries that I can view throughout different parts of the world. For example, installations of sculptures, paintings and photographs.

Complete Sentences, Level 3

NAME _____

Underline all complete sentences below. Then correct all the fragments, adding or changing words or punctuation where necessary.

1. Musicals with bright lights and fancy costumes, filled with romance and energy. Actors and dancers doing what they love most: performing. Dance centres on Broadway taught by great people of the dance world. The dreams of my future coming almost within my grasp.

2. A friend of mine who was eating at the school cafeteria for one year, and in that time he gained 50 pounds.

3. After the World Cup soccer matches were finished, the tennis tournament of the American Open came. In fact, I slept only about 20 hours the whole week. No more homework, housework, shopping, meal schedule or other things on my mind. Only the matches, the scores and the players.

4. Irate clients wanting their cheques cashed, unsatisfied customers requesting closure of their accounts, couriers picking up banking statements for companies. Just another uneventful day at the bank.

5. The richness of the city's exciting past when celebrities were actually seen and admired by the public of New York. Proof of it on the walls of every restaurant in the framed black-and-white photos. Famous people like James Dean and Marilyn Monroe.

6. Before us was a 15-foot hydraulic rapid waiting to consume our raft. Everyone paddled wildly, then, pow, we hit, and hundreds of gallons of water rushed over my body. Crushing my chest against the front of the raft, my head bouncing around as if it were in a washing machine.

7. Sooner or later almost everybody buys a car. A choice that is difficult to make. An investment that loses money, because the value of the car decreases day by day. A decision that leads to environmental tragedy as well.

8. I believe adoption is good because it has double aims. First, for parents who are unable to have children can fulfill their desire and have families. Second, for children without parents can have a family and warm feelings in a good home.

9. As you walk down Princess Avenue, the main street of downtown Kingston, you discover the street is full of specialty shops. Army surplus, mountain equipment, art galleries, athletic stores, computer shops all packed onto one long street that flows down to the harbour.

10. Every parent and child when I was growing up knew each other on the streets where I lived. It was a safe place where children could be innocent and free. Where it was safe to let children out on their own and not have to worry about them, because one parent was always keeping an eye on all the kids around.

11. Acid rain, thousands of dead or dying lakes, pollution in the atmosphere, water and food contamination, disease, birth defects, land and wildlife devastation, the deteriorating economy, war as well as hunger in Third World countries, the Middle East crisis, and the possibility of nuclear war.

12. As the plane hovers over Pearson International Airport all new immigrants get their first real glance at the city of Toronto—a city of lights, excitement and opportunity. Their emotions are now heightened with both fear and excitement. The fear of finding their way around this maze of a city, and the excitement of starting a new job.

13. Over the next few days I took numerous tours of the island. The sugar cane fields full of people cutting the canes down by hand to make sugar and sell to the local islanders. All of the banana trees full of ripe bananas ready to be picked, and fields of pineapples growing on the ground in clumps. Driving by on the bus and seeing the cattle along the side of the road, with no fences or restrictions on where they wandered and grazed.

14. I took stupid risks with my life and the lives of my friends while behind the wheel of a car. Running lights while my fans in the back chanted Go! Go! Go! Why do we do it? Just being an awkward 16-year-old is pressure enough, but when the status of driving comes along, we all perk up and accept the challenge. For this is just another thing to compete for to achieve that dreamed-about image of "coolness."

15. Hong Kong ranks high in the world of tourism because it has so many places that are worth seeing. Such as the 90-year-old restaurant and shopping centre at the Peak which is decorated like a castle in Germany; the 360 half-sphere theatre in the Space Museum which can make the audience feel like they are sitting in a space shuttle and travelling in the solar system; the Central Plaza commercial building, which is ranked the fifth-highest in the world and is worth 10 billion; the biggest ocean park in Southeast Asia, where rare whales, dolphins and fish can be seen; and the most characteristic jumbo seafood restaurant where you can bring your own freshly caught fish for supper.

EDITING OUT THE COMMA SPLICE AND FUSED SENTENCE

To "splice" a rope is to fasten two or more parts into one. To "fuse" pieces of steel is to melt them to each other, as in welding. Such procedures are good in manufacture and repair, but not in writing the sentence. **Joining independent clauses (or, roughly speaking, "sentences") with nothing but a comma produces a COMMA SPLICE. Jamming the sentences together with no punctuation or connecting word at all creates a FUSED SENTENCE.**

Why do most readers perceive these as serious errors? Because by omitting the right punctuation or clear joining words, *we fail to show the relationship between thoughts.* The result is confusion. How would you like to read an essay made of sentences like this?

> Cuba is my favourite holiday spot before I went to Barbados.

In this double sentence melted together, we can hardly tell whether the writer went first to Cuba or to Barbados. Signalling the logic with punctuation makes all the difference:

> Cuba is my favourite holiday spot. Before, I went to Barbados.

It is true that some readers no longer object to the comma splice in informal writing. Sometimes a novelist, such as Margaret Atwood, will even use it on purpose for special effects. But most experienced writers of essays will be sure to edit the *comma splice,* and its cousin the *fused sentence,* out of their drafts.

Though these two defects are widespread, you can avoid them if you learned in the previous section to identify independent and dependent clauses (review now if necessary). *This section now examines four main ways to edit a comma splice or fused sentence out of your writing.*

COMMA SPLICES

1. Spanish is easy, German is hard.
2. I applied early, I got the job.
3. Income tax favours the poor, sales tax favours the rich.

FUSED SENTENCES

1. Spanish is easy German is hard.
2. I applied early I got the job.
3. Income tax favours the poor sales tax favours the rich.

Apart from rewriting the whole thing, there are four easy ways to correct a comma splice or fused sentence:

A. Put a *period* between the independent clauses:

1. Spanish is easy. German is hard.
2. I applied early. I got the job.
3. Income tax favours the poor. Sales tax favours the rich.

This method may be easiest but is not always best. Rather than joining the independent clauses, it separates them, which can hide the logic of their relationship to each other. Besides, having many short sentences produces a choppy style.

B. Join the independent clauses with a *coordinator* (*and, but, for, or, so, yet*):

1. Spanish is easy, *but* German is hard.
2. I applied early, *so* I got the job.
3. Income tax favours the poor, *but* sales tax favours the rich.

Your writing improves when you choose the joining word that best displays your meaning. Do not always reach for "and"; it may be easy to use but is so vague that it can mean almost nothing. Instead, choose "but" to show contrast, "or" to show alternatives, "so" to show cause and effect, etc.

(See above how the comma goes *before* the coordinator, not *after*. If the "sentence" before the connecting word is short enough, the comma can be left out. For example, this might be done in numbers 1 and 2, but probably not 3.)

C. Reduce one of the independent clauses to a dependent clause by putting a *subordinator* before it:

1. *Although* Spanish is easy, German is hard.
2. *Since* I applied early, I got the job.
3. Income tax favours the poor, *while* sales tax favours the rich.

(Note that a comma usually joins the dependent and independent clauses, though it may be left out when the first word group is short.)

Choose the subordinator that most exactly shows your logic. Here are more, with some of the most useful in bold print:

after	before	so that	when
although	**even though**	**though**	where
as	except that	till	whereas
as long as	**if**	**unless**	whether
because	**since**	until	**while**

(For more on using subordinators, review pages 108–109.)

D. When two independent clauses (stand-alone sentences) are closely related in meaning, and especially when they are also balanced in form, join them with a *semicolon*:

1. Spanish is easy; German is hard.
2. Income tax favours the poor; sales tax favours the rich.

For most people the hardest comma splices and fused sentences to avoid are those followed by certain joining words called *conjunctive adverbs*:

also	instead
anyway	likewise
besides	nevertheless
consequently	otherwise
furthermore	similarly
however	still
indeed	**therefore**
in fact	thus

(The three worst offenders, which together cause up to half of all comma splices, are boldfaced. Memorize them.) The words in this list do not *subordinate* what follows them, so there is no problem when they begin a sentence. But be careful when they *join* sentences: if you punctuate them like subordinators, with a comma before, you will make comma splices. If you put no punctuation at all before, you will make fused sentences. Instead, the more accurate punctuation is a semicolon *before* and a comma *after*:

1. Spanish is easy; *however*, German is hard.
2. I applied early; *therefore*, I got the job.
3. Income tax favours the poor; *however*, sales tax favours the rich.

Though these conjunctive adverbs signal your sentence logic clearly, use them sparingly to avoid a slow and heavy style that puts readers to sleep. Would you want to read an essay with a "consequently," "furthermore" or "nevertheless" on every line? Use the semicolon sparingly, too, for it too is heavy and slow. (See page 134 for more discussion of these words and of semicolons.)

Finally, in identifying comma splices and fused sentences in the worksheets that follow, concentrate on the independent clauses and their proper joining or separation. Do *not* be distracted by phrases or dependent clauses that may occur before, between or after the independent clauses. These expanded versions of example 1 still contain independent clauses improperly joined:

COMMA SPLICE

Spanish is easy, *because the grammar is uncomplicated,* German is hard.

ONE POSSIBLE CORRECTION

Spanish is easy, *because the grammar is uncomplicated;* German is hard.

FUSED SENTENCE

Spanish is easy German is hard, *because its grammar is complex.*

ONE POSSIBLE CORRECTION

Spanish is easy, but German is hard, *because its grammar is complex.*

Remember: If you change a comma splice by just removing the comma, you create a fused sentence. If you change a fused sentence by just adding a comma, you create a comma splice.

A Special Case: Punctuation and Quotations

Many people whose punctuation is otherwise good may suddenly "lose it" when writing research essays. They think that somehow, when they add quoted words to their own sentences, the principles of punctuation are suspended.

Nothing could be further from the truth. Except for adding the required quotation marks, when you join a quotation to your own sentence *you should in most cases punctuate as if all the words were yours.*

A typical case from an actual essay:

Raoul Cedras gave a challenge to the Americans "We are ready for combat."

It is not hard to identify two independent clauses (or "sentences") here, jammed together at the first quotation marks. But the fact that the right half was said by someone else, a Haitian general, makes no difference: the lack of punctuation is still an error, a *fused sentence.* Could we put in a comma?

Raoul Cedras gave a challenge to the Americans, "We are ready for combat."

No. Despite still having the quotation marks, it is clear that now we have only traded one error for another: the same two "sentences" are now joined by nothing but a comma (*comma splice*).

When choosing punctuation to use with a quotation, do not take as your model the "speech tags" found in dialogue. Though in fiction a comma does often introduce a quotation ("Then she said, 'Drop dead'"), this is a special case used mainly to identify the speaker.

And though we know a period can go between independent clauses, surely something different is needed here, to signal how the writer's words *introduce* the general's words. Try a colon:

Raoul Cedras gave a challenge to the Americans: "We are ready for combat."

Here is another typical example, from a literary paper:

On page 121 Shields sums up the whole novel, "The real troubles in this world tend to settle on the misalignment between men and women. ..."

Again the problem occurs where the essay writer's words meet those of the quoted person, in this case the narrator. Quotation marks do not hide the fact that two "sentences" are just jammed together with a comma. Again, it is a colon that makes most sense, whether or not there are quotation marks:

On page 121 Shields sums up the whole novel: "The real troubles in this world tend to settle on the misalignment between men and women. ..."

DIAGNOSTIC

Comma Splice and Fused Sentence

NAME _____

Write "CS" in the blank beside each comma splice and "FS" in the blank beside each fused sentence. Some examples are correct.

1. I was always an open-minded person when it came to my social life, I was game for anything. _____

2. The weather in Thunder Bay was not that great for both semesters, because of the snow and ice, we always faced cancellation of lectures. _____

3. Children with permissive parents seem to be wild and crazy. _____

4. The streets were full of blood and dead bodies, houses were being burned. _____

5. Let's imagine that you are employed by a strict and stingy boss, would you work hard for this person? _____

6. Jennifer and Tony were high school students they quit school and got married. _____

7. The scene was horrible and unbelievable, people screamed and were helpless. _____

8. With credit cards we have no need to carry large amounts of cash in our wallets hence we don't lose much if the wallet is misplaced or stolen. _____

9. Finally we arrived at the hospital we checked into the birthing area. _____

10. In high school I had no respect for books, I wrote in them and ripped pages out for reference. _____

11. I swung around to catch a guy charging at me, I grabbed him and threw him to the ground. _____

12. In the past, the computer could not do as many things as it can today. _____

13. I happened to witness a drunken young man who was about 18 years old, his face and right arm were covered with blood and severe cuts. _____

14. With a part-time job I have less time to dedicate to my studies, therefore I have gone from a B plus student to a C student. _____

15. Children are spending too much time in front of the television, therefore they want the latest in toys and clothing. _____

16. My neighbourhood has changed dramatically drug dealers, robberies and conditions in the building are major problems. _____

17. The clock was ticking away with two minutes left in the game we were on our own five-yard line. _____

18. An old woman fell as she crossed the street, but the New Yorkers near her kept walking; it was only when I offered a hand that she got back on her feet. _____

19. During rush hour the streets of Canton are full of bicycles, the buses travel slowly to avoid hitting them. _____

20. Living on my own gave me all the freedom I had ever wanted in my life, for example, I was able to go out whenever I wanted without the consent of my parents. _____

21. When we go to the cottage it's a totally different life than at home in the city everything runs at its own pace, we wake up at about nine, sit outside and listen to the waves crash against the shore. _____

22. Abusive men become angry when they lose control, "violent men often try to track down their wives and threaten them, or their children, if they don't come home" (Gibbs 39). _____

23. In law class we study about people's rights, the richer the people are the more rights they have. _____

24. As we age, our metabolism slows down however, many women and men keep on eating as much food as when they were young. _____

25. The day my cousin began high school, she came home and told her parents she needed a computer. _____

26. Hail is nothing to be afraid of however, caution is always a good thing. _____

27. Many people do not know how to cook, therefore they end up eating junk food. _____

28. Driving a car makes people lazy, they no longer walk anywhere. _____

29. The lake was frozen over, some boys had cleared a spot of ice and were playing hockey. _____

30. Sickle-cell anemia is passed genetically therefore it is not contagious. _____

31. I never inherit money from a rich uncle it is always the person next door who has all the luck. _____

32. There are some good things about living in a big city, but they don't outweigh the bad things. _____

33. My friend Carole and her partner lived together, they shared everything from appliances and furniture to a joint bank account. _____

34. On April 27 of each year since the accident, I have held a party to celebrate being alive. _____

35. Date rape is a serious crime in our society, however, it can be prevented by education. _____

36. Dealing with the public can be a very rewarding experience, it can also be trying. _____

37. The night before my driver's test I couldn't eat or sleep, I was in a stupor. _____

38. Indonesia is very large, it consists of more than 13 600 islands. _____

39. The basement was dark, a mouldy smell filled the air. _____

40. Ten years ago it was safe on my street even at night, that's when all the fun would happen. _____

W O R K S H E E T

Comma Splice and Fused Sentence, Level 1

N A M E _____

Correct the comma splices and fused sentences below. If an item contains no error, write "Correct" after it.

1. Winter came, the wind was howling outside.

2. There are many ways of exercising, different things work for different people.

3. Some hockey clubs have three or four goon players; however, this strategy may not win games.

4. I looked at my fingers they were covered with blood.

5. I screamed for help but it was in vain, the echoes just faded away into the surrounding jungle.

6. The night was silent, time stood still, I had no thought of the events going on around me.

7. Night people simply like to accomplish their tasks at night therefore, they need more sleep in the morning.

8. I ran toward the back of the house to see what had happened.

9. It was five in the morning the street was filled with broken glass.

10. We worked, and worked, the day got hotter, and hotter, longer and longer.

11. Now Prince Edward Island is my favourite vacation spot before I used to go to Maine.

12. The rooster crows at five o'clock, the farmer gets up and does the chores.

13. I came home from school, at the door lay a man covered in blood.

14. I was shocked I didn't know what to do.

15. The town is in a valley, there are snow-covered mountains on both sides.

16. The buildings were destroyed, people were killed, others were taken hostage.

17. In the past, bicycles were made to last a lifetime.

18. I wasn't sure of myself, I thought she would laugh at me.

19. In a few minutes the dentist came in she put on a mask and a pair of gloves.

20. I knew I was caught. The cops came over to where I was hiding, they were very large and very angry.

21. It was a beautiful July day in Edmonton there was no sign of rain and not a cloud in the sky.

22. In winter the Northern Hemisphere is tilted away from the sun, spreading the rays over a greater distance; therefore, the temperature falls.

23. I had to sit in the front seat next to the driver this is the most dangerous seat on the bus.

24. Lies have a snowball effect, they get larger and larger.

25. There are four seasons in Japan each has its own colours.

26. After a few minutes I heard her asking for help, I ran to see what was going on.

27. Many business people wear glasses to give them a more professional look; some wear them even if the glasses are nonprescription.

28. New York City was just a mess, there were people living in broken-down houses and run-down apartments, there were potholes in the street and there was garbage all over the sidewalks.

29. We were a quarter of a mile away when we heard ten or fifteen shots we turned around to see a wave of human beings headed in our direction. We heard more shots and the wave built, there were women screaming and men shouting as a cloud of dust rose behind them.

30. In the theatre there was a middle-aged man who had a bag of chips and was making a lot of rustling noises Anne was very annoyed because she had trouble hearing.

W O R K S H E E T

Comma Splice and Fused Sentence, Level 2

N A M E _____

Correct the comma splices and fused sentences below. Don't bother to recopy the passages if you can just change punctuation or add the right joining word above the line. If an item contains no error, write "Correct" after it.

1. We took the F train to downtown Manhattan, when we got off I was almost run over by a police officer he told me to get out of his way the next time.

2. For a thrill, a laugh, a lesson or a reason for a date, go to the movies.

3. One new driver, only 16 years old, decided to take his friends for a joyride to celebrate his new licence, now three of his friends are dead.

4. Country music fans have suffered, many people consider them "hicks" and think the lyrics are always about drinking and leaving lovers.

5. It does not matter how successful you are if your luck turns bad you may be the next homeless person.

6. Some people drive like maniacs, they do not stop at red lights, they speed as if to win an award.

7. When you go to the Tai Ping Peak at night, you will see the lamps of the shops and buildings of Hong Kong, they look like millions of pearls floating in the dark.

8. You can't hide; as long as there is wind, acid rain can reach you.

9. Trees are the anchors of the earth when they are cut down the soil is washed away.

10. I was sitting in the front of the stalled van when I saw the train, with my heart pounding I shouted to the others to get out.

11. In Somalia our home was close to the beach I knew quite well how to swim the raging waves, the technique I used was not to struggle with the waves, I just followed them.

12. Every mountain rose out of the valley, yet each was distinct; some had faces where avalanches had wiped out all the trees, others were bold bare windblown slopes.

13. Solitude scares the narrator and leaves her feeling shallow inside, "The river slips past, unperturbed by our coming and going."

14. I loved the scent of the double cheese spewing from the sides of the pizza box, and the grease dripping from my fingers was enough to drive me into a frenzy.

15. Banff is a postcard paradise, it is an incredible place to see, but don't just take my word for it ask the seven million people who visit each year.

16. My mother arranged for me to escape from Iran, she paid an enormous amount of money to a smuggler to get me past the border and on my way to Canada.

17. We drove as far as we could, the smuggler said it would be safer to spend the day in Tabriz and leave for the border at night.

18. Finally we reached the border, from that point we could no longer drive the journey was now by foot. The howling of the winds answered the cries of the wolves that roamed the mountains. Many hours later we reached a village in Turkey, we were to endure yet another night before we reached our next destination, Istanbul.

19. Some critics felt the novel lacked sustained power, it had inconsistent ideas, some went so far as to say it was a dull book.

20. When I saw 12 members of the Hells Angels stop, I was scared to death, they asked what had happened and helped to fix the bike. Then I rode with them to the next town and offered them a couple of drinks, the only problem was that their couple of drinks ran my bill up to a hundred dollars.

21. I could not put pressure on my foot; therefore, I could not walk, run or dance.

22. We called the police immediately when we discovered we were robbed, this was at 6 a.m., the first police vehicle arrived at 11 a.m., five hours later.

23. The officer in charge rubbed out his cigarette with his foot and slowly ambled up to us. After reminding us that his lunch break was just one hour away, he began to look around the crime scene, the rest of the officers remained outside, uninterested in the proceedings.

24. I was talking to another student about the protest when two explosions sent clouds of tear gas into a scattering crowd. This was the little spark that ignited the fury of the people they charged the army with bottles, stones and any piece of metal they could put their hands on.

25. Finally, I executed the test without any flaw in my driving and we returned to the police station, the officer just stared at me and slowly shook his head from side to side. I had failed the driving test. I was left in disbelief until my friends explained to me why I had failed, apparently I had to enclose a large amount of money in the test booklet, and when we executed the parking, I was supposed to invite the officer into the nearby restaurant for a meal and a drink, only then would I pass.

EDITING FOR PUNCTUATION

The tiny dots and squiggles of punctuation on your page may look insignificant. They may seem like minor details. In fact some people view them as mere decorations, ornaments to be strewn here and there ("Let's throw in a comma because the last sentence didn't have one"). But how would you like to read an essay made of statements like this one found in a student paper?

> I don't smoke myself because I've tried it and don't get anything out of it.

While it may be true that few people enjoy smoking themselves, what the author had in mind was probably something more like this:

> I don't smoke, myself, because I've tried it and don't get anything out of it.

The small change in punctuation signifies a great change in meaning. And this is what punctuation is all about: the period, comma, semicolon, colon, question mark and exclamation point are above all *logic signals*: like road signs by the highway, they show us where we are going.

One problem arising from the tiny size of punctuation marks is that, if you write by hand, they may or may not end up looking like what you meant them to be. For example, if you form a period by jabbing at the paper, as people in a hurry do, it might come out so long that your reader will see it as a comma. Always proofread closely for punctuation, but especially if you write by hand.

In reviewing the following summary of the main uses for punctuation, keep in mind that these small marks powerfully influence your writing for better or worse. If you select among them to highlight your logic, you are taking one of the most important steps on your writing journey.

Period (.)

A. Use a period to end a *statement* or *command*:

STATEMENT

> There is no status quo.
>
> —Diane Francis

COMMAND

> Just do it.

B. Use a period after most *abbreviations*:

> At 3 p.m. Dr. Rubright removed Mr. Gagnon's appendix.

(See also "Abbreviations," pages 210–211.)

Apostrophe (')

(See "Apostrophes," pages 201–202.)

Comma (,)

The period and comma are both heavily used. The period, though, is easy to manage, while the comma takes some real thought: it can serve in many more situations and mean many different things. The old folklore that a comma is a "breath" is to some extent true, but provides a risky guide for the writer (is a period not a "breath" as well?).

Another complication: some commas are optional. One person will stuff every possible comma into a paragraph, while another will use as few as possible. Though the first preference is more traditional and the second more modern, both are correct—which means that in using commas you need to develop your own style.

As you begin this section on commas, start by reviewing pages 119–121 on the "**comma splice**," the most important matter of all: If you place a comma where a period should go, your reader cannot sense where one statement ends and another begins.

A. Use a comma to separate items in a *series*:

> Among the many kinds of mutual funds now available to the investor are growth funds, value funds, index funds, sector funds, country funds, balanced funds, bond funds and money market funds.

A gardener's rewards are the glow of outdoor exercise, the pleasure of fresh air, the satisfaction of honest work, and the freshest vegetables in town.

Most people now omit the optional comma between the last two items of a series, especially if the items are short (as in the first example above). In the second example, though, see how the final comma contributes by separating larger word groups that might otherwise run together.

B. If an *introductory word group* is long, use a comma to separate it from what follows. If it is short leave it unpunctuated. (Examine the two sentences you have just read as examples of the rules they state.)

C. Place a comma before the *coordinator* of a *compound sentence*, unless the first independent clause is short:

The Laplanders have retained the most traditional culture of any European society, *but* modern Scandinavia has now begun to assimilate them.

A canoe is fast *but* a kayak is faster.

(Note how the comma occurs *before*, not *after*, the "but" or other coordinating word.)

D. Modifiers (to review briefly) are word groups that elaborate on a more important part of the sentence. Not everyone understands their relationship to commas. First of all, a modifier is said to be "restrictive" if it is crucial to the basic meaning of a sentence, and "nonrestrictive" if it is not. *Set off a nonrestrictive modifier with commas* to show its limited relationship to the sentence, but *leave a restrictive modifier unpunctuated* to show how its importance integrates it into the sentence.

RESTRICTIVE

Some people *infected with the HIV virus* live more than ten years.

We sense that "infected with the HIV virus" is a restrictive modifier, because without it the whole point of the statement is lost:

Some people live more than ten years.

This modifier, then, is so important that we do not want commas to distance it from the rest of the statement.

NONRESTRICTIVE

The HIV virus, *unknown a generation ago,* is changing the nature of our relationships.

Although the words "unknown a generation ago" do add information to the idea, taking them out does not drastically change the statement:

The HIV virus is changing the nature of our relationships.

Thus we do need commas at each end of this modifier (like parentheses) to signal its more distant relationship to the main idea.

E. Put a comma after the *salutation of an informal letter*:

Dear Brandon,
Dear Mom,

Use a colon, not a comma, if the letter is more formal:

Dear Ms. Jessamy:
Dear Sirs:

F. Put a comma between the date and year. A comma is optional between the month and year:

July 19, 1941
July, 1941
July 1941

G. Use a comma wherever necessary to *avoid a misreading or other ambiguity*:

AMBIGUOUS

After drinking the three men played cards. (Did the three men drink or did something drink them? We are distracted for a moment, losing time and attention, while deciding what the statement means.)

CLEAR

> After drinking, the three men played cards.

AMBIGUOUS

> What I really dislike is the size of the city and the people. (Are the people the wrong size?)

CLEAR

> What I really dislike is the size of the city, and the people.

AMBIGUOUS

> Alcohol in my eyes only adds to people's troubles. (Where is the alcohol?)

CLEAR

> Alcohol, in my eyes, only adds to people's troubles.

Of course feel free to revise more thoroughly, when this produces an even clearer and more graceful version:

> What I really dislike is the size of the city and the rudeness of its people.

> I think alcohol only adds to people's troubles.

H. Normally, *do not place a comma between a subject and its verb.* Many student writers suffering from a condition that could be called "comma-itis" put commas in places such as this:

> The ever so popular Madonna, is known for her sense of style.

Note the effect of this extra comma: it actually separates the two parts of the sentence that should be most closely connected: the subject "Madonna" and the verb "is ..." which goes on to tell what we want to know about the subject. Another example:

COMMA-ITIS

>   S   V
> Our neighbour's *dog, ran* away.

REVISED

> Our neighbour's *dog ran* away.

On the other hand, if expressions such as a nonrestrictive modifier (review item D) interrupt between subject and verb, of course use a comma at both ends of the interruption (like parentheses) to separate it from the core sentence:

CORRECT

> S   V
> *Vultures,* the scavengers of death, *circle* their prey before moving in.

W O R K S H E E T

Commas

NAME _____

The passages below all appeared in actual student essays. Where you see a comma that does not belong, cross it out. Where you see that a comma is needed, add it. If a passage already uses commas well, write "Correct" after it.

Example: Patients must be fed when they are too weak to eat , themselves.

1. As I put my coat on the dentist and receptionist had a brief discussion.

2. Sharon flirted outrageously with Michael and Kenny and Jason flirted with her.

3. My brother grandfather and I had been going to the races since before I could remember.

4. North Americans, believe in eye contact.

5. The fastest sports are soccer, hockey football, rugby and basketball.

6. Some researchers say, that the few precious moments after birth are critical in forming a strong bond between parent and child.

7. O. J. Simpson the famous athlete, a hero to many was an abusive husband.

8. Once, I placed, a couple of lines on the paper, some thoughts, began to appear.

9. The Chinese way of life, stresses education.

10. Our media especially television are to blame for sexism in society.

11. If you can use cash or make your payments promptly.

12. While Dad was putting the lights on my brothers and I started to place the star on the Christmas tree.

13. Adoption, is an event that dramatically changes a child's life.

14. Children, who were victims of their parents' violent outbursts, may undergo mental illness or personality disorder when they grow up.

15. Our diet should contain dairy products rich in protein and vegetables.

16. I am amused by how fast Hollywood stars fall in love, get married, have affairs, get divorced, fall in love again, get married again and so on.

17. Clinging to their old culture, gives immigrants a sense of security.

18. Marriage, is a big commitment.

19. Hard work, can pay off.

20. For hundreds of years English Canada, had social and political control over Quebec.

21. Although stubborn Hagar is one of Margaret Laurence's most admirable characters.

22. As I mentioned before Ontario has a low level of education.

23. When planning your holiday visit or phone the tourist information centre in your city.

24. It's no secret that a life of freedom, especially in small and less powerful countries, is a rare commodity.

25. A student, such as myself, who has a part-time job, while attending university full-time, is bound to, sooner or later, pay the price.

26. Once the needle is in the plunger is retracted to check for blood.

27. One thing that really bothers me, is the idea of a large dog being kept in the city.

28. I love to play hockey but, studies come first.

29. Alcohol has become a problem for our schools and teachers are deeply concerned.

30. The truth is that many alcoholics never seek help resulting in their own destruction.

31. As society becomes more and more prosperous, and small cities become big cities, the crime rate also increases.

32. Ham radio, has become my obsession.

33. Our friendship lasted for years, within which time we sinned, lied, cried, laughed, argued, shared and grew together.

34. Harsh lighting, produces harsh photographs.

35. My problems in math started the day I began school.

36. One of my math teachers, helped me learn, to achieve my goal, in the subject, by spending a great deal of time working with me.

37. When rivers lose their velocity suspended particles of clay and silt are deposited creating fertile soils in river deltas.

38. Brian McDonald, a youth worker in Vancouver says one of the major reasons for school violence is the "slow response of a clogged court system."

39. The last step is to record the time drug and dosage on the patient's chart.

40. I love to cook myself and eat at home.

Semicolon (;)

It is possible to live your whole life never using a semicolon. Many people do. After all, the uses of this punctuation mark are not as easy or clear as those of commas or periods. Further, some people who do use the semicolon abuse it, sprinkling five or ten of these very heavy items on each page, creating a style that feels like a herd of elephants marching through the forest. Clearly it is better not to use this punctuation mark at all than to misuse it.

On the other hand, in the right places it is eloquent and powerful. If you wish to use the semicolon, study the examples that follow:

A. Use a semicolon between independent clauses (or, roughly speaking, *between closely related "sentences"*), when there is no joining word:

> Keenly, for the first time, I felt that I was a stranger in a strange land; my heart yearned intensely for my absent home.

> —Susanna Moodie, *Roughing It in the Bush*

Note how the semicolon, in the middle, pulls the two parts together, emphasizing their close relationship. The effect is even stronger and more eloquent when the two "sentences" are not only related, but mirror each other in form:

> Becoming independent is the easy part of a revolution; staying independent is the hard part.

> Americans make money; Canadians count money.

B. Use a semicolon between independent clauses (that is, between "sentences") that are joined by one of these *conjunctive adverbs*. (The ones you probably use most often are boldfaced:)

anyway	instead
besides	likewise
consequently	**nevertheless**
furthermore	otherwise
however	similarly
indeed	still
in fact	**therefore**

> The most heavily exposed parts of the negative receive the thickest deposit of silver; *therefore,* these areas appear darkest.

See how the semicolon comes *before* the joining word and the comma *after*. **Remember that putting a comma *in front of* one of these conjunctive adverbs creates a serious error: the comma splice (if necessary, review pages 119–121 now).**

C. Use a semicolon between *items in a series* if these items have internal punctuation:

> If you borrow a garment of any kind, be sure that you will tear it; a watch, that you will break it; a jewel, that you will lose it; a book, that it will be stolen from you.

> —Susanna Moodie, *Roughing It in the Bush*

D. Incorrect semicolons will harm your writing more than correct semicolons will help it. Remember that apart from separating internally punctuated items in a series, *the only normal function of a semicolon is to join independent clauses*. Avoid other uses:

■ Except for the case of item C above, *do not use a semicolon as a comma*:

WRONG

> As the guitar and the drums began to roar; the crowd began to scream.

BETTER

> As the guitar and the drums began to roar, the crowd began to scream.

WRONG

> Only two problems; the cost and the danger, limit skiing as a sport.

BETTER

> Only two problems, the cost and the danger, limit skiing as a sport.

■ *Do not use a semicolon as a colon*:

WRONG

> There are two groups of unemployed; the undereducated and the overeducated.

BETTER

There are two groups of unemployed: the undereducated and the overeducated.

Colon(:)

The colon is a lively punctuation mark that strongly pushes the reader's attention forward. Most student writers could exploit it more fully, adding force to their writing. Use it more often than the slower semi-colon.

A. *Use the colon to formally introduce a statement,* whether your own or a quotation:

This is the main point: censorship is dangerous.

The main question is this: do taxes increase inflation?

Goethe's most famous words are his last: "Light—more light!"

This is Talleyrand's recipe for coffee:

Black as the devil,
Hot as hell,
Pure as an angel,
Sweet as love.

Of course quotations, especially short ones worked into your own sentence, may also be introduced by the comma:

On his deathbed Goethe said, "Light—more light!"

B. For *emphasis,* use a colon to introduce even a single word:

Scrooge loved only one thing: money.

C. Use a colon *when a second statement explains a first:*

The climate is changing: by the year 2050 our winters will be noticeably warmer.

D. Probably the best-known use of the colon is to *formally introduce a series:*

The cylinders of a V-8 engine fire in this order: 1, 8, 4, 3, 6, 5, 7, 2.

Here is one point of style commonly ignored, but usually followed by careful writers: in introducing a series, do not place a colon right after the verbs *is, are, was* or *were,* or after the words *of* or *to,* because this separates closely related parts of the sentence:

WEAK

The causes of inflation *are*: low productivity, high wages, depletion of resources, and government debt.

BETTER

The causes of inflation *are* low productivity, high wages, depletion of resources, and government debt.

BETTER

These *are* the causes of inflation: low productivity, high wages, depletion of resources, and government debt.

BETTER

The causes of inflation *are* as follows: low productivity, high wages, depletion of resources, and government debt.

E. Put a colon *after the salutation of a formal letter:*

Dear Ms. Vargas: Dear Concha,

BUT

Dear Sir: Dear Grandpa,

Question Mark (?)

The question mark may seem easy to use, but actually it causes many little errors. Be sure to put it where it belongs, and guard against putting it where it does not belong. *Place a question mark after a direct question but not after an indirect question:*

DIRECT QUESTIONS

What time is it?

I asked myself, "Would I help a person being attacked on the street?"

INDIRECT QUESTIONS

I wonder what time it is.

I asked myself whether I would help a person being attacked on the street.

Notice how the direct questions are the *exact words of a question*, while the indirect ones merely *report* a question. If you would not ask "What time it is?" or "Whether I would help?" then you know they are indirect, and therefore do not require question marks.

WRONG

When I reached home I asked my mother what was happening? (Omit the question mark after this indirect question, *or* make the question direct.)

BETTER

When I reached home I asked my mother, "What is happening?"

WRONG

Why is car insurance so high. (The person who wrote this may have sensed it was a direct question, but just forgot the question mark. Many little errors are made like this: proofread to catch them.)

BETTER

Why is car insurance so high?

Exclamation Point(!)

In the comics, even the most ordinary statement by Mickey Mouse or Superman or the latest alien or monster will end with an exclamation point—or even a whole row of them. At first this tactic may heighten the readers' attention (!!!!!), but soon these punctuation marks become so common, so cheap, that they mean nothing at all. It is better to save this strongest of all punctuation for the strongest expressions of feeling. To end an ordinary statement with an exclamation point is to swat a fly with a sledge hammer.

A. Use an exclamation point to express *strong emotion* such as fear, anger or sorrow:

"Save me!" he cried, "I'm drowning!"

Ruin seize thee, ruthless King!
　　　　　　　—Thomas Gray, "The Bard"

Alas! alas! that ever love was sin!
　　　　—Chaucer, "The Wife of Bath's Prologue"

B. Do *not* try to make an ordinary statement exciting by adding an exclamation point. Avoid excesses such as this:

When the fair is about a month away, farmers begin to clean their livestock. First the cows are hosed down with warm water and soap in order to get their hair as clean as possible! After the hair is rinsed, a blow dryer is used, along with a comb, to get the hair as fluffy as possible! In some places, styling is needed to make the hair go the right way!

WORKSHEET

Semicolon, Colon, Question Mark and Exclamation Point

NAME _____

These examples were found in actual student essays. Wherever a semicolon, colon, question mark or exclamation point is wrong, or wherever it is needed but missing, fix it. (Sometimes there is more than one item per sentence to change.) If a passage is already well punctuated, write "correct" after it.

1. Why go all the way to Paris when Montreal has it all here.

2. Since I had arrived early and knew the area well; I went to a nearby doughnut shop for a cup of coffee.

3. A person cannot get AIDS from: telephones, toilet seats, swimming pools, whirlpools, hugging, sharing glasses or dishes, buses and subways, kissing, or mosquitoes.

4. How can a teenager resist wanting to look as great and as happy as the models in magazines.

5. The computer will ask if you are ready to send your message?

6. I have felt many results of not being able to speak Punjabi fluently, in the following areas; communication problems, reduction of job opportunities and the loss of my heritage.

7. Traits of violent children include: low self-esteem, impulsive aggression, short attention span, and, in many cases, high intelligence.

8. Living with four people I learned two things compromise and respect for others.

9. Permissive parents always say "yes"; strict parents always say "no."

10. Seven is the most popular lucky number, while 13 is considered extremely unlucky!

11. Banning guns from the public does not necessarily mean that a person who really wants a gun won't get one, however; it does prevent crimes of passion.

12. University students have many responsibilities that take a great deal of time: major research papers; employment; and family matters.

13. Some serious effects of overindulging in candy are; cavities, malnutrition and death.

14. Try to analyze what kind of car you need? Is it for city driving? Are you going to use the car in your work? Do you mind the gas money, or is convenience all you care about?

15. I wonder how bus drivers put up with the rush-hour crowd every day.

16. The main advantage of working while being a student is: learning effective time management!

17. Although I was swamped with projects, essays and homework; I now know that the workload could have been worse.

18. There are five major types of energy. Mechanical, chemical, electrical, atomic and solar.

19. As soon as I saw my brother; I knew that something was wrong.

20. Wife abuse crosses geographic and income lines; can be found in both rural and urban households, and spans the diverse cultures of any given society.

21. The girls' uniform consisted of five pieces; white shirt, a tie, a green vest, a plaid skirt and a pair of green socks with the school logo embroidered on them.

22. Nowadays the thought of a couple happily married after 50 years is incomprehensible to many people; however, my Grandma and Grandpa Wilcox are living proof of a happily married couple after 50 years of togetherness.

23. "Hey buddy, got any change," is the most frequent question asked today in Halifax.

24. Bank robberies are meticulously planned to the finest detail to include: the time of the operation; the getaway route; disguises; choice of bank; and a look at police surveillance in the area.

25. On page 71 Dickens describes Stephen "He was a good power-loom weaver, and a man of perfect integrity."

26. In prison we could play: volleyball, soccer and table tennis.

27. Elder abuse may take many forms such as: neglect, isolation, physical abuse, emotional abuse and financial abuse.

28. Even little children who can hardly skate are seen trying to copy the methods and techniques of their favourite hockey player; which usually involves some form of violence.

29. At a wedding you see bright happy colours such as: red, white, purple, green and pink. At a funeral you see dark depressing colours such as: blue, brown and black.

30. As speeders roar past, we wonder what they will hit or whose life they will take today?

31. How we all love to eat!

32. I wonder how families can afford more than one car?

33. Why is it that Canadians go south for the winter, instead of looking for something in their own back yards.

34. If I don't stop eating chocolate bars, I will soon have to be rolled around from place to place; just like a big ball.

35. "How long do I have to stay here," I asked one soldier. He turned to me, hit me on the face with his gun, and told me, "Very long, probably forever."

36. A hundred years ago a person looking for entertainment could not: turn on the TV, go to a movie, play a couple of hours of racquetball, or lie back and listen to the stereo.

37. In Canada we encounter four different seasons spring, summer, fall and winter.

38. Before you even start looking for a car, decide exactly how much money you are able to spend?

39. The younger students walk down the long school halls with open ears, hearing what decisions the graduating students have made; dreaming that someday they will be doing the same thing.

40. I crave the night life of the city; the bright lights, concerts, movies, cafés, shows and nightclubs.

Dash (—)

The dash, like the exclamation point, is dramatic—and, like the exclamation point, often abused. Since the dash can fit almost anywhere, some writers use it as an escape from the bother of choosing more exact punctuation. ("Let's see, do we put a colon or a semicolon here?—oh well, let's just throw in a dash.") Some people routinely scrawl dashes between phrases, between sentences, anywhere, because this punctuation is lively, fast—and, above all, easy. Such a strategy may be fine for very informal writing such as personal letters. In essays, though, strewing dashes left and right makes the logic harder to grasp, giving a breathless and even scatterbrained impression.

On the other hand, there are times when the dash achieves an effect better than any other punctuation can. These are probably its best uses:

A. A dash can set off *parenthetical material* (extra explanation that is not crucial to the sentence) more dramatically than commas or parentheses can:

> And then—was it hours or minutes after I arrived?—he opened his eyes.
>
> —Margaret Laurence, *The Stone Angel*

B. A dash can set off and thus emphasize *a key word or phrase at the end of a sentence*:

> Only one investment will endure forever, cannot be taken from where it is, and over time will almost always increase in value—land.

Parentheses and Brackets ( ), [ ]

Like dashes, parentheses are almost too convenient. Some writers rely on them as substitutes for more specific punctuation, while others use them to legitimize irrelevant matter that should be cut from their writing. For these reasons, and because the clutter of parentheses can slow down your reader, this device should be used sparingly.

Note that, although square brackets appear on computer keyboards, they are limited to certain specialized situations. It is the rounded parentheses that are used in the traditional manner:

A. Use parentheses to *enclose matter that does not fit into the grammatical structure of a sentence:*

> Caligula (A.D. 12–41) was the most corrupt and tyrannical of all Roman emperors.

B. Use square brackets *in quoted material* as you would use parentheses in unquoted material:

> "Angling [fishing with line and hook] may be said to be so like the mathematics that it can never be fully learnt."
>
> —Isaak Walton, *The Compleat Angler*

Since "fishing with line and hook" is an editor's explanation, it is placed in square brackets so we will not think Isaak Walton wrote these words.

EDITING TO AVOID THE RUN-ON SENTENCE

When a sentence is a monster in length, it is a run-on. Even if it is short, but has word groups too casually stuck together with loose connections such as "and," it is a run-on.

Some people also label as run-ons the "comma splice" and "fused sentence" which we discussed on pages 119–121; while there is some overlap, in the present section we focus more on sheer length and on flabby connecting words.

While not as serious as its opposite error, the sentence fragment, the run-on is not good: its logic may be hidden, and in extreme cases its length will totally confuse the audience.

A. Change monster sentences by *breaking them into parts,* by *avoiding overuse of coordinators* (*but, for, or, so, yet,* and especially *and*) and by *cutting out deadwood.*

The following monster, found in a student essay, could be called an "extreme sentence." How would you like to read a whole essay made of these?

> A hundred years ago people were not as busy as they are today, *and* they could sit down *and* write letters *and* send them to their friends *and* their business associates, *but* in our modern times people are really busy, *and* they find that writing is too much work, *so* they just pick up the telephone *and* make a call to someone else. (63 words)

Joining many thoughts loosely in one statement is something we do in speech, because we often talk faster than we think. When we write, though, the opportunity to revise leaves no reason for unorganized and wasteful language.

In our example above, not only does the repeated word "*and*" sometimes fail to make logical connections between parts, but the confusion has also allowed *deadwood* to come in. First let's look at a revision that improves only the connections:

> A hundred years ago people were not as busy as they are today: they could sit down and write letters to send to their friends and their business associates. But in our modern times people are really busy. They find that writing is too much work, so they just pick up the telephone and make a call to someone else. (60 words)

So far, so good. We have cut the monster into three manageable parts. We have also replaced some of the "ands" with more exact connections such as good punctuation or more specific connecting words. But now let's look at a more radical revision that also cuts out the deadwood that was smothering the meaning:

> A hundred years ago people had time to write letters, but today we are so busy that we just pick up the telephone. (23 words)

Now we have one sentence of medium length whose parts are so tightly joined that the vague word "and" never occurs at all. In addition, the message has been shortened and concentrated by removing self-evident facts. For example when we "pick up the telephone" it is obvious that we are going to "make a call to someone else" (have you ever called yourself?). So why write it if your audience already knows it?

In revising monster sentences, do whatever you have to: adding periods or better connecting words may sometimes be enough, while other times only a full rewriting will do the job. (See "Editing for Economy" on pages 65–70 for more on cutting deadwood.)

B. *Join the parts of even short sentences accurately.* Above all, never write "*and*" when a more exact connection can be made. Our first example had 63 words. This one from a student essay has only 18 but is still a run-on:

> The goalie has only one job to do and that is to keep the opposing players from scoring.

Here the word "and" is illogical: it implies that keeping the opposition from scoring is *in addition* to the goalie's job, when actually it *is* the job. A better connection than "and" would be a colon, since the beginning word group introduces the rest of the sentence:

> The goalie has only one job to do: keep the opposing players from scoring.

Almost all word processing software contains a strong tool for detecting overuse of "and"—or of any other term.

Learn to use the "search" function of your system, entering "and" as the word to find. (Your software may work better if you enter a space both before and after the term, so that larger words such as "sand," which contain "and" within them, will not also be identified.)

As the cursor comes to rest at each occurrence of the word, ask yourself whether this particular "and" signals a logical joining of two items (like "bacon and eggs") or whether it was applied like Crazy Glue just to hold stuff together. If it was, now replace it with a more logical word or with appropriate punctuation.

. . . AND . . . AND . . . AND . . . AND . . .

AND . . .

"And" is the most overused word in English. Avoid it except to show that one thing is genuinely *in addition to* another.

Run-on Sentence

NAME _____

Which of the following are run-on sentences? Write "ROS" in the blank beside them. (Remember that not all run-ons are long; many are short, caused by loose connections such as the often vaguely used "and").

1. A breakfast of bacon and eggs is filled with cholesterol. _____

2. I work in a store and some people come in and charge for items under one dollar. _____

3. It is often thought that old people are unable to manage a household and end up in nursing homes and other long-term care institutions. _____

4. I ordered a Hawaiian pizza and I found only four pieces of pineapple and the cheese covered only the middle of the pizza, leaving the edges with nothing but sauce. _____

5. He threw a punch at me trying to catch me off guard, and seeing it coming I ducked and gave him a shot in the ribs, and feeling him buckle under the punch I knew I had won the fight. _____

6. When inspecting your home for places where burglars may break in, check the basement windows carefully. _____

7. In one day I went through two interviews and I was hired and asked to start the next day at six in the morning. _____

8. I know of an employee who had worked faithfully for a number of years for the company and a pay raise had never been granted. _____

9. How is it that we spend one-third of our lives in sleep, yet we still know so little about it? _____

10. I am somewhat clumsy and tend to miss the pass and the ball goes off the field and out of bounds. _____

11. In the police stories we watch on television, a crime is committed and the police have a car chase and a shootout and capture the criminal. _____

12. I saw one thing in Thailand that still gives me the shivers, and that was lizards. _____

13. In New York City people cannot walk the streets after nine o'clock at night, because they might get mugged. _____

14. One day I decided to try and get a job and about three weeks later I was doing dishes. _____

15. My niece is in grade two and all they do in school is drawing, playing music and twice or three times a week they have spelling and math for one hour. _____

16. I passed the first semester of chemistry, but failed the second semester. _____

17. The brakes failed, and suddenly the driver knew his only chance to try and save us from going over the cliff was to steer the van toward the side of the mountain. _____

18. There was only one problem with my teachers, and that was that they did not know how to teach. _____

19. At age 14 I decided I was ready to become part of the real world. I felt I was maturing and ready for a part-time job, and so I got one. _____

20. The youngest of my roommates is called Sue and is still in her teens, and keeps confessing that this is her first time on her own, away from home. _____

21. When farming was the way of life, a family would have six or seven children. _____

22. Cats are much smaller than dogs and belong more in a home and they're not vicious little things like dogs. _____

23. Our car slid into an embankment and the shock threw us forward as if we were rag dolls in the seats and fortunately for us we had our seatbelts on. _____

24. I had my first date when I was 15. _____

25. There is only one sign of my grandfather's aging, and that is a hearing problem. _____

26. I called the lab advisor over and she took a careful look at the situation and apologetically informed me that the printer was now out of order. _____

27. A dog knows when you're happy and it shows it's happy too and it knows when you're sad or hurt and it tries to show that it understands. _____

28. The purpose of e-mail in business is to improve communication and make management more efficient and it can release the manager from the boundaries of traditional office time. _____

29. I strongly believe that, to have a better world, men must make up their minds to learn to share ideas, household duties and child-care duties, and let women become more active in social and political life and accept women as their equal partners. _____

30. In order for multiculturalism to work, society needs to deal with equity, so that people of colour will hold high positions in Parliament and other institutions, and they will be directors, vice-presidents and so on, and this will enable people of colour and white people to work together as partners, and they will share power, information, resources and decision-making regarding the systems and structures. _____

W O R K S H E E T

Run-on Sentence, Level 1

NAME _____

*Inaccurate use of the word "**and**" is one of the main causes of run-on sentences. Below, cross out all the "ands" you can. Replace them with more exact **coordinators** (review page 139), with well-chosen **subordinators** (review pages 108–109), or with appropriate **punctuation**. Where necessary, rewrite in the space.*

but

Example: I flicked the switch several times A̶N̶D̶ no light came on.

1. Basketball is extremely popular around the world AND it's a court game played by two teams of five players each.

   _____

   _____

   _____

2. People in the city do not try AND make contact with others.

   _____

   _____

3. I applied for a job AND was anxious to talk to my mom AND when I received the job I could not wait a couple of hours AND call when the rates were cheaper.

   _____

   _____

   _____

4. If you want to double your money at the races, fold it in half AND put it in your pocket AND just watch.

   _____

   _____

5. My father and mother helped me collect some money AND I began my escape AND headed for the mountains of Turkey.

   _____

   _____

   _____

6. The audience simply adores action AND excitement AND hockey has it in every game.

   _____

   _____

7. My car is eight years old, AND it still looks and drives like new.

   _____

   _____

8. Mom doesn't like it when I talk back AND she gets upset AND I know I have it coming.

9. I tried with difficulty to tell the cab driver where to go, AND the cab driver did not understand me.

10. Love is true AND lust is false.

11. I went up AND down all the halls, AND I still couldn't find the room.

12. I know one thing AND that is to fight.

13. Sometimes in the middle of the night Granny can cough for an hour AND the next day she will be walking around the house with a cigarette hanging from the corner of her mouth again.

14. In the social work program more than 1000 people applied, AND fewer than 300 were accepted.

15. Good coaches motivate their athletes AND reinforce their good behaviour AND punish their bad behaviour.

16. The old man tried to cross the street at a crosswalk AND the cars did not even stop.

17. Each day a great miracle occurs AND a newborn child enters the world.

18. If you feel you are hungry enough to eat a horse AND do not want to gain any weight, a Chinese restaurant would be best.

19. One officer pulled his gun AND said not to move AND hearing this AND having a gun pulled on me I didn't even want to breathe for fear of my life.

_____

_____

_____

20. Now it is evening AND the sun is setting in the west AND the sky is changing to a clear bright blue.

_____

_____

21. As a male driver I would have to pay $4500 for insurance AND my sister would have to pay approximately five times less.

_____

_____

22. Soon after the accident, a woman who was driving by stopped AND asked if she could help AND my neighbour put me in the car AND the woman took me the rest of the way home, AND my neighbour brought my dog home.

_____

_____

_____

_____

23. On the bus we started to talk AND he asked about my daily routine AND what I was doing tonight AND what I liked to do during the weekends.

_____

_____

_____

24. The problem of garbage has existed since the beginning of time, AND only now has it become enormously multiplied.

_____

_____

_____

25. My little brother AND I got into a hundred play fights when we were little, AND some when we were not so little, like the time when I was in grade nine AND he was in grade seven AND I picked a fight with him AND beat him up AND chased him to his room.

_____

_____

_____

_____

WORKSHEET

Run-on Sentence, Level 2

NAME _____

*Revise these run-on sentences by substituting more accurate **connecting words** or **punctuation**, by crossing out all **deadwood**, or, if necessary, by completely rewriting in the space.*

1. I started to panic because I knew the stop sign was too close for me to make a safe stop, and I did what any inexperienced driver would do in my situation and that was to slam on the brakes.

   _____
   _____
   _____
   _____

2. It rained that afternoon, and planning to get a suntan on the beach was out of the question.

   _____
   _____

3. In five minutes a slow song came on and I walked across the dance floor and asked her to dance and she said, "Sure."

   _____
   _____
   _____

4. It is very difficult to judge what type of television show is good for each individual, so I believe it is important for people to identify the programs that have a bad influence on them and on society, and restrictions can reduce the amount of time people spend watching the violent scenes.

   _____
   _____
   _____
   _____

5. Let's look at the Philadelphia Flyers, a hockey team that plays a very aggressive game whether winning or losing, and when they're losing they maintain their aggressiveness and you notice signs of hatred and revenge in their game, such as the cheap shots and especially the stick coming down on their opponents.

   _____
   _____
   _____
   _____

6. We left my house around eleven, because it's just before midnight when the strip really becomes crowded, because that's when the theatres close, or if there's a concert on at the Gardens, it usually ends around midnight, and not many people go home right away, because they go for a walk on the strip and meet all the lunatics they can find.

---

7. The topic of rape is not a pleasant one, and the majority of individuals would rather not think about it, or if they do, they usually envision a stranger with a knife hiding in the bushes or in a dark alley waiting for unsuspecting prey to come along, but statistics tell us that 80 percent of all rapes are carried out by people the victim knows.

---

8. When I looked to see the other driver, he was still in his car. A group of people ran over to this car and tried to talk to him, but they couldn't figure out if he was all right or not, and they tried the door and it wouldn't open. So they kept on trying till the door opened and the driver came out and he had only minor bruises and he was in a state of shock. Oh, I forgot to mention that when the accident happened one of the women waiting outside with me went and phoned the police and they didn't show up till everyone seemed to be fine.

---

9. Up ahead my favourite high-speed bend was coming, so I clicked her in 80 and opened the throttle and without warning my bike was all over the place. My back wheel had come loose and before I could stop, it fell off and I went flying over my handlebars and right over the cliff, and I landed in the water next to a big sharp rock, so I feel lucky to be alive today, because when you come that close to death it really makes you think how easily you can be killed through no fault of your own.

---

10. Many well-known companies have undergone extensive economic hardship as a result of unions demanding higher incomes, superior benefit packages, overtime and shift premiums and incentives that give employees a false sense of being indispensable, for example, employees tend to slow down their work, take advantage of overtime and sick leave and when supervisors try to discipline the employees, the union will step in and take control of the situation, usually not to the benefit of the employer.

_____
_____
_____
_____
_____
_____
_____
_____
_____

11. The story is told in a narrative way with Frederick Henry narrating for us, and giving us a good literary description of the surroundings and happenings at the present time period of World War I by speaking of common occurrences during the war, such as shell-marked iron of different structures which were hit by enemy artillery during the war, which, in part, is being described generally and fluently by our narrator, who is an ambulance driver for the Italian army, who is also an American who, as mentioned earlier, donated or sold his skills and techniques to the Italian Army during this time of hardship for the Italians and other warring peoples who are taking part in the war which is spoken of in the story.

_____
_____
_____
_____
_____
_____
_____
_____
_____

12. I asked one of the soldiers how long I would have to stay. He turned to me and hit me in the face with his gun and said, "A very long time, probably forever." I fell down on the ground, and he made me stand up. He covered my eyes and forced me to walk. After we walked for a few minutes he told me to stop and he hit me with his gun again and I fell to the ground. It was one of the coldest months of winter and the temperature was about 25 degrees below zero. I was freezing to death and I was sure it was the end of my life.

_____
_____
_____
_____
_____
_____

EDITING FOR PRONOUN REFERENCE

Pronouns are handy. In substituting for nouns, they save time and spare our readers clumsy repetition. But like shortcuts on a journey, pronouns can also waste time, or even stop us from reaching our destination. So use these shortcuts wisely: **make a pronoun refer clearly to the word for which it substitutes.**

A. Most pronouns need to refer to another word (this is usually called the *antecedent*). Without a noun or sometimes another pronoun to refer to, isolated pronouns such as "she," "he," "they" or "it" cause confusion because the reader does not know what they mean:

> In the far North, *they* do very little in winter. *They* stay inside *their* shelters because the weather can kill.

Here the pronoun "they" has no antecedent. Does "they" refer to polar bears? To First Nations people? To Southerners stationed in the North? To those who live off the land? Or to those who search for oil, gas or minerals? *The easiest way to correct such confusion is to replace a vague pronoun with a noun:*

> In the far North, *prospectors* do very little in winter. *They* stay inside *their* shelters because the weather can kill.

Now the pronouns "they" and "their" make sense, because they can refer to the noun "prospectors." Of course if the author had placed the "prospectors" in the sentence before, or maybe even earlier, we would have an antecedent to explain the pronouns. But *the antecedent should not be very far away.* The noun "prospectors" at the opening of an essay will not explain the pronoun "they" in the tenth paragraph!

■ Sometimes a pronoun merely *seems* to have an antecedent, as in this example from a student essay:

> Smoking is an expensive habit. *It* burns away as soon as a person lights *it* up, even when *it* is not being smoked.

Can "smoking" burn away, be lit up or be smoked? By substituting the noun "smoking" for the pronoun "it," we find that "smoking" has only disguised the lack of a real antecedent. Now let's add one:

> Smoking is an expensive habit. A *cigarette* burns away as soon as a person lights *it* up, even when *it* is not being smoked.

Here is another typical way of misusing a pronoun:

> In the newspaper, *it* says we will have a spring election.

"It" seems to refer to "newspaper"—until we check it by substituting the noun:

> In the newspaper, the *newspaper* says we will have a spring election.

Since a newspaper can hardly be *in* itself, we see that there is in fact no antecedent. Let's avoid the problem by removing the pronoun:

> The newspaper says we will have a spring election.

■ Note that of course *the pronoun "I" needs no antecedent*, because it refers to the person writing. "We" should be explained, though, so readers know who else is included.

■ Note how *the pronoun "it" is sometimes used in a general sense without an antecedent:*

> *It* snowed last night.

> *It* takes two hours to eat a good French dinner.

> No one but the writer knows how difficult *it* is to fill up blank pages day after day.

B. A singular pronoun should not refer to more than one antecedent. The reader feels uneasy having to guess at the meaning of a sentence such as this:

> I watched the old man walk out to his car, open the door, start *it* up and drive away.

What does he start up and drive away, the *door*? Though common sense tells us this is ridiculous, we waste effort having to interpret the message—because there are two possible singular antecedents, "car" and "door," and the second one is closer to the starting and driving.

One common way around this problem is to replace the unclear pronoun with the noun:

> I watched the old man walk out to his car, open the door, start the *car* up and drive away.

Now what happens is clear, but the word "car" occurs twice, weakening the style through repetition. Let's find a different noun, then:

> I watched the old man walk out to his car, open the door, start the *ignition* and drive away.

■ *Be especially careful to make the pronouns "which," "that" and "this" refer to only one specific antecedent.* Since these pronouns can refer to many things—from a single noun to a group of words to a whole sentence or even a paragraph—they must be used with precision. Is the following passage clear?

> My boss accused me of taking extra breaks. *This* was ridiculous, because all day long the store was packed with customers.

So which was ridiculous, the employer's accusation or the author's taking extra breaks? We can only guess. Now let's look at a clearer version of both possibilities:

> My employer's accusation that I took extra breaks was ridiculous, because all day long the store was packed with customers.

> OR

> My employer called my extra breaks ridiculous, because all day long the store was packed with customers.

C. **The pronoun "who" refers to a human antecedent. The pronouns "which" and "that" usually refer to nonhuman antecedents.** Most of us do not make this distinction when we talk, but in the space of an essay we are expected to be more exact: do not refer to a human as a nonhuman or a nonhuman as a human. Here are some typical cases:

> A student *that* cheats may not have a good self-image.

> People *which* lack interest in exercise are lazy in their bodies and minds.

> A pup is easier to train than an old dog, *who* cannot learn new tricks.

In essays, let's substitute the more exact pronouns:

> A student *who* cheats may not have a good self-image.

> People *who* lack interest in exercise are lazy in their bodies and minds.

> A pup is easier to train than an old dog, *which* cannot learn new tricks.

D I A G N O S T I C

Pronoun Reference

NAME _____

Write an "X" in the blank beside each passage that contains unclear pronoun reference, and underline each faulty pronoun.

Example: Many dog owners feel <u>they</u> are real companions.　　　　　X

1. In the travel brochures, they will say anything to convince you to go to their resort.　　_____

2. In Quebec City it is very romantic.　　_____

3. Today many travellers visit Vietnam for their wonderful scenery.　　_____

4. Public transit is readily available to anyone who wants to ride it.　　_____

5. The individual that wants to be successful must have a dream.　　_____

6. Just because most Americans I have met are ignorant about Canada it does not mean they all are.　　_____

7. Plumbing was a profitable trade, but I didn't want to be one all my life.　　_____

8. A person can learn much about a culture through their diet.　　_____

9. Crack addicts may kill their parents because they refuse to give them money for their drug habit.　　_____

10. Shy people are often misunderstood, because they do not express their emotions.　　_____

11. By limiting the hours of TV viewing, it will hopefully increase time spent on more worthwhile activities.　　_____

12. When a thorn scratched my knee, it became infected with gangrene.　　_____

13. The Chinese language is not easy at all. Since they do not have an alphabet, I do not understand how one manages to learn every word when it seems like the words are endless.　　_____

14. By talking, it will bring emotions into the open.　　_____

15. A computer does what it is told.　　_____

16. Today employers like to hire an applicant that can speak either Cantonese or Mandarin.　　_____

17. Unions are dreaded by large companies, and they do everything in their power to keep them out.　　_____

18. At every high school they have a guidance counsellor.　　_____

19. Children's drawings are very important to some child psychologists because, to them, they are signs of their mental and emotional states.　　_____

20. Why do some people have back problems while others do not? Let us consider them.   _____

21. After the city health department did many studies, it decided to ban smoking in bus terminals, subway stations, airports and governmental offices.   _____

22. Teachers should tell students how to be more responsible when they sit behind the steering wheel.   _____

23. An underground economy is created when taxes are so high that people cannot afford it.   _____

24. Canada cannot raise the drinking age when keeping in consideration the responsibilities we hand them at 18—the right to vote, and the right to defend their own country.   _____

25. If I won a million-dollar lottery, there are several ways I would spend it.   _____

26. Women have been sending a clear message to men that they are as good as they are.   _____

27. The next generation of parents will probably be the same as their parents unless they learn from their mistakes.   _____

28. In British Columbia, trees are their main resource.   _____

29. The people that really get me are those that run up the escalators.   _____

30. If we were to learn how to speak Japanese, we would be more interested in the way they operate and reduce the barriers between our two very different cultures.   _____

31. There are many athletes who would risk their lives to use steroids, in order to win.   _____

32. When writing a report, it should be totally clear.   _____

33. Sometimes if parents have to discipline their children at home, they feel threatened by them.   _____

34. If there is a civilization elsewhere in our galaxy, they might be advanced beyond our imagination.   _____

35. Do most people who buy homes actually own them?   _____

36. When the health authorities came to inspect the restaurant, they told Myra and Carol that they needed special permits to operate.   _____

37. Teenagers all need independence, and working is a form of it. It is their own income, and they may spend it any way they wish.   _____

38. Some people will cash their pay cheques and spend it all on lottery tickets.   _____

39. In my country, the children grow up totally dependent on their parents even after they are married.   _____

40. Parents may sometimes go wrong in their children's upbringing. Of course, nobody is perfect. We cannot expect parents to be right always. How would they know that their children would grow up in the wrong way? They tried to give the best for them, and now they are having problems.   _____

W O R K S H E E T

Pronoun Reference, Level 1

NAME _____

Wherever you see a pronoun used unclearly, replace it or even revise the whole passage so everything makes sense. When you find an example with no pronoun problem, write "Correct" in the blank.

Example: At the hospital t̶h̶e̶y̶ *doctors* put ten stitches in my head.

1. My first kiss with a new person is exciting, because it shows how the person feels about you.

   _____

   _____

2. One of my favourite restaurants is Twiggy. They serve a juicy rack of lamb with a tangy mint sauce.

   _____

   _____

3. During the final exam, a guy sitting in front of me took a pack of cigarettes out of his pocket and lit it up.

   _____

   _____

4. There are many programs on TV unsuitable for children, and parents should always make sure to keep them away from them.

   _____

   _____

5. By building tall buildings, it can save space.

   _____

6. Under current law, homeowners that use firearms to defend themselves can be arrested.

   _____

   _____

7. Not all people who diet have an eating disorder.

   _____

8. For consumers, credit cards are useful because they do not have to carry large sums of money.

   _____

   _____

9. The English promised the French that if they joined them they would give them the same powers, but they didn't.

   _____

   _____

10. In big cities the traffic is unbelievable! They drive recklessly. They disobey rules, don't stop at red lights, and speed as if to win an award.

_____

_____

11. People are becoming unemployed because now a computer can do it faster and better.

_____

_____

12. Men no longer have to open doors or light cigarettes for women, because they are equal.

_____

_____

13. Suddenly, out of nowhere, a car came swerving around the corner before their light had changed to green.

_____

_____

14. There are still companies that do not use robots.

_____

15. Parents want to have children that will graduate from university.

_____

_____

16. Have you ever asked yourself why they manufacture products that fall apart?

_____

_____

17. When people hear the judge sentencing a criminal, they do not realize that they will probably not spend all this time in jail.

_____

_____

18. During the snowy season, it can make life hard for country dwellers.

_____

_____

19. The only person that could talk to me was my father, who could speak my language.

_____

_____

20. Hong Kong lies in the subtropical zone. They have never dealt with snowstorms or vehicles stuck in drifts. How lucky they are!

_____

_____

WORKSHEET

Pronoun Reference, Level 2

NAME _____

Revise all faulty pronoun reference below. In some cases you can just substitute a clearer word, while in other cases the whole passage needs rewriting.

in old age

Example: In earlier times, children were the only security parents had ~~when they became old and helpless.~~

$\wedge$

1.   My father is a paramedic, whose job is to pick up limbs that have been severed in teenagers' drag races that weren't quite as cool as they thought it would be.

   _____
   _____
   _____

2.   Parents buy the latest clothing in order for their children to fit in at school. What happens next? They get beaten up by the next kid, whose parents could not afford them.

   _____
   _____
   _____

3.   According to one study, 30 000 businesses in Canada survive by avoiding the GST in underground deals. These employ about 90 000 people.

   _____
   _____
   _____

4.   The maid of honour and best man carry the rings to be exchanged by the couple as a token of their love.

   _____
   _____

5.   After World War II the soldiers that returned gave rise to the "baby boom."

   _____
   _____

6.   Under the Duvalier dictatorship they employed up to 55 000 civil servants, who had little to do, but took up 80 percent of Haiti's budget.

   _____
   _____
   _____

7. We turned on the radio to find out what was happening. There was a tornado warning and it was coming in our direction.

_____

_____

_____

8. There are parents who think their children will appreciate the fact they are trying to provide for them a better life than they had themselves, even if they never spend any time with them.

_____

_____

_____

_____

9. By adding a camper to a pickup truck, it can be used for summer enjoyment.

_____

_____

10. I distinctly remember how I felt in grade eleven math when experiencing difficulties with a question. I called upon her for her assistance. In turn she looked at the question, wrote it on the board, then wrote the answer, and walked away without explaining the process at all.

_____

_____

_____

_____

_____

11. Take politics, for example. Most of them can warp language to their advantage, because they can word campaign promises to solicit a variety of interpretations.

_____

_____

_____

12. It rained all night and, as a result, caused the tent to collapse.

_____

_____

13. Many people choose to have a dog as a pet because they are good companions.

_____

_____

14. The rent of the store site was extremely expensive, since it was located in the centre of Vancouver.

_____

_____

15. After 30 minutes in the oven, the cake is tested by sticking a knife into it. If the knife blade remains clean, then the cake is done. If the knife blade has some batter on it, then it needs cooking for another 10 minutes.

_____

_____

_____

_____

_____

16. The biggest problem with teenage drinking is not that they do it, but that they do it illegally, behind their parents' backs.

_____

_____

_____

17. The two years' difference between Canada's drinking age and the legal age in the United States seems small, but consider the following factors. In Canada they cannot drink at graduation, while in university, or possibly while holding a job. They are treated as adults in every other way except making the choice to drink.

_____

_____

_____

_____

_____

_____

18. Not only do young drivers risk their lives, but they also risk the lives of all the other people who are with them. I believe the only way we can save these lives is by giving them more time so that they can understand the bloodshed of drinking.

_____

_____

_____

_____

_____

19. In Quebec City they have buildings that attract crowds of tourists, because they are hundreds of years old.

_____

_____

_____

20. Miss Scatcherd accused Helen of not washing her fingernails, which was impossible to do since the water was frozen.

_____

_____

_____

21. Poverty, homelessness, child hunger, unemployment, exploitation of children in the workplace and increased crimes are all alarming issues that seem to be a part of our daily lives, but what is being done about it?

22. On Yonge Street a production crew was filming a movie called *Forever Night.* A set member told us that more and more films are produced in Canada because it costs a lot less.

23. When crimes are committed by young people, they are usually placed in a detention centre or group home.

24. The Canadian immigration office in Singapore set an interview appointment with my parents. They asked them some general questions about employment, health and criminal records. Then they informed them that they would get in touch with them in a couple of weeks. When they did get back to them, they sent all of my family to various departments for medical and criminal clearance. After all the results were in, they then summoned my whole family for the final interview.

25. Most parents want their children to have their own licences as soon as possible because they do not want to drive them everywhere. If they have their licences, they will not have this kind of trouble. However, they have the responsibility of driving with them for at least a few weeks once they get the licences.

EDITING FOR AGREEMENT

The English we speak and the English we write can be as different from each other as the clothes we wear to the beach and the clothes we wear to the prom. In editing for agreement, this contrast can grow so sharp that sometimes it almost seems that what is natural in speech is wrong on the page, and what is correct on the page is unnatural in speech.

But there is really no problem unless we blindly take speech as our model for writing. We would all *say* "Everyone ate their lunch," and our listeners would regard this as normal speech. But the same words in the more formal space of your essay would seem illogical, because "everyone" is singular while "their" is plural.

This could change. In fact, some newspapers and magazines already use the speech-like approach of the example we just looked at, "Everyone ate their lunch." In a few more years most readers may agree.

For now, though, the customary approach to agreement is safer for those writing in school—because many readers, especially teachers, still see these more conversational usages as errors. Especially in the more formal kinds of writing, such as literary papers or research papers of all kinds, stay with the techniques explained below.

> *Of the ten parts that follow, items A, E, F, H and I will cover about 90 percent of all cases. Highlight them in your book.* Pay special attention to the best technique of all, the *pluralizing* suggested at the end of item H, because it avoids the whole problem of informality vs. formality.

A subject and its verb must agree in number; that is, they must both be singular or both be plural. A pronoun and its antecedent—the noun to which it refers—must agree in number and in person.

A. *Make a **verb** agree with its **subject**, and a **pronoun** with its **antecedent**, **no matter how many words separate them.*** Sometimes it helps to imagine brackets around interrupting word groups such as dependent clauses, to make items that must agree easier to identify.

> S
> My first *impression* [of downtown Vancouver
> with its noise, traffic jams, crowded buses and
> V
> thousands of pedestrians] *was* frightening.

> S
> The *slaughter* [of rare species, not to mention
> V
> many more species still undiscovered], *is* still
> continuing.

B. *Make related nouns, pronouns and verbs agree even when one or more is **outside the independent clause*** (to review independent clauses, see page 105):

> N V P
> I took the job because the *company pays its* employees well. (Here the related noun, verb and pronoun are all in a dependent clause.)

> N V
> The film left out many *parts* that *were* covered in the book. (Here a verb in a dependent clause is related to a noun in the independent clause.)

> N P
> A *factory* leaves its workers unemployed when *it* closes down. (Here a pronoun in a dependent clause is related to a noun that is the subject of the independent clause.)

C. *Make the **subject and verb** agree even **when their order is reversed**.* Once in a while the verb occurs first, which makes the subject harder to identify. Just remember that the subject is what the sentence is *about*, while the verb tells what the subject *does* or *is*. Once you identify the two, making them agree is easy.

> V S S
> On the desk *are* [not *is*] the keyboard, monitor,
> S S
> mouse and printer.

To double-check your sentence, just think of it in the normal word order with the verb following the subject:

> S S S S V
> The *keyboard, monitor, mouse* and *printer are* on the desk.

D. *Singular subjects joined by* **or** *or* **nor** *take singular verbs and pronouns.*

> Butter or margarine *is* [not *are*] fattening.

> Neither salad nor fruit *is* [not *are*] fattening.

Of course if the items were joined by "and," they would form compound subjects that would call for plural verbs:

> Butter and margarine *are* fattening.

Where two subjects are habitually treated as a unit, though, the two together are singular:

> Bacon *and* eggs *is* my favourite breakfast.

E. *Collective nouns take singular verbs and singular pronouns when the group is seen as a unit:*

> The company *wants* [not *want*] to lower *its* [not *their*] costs.

> The government *was* [not *were*] ready to defend *its* [not *their*] decision.

> The team *loses* [not *lose*] more than *it wins* [not *they win*].

Although a company, a government or a team is made up of many people, we are discussing one company, one government and one team—so each is singular. But if the members of a group act separately, the group may be treated as a plural:

> The jury *were* arguing about the verdict.

F. *"Indefinite pronouns" are usually singular, even though some may seem plural.*

- *anybody, everybody, nobody, somebody*

- *anyone, everyone, no one, one, someone*

- *anything, everything, nothing, something*

- *another, any, each, either, neither*

> Everyone *is* [not *are*] going to the club.

> Anyone who *is* finished may hand in *his or her* [not *their*] essay.

When we talk, it feels right to say "Someone has left their notebook." But though this is what most of us would say in casual conversation, it actually makes no sense. Why? If we begin with "someone *has*," we've signalled that "someone" is singular—otherwise we would have said "someone *have*." But we knew that didn't sound right, so we didn't say it. Yet once having established "someone" as singular by saying *has*, we might rush right on and say *"their* notebook"—yet *their* tells us that "someone" is plural. A word can't be both singular and plural at once. And that is why, in the more logical and exact space of the page, we would write "Someone has left his or her notebook."

The moral of the story: writing is more logical and exact than speech. Don't let that "voice" in your ear dictate all the words that end up on the page. Take as your model for writing not how others speak, but how other good writers write.

> Someone *has* left *his or her* [not *their*] notebook.

G. **(For ESL Students:)** If you're not sure whether a verb is singular or plural, remember that *although the final "s" makes a* **noun plural,** *it makes a* **verb singular:**

SINGULAR

>   N   V
> The bird flies.

PLURAL

>   N   V
> The birds fly.

If you're still in doubt about the number of a verb, apply the "it-they" test. Place the words "it" and "they" before the verb. If singular "it" sounds right with the verb, the verb is singular; if plural "they" sounds right, the verb is plural:

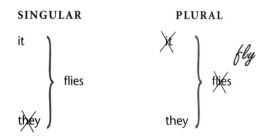

H. *Be consistent in pronoun use.* Do not change in the middle of a passage from singular "he or she" to plural "they":

WRONG

> The sensible drinker will have only one or two beers, so *he or she* will not lose *their* self-control.

(The student who wrote this sentence forgot that singular verbs joined by "or" take singular verbs and pronouns.) Other writers grimly exchange bad grammar for bad style by repeating pronouns:

> The sensible drinker will have only one or two beers, so *he or she* will not lose *his or her* self-control.

When you read writing from earlier times, sometimes you'll find "he" used to mean people in general. Today this usage is no longer an option, for it ignores women. In the following example, it could also imply that only men drink beer!

> The sensible drinker will have only one or two beers, so *he* will not lose *his* self control.

(A better solution is to rewrite the sentence so as to avoid all problems of grammar, style and prejudice:)

> The sensible drinker will have only one or two beers, to avoid losing self-control.

Note how the statement now has no pronoun problems—because it has no pronouns! Solutions like these are direct but not always possible. You'll find that **the most widely useful solution of all is to** *pluralize* **from the beginning. Use this method often:**

> Sensible *drinkers* will have only one or two beers, so *they* will not lose *their* self-control.

I. *A pronoun and its antecedent* must *agree in person:*

FIRST PERSON

> I, me, we, us

SECOND PERSON

> you

THIRD PERSON

> he, him, she, her, one, it, they, them

In speech and informal writing, the second-person "you" is often used to mean people in general. Yet "you" is in the second person while "people" is in the third person. "You" may even be understood by the reader to mean herself or himself, personally:

> In the two years *I* worked at the restaurant, *I* was always given a meal, a break and all the pop *you* could drink.

(Unless the reader is the person who drank the pop, the writer should stay in the first person:)

> In the two years *I* worked at the restaurant, *I* was always given a meal, a break and all the pop *I* could drink.

There is no such word as *"themself"* or *"ourself,"* because "them" and "our" are plural, while "self" is singular. Instead, write the logical and standard terms, *"themselves"* and *"ourselves."*

J. *The words "media," "phenomena" and "criteria" are plural; their singular forms are "medium," "phenomenon" and "criterion."* Examples:

PLURAL

> Television, radio and the other mass *media are* turning Canadians into Americans.

SINGULAR

> Film *is* a *medium* of great cultural power.

PLURAL

> Centrifugal force and centripetal force *are* two opposite *phenomena.*

SINGULAR

> The falling of snow *is* a *phenomenon* that most of the world's population has never seen.

D I A G N O S T I C

Agreement

NAME _____

Put an "X" in the blank after each passage that contains any fault in agreement. (Remember: the informal way we speak is not always right for the more formal and exact space of an essay.)

1. You can tell a lot about a person by the way they kiss. _____

2. I detest hot and humid days when you sweat and get headaches from the heat. _____

3. It is essential to comfort your ex and tell them they are an exceptional person. _____

4. In time, your former partner will come to see that you were being truly honest with them. _____

5. The mass media are very popular today. _____

6. One day while I was in a bus going to school, a soldier came in and asked for everyone's identification. They made many passengers get out, including me. _____

7. A pregnant person would start asking themselves questions such as "Is it a girl or a boy?" _____

8. One cannot enjoy listening to your CD as you exercise. _____

9. Computer viruses can duplicate themself and move to another system, then duplicate themself again. _____

10. In prison I dared not pick a quarrel with anyone, because they could beat me at any time. _____

11. A series of studies has shown that addiction to TV kills the imagination. _____

12. One wants to look their best for formal events. _____

13. Will the people of Hong Kong have a say in what the government do? _____

14. If you're sitting and a pregnant or elderly lady is standing, you should give them your seat. _____

15. I have both a high school diploma and a community college diploma, but neither of them has helped me get a job for the summer. _____

16. At the foot of the bed are a desk and a chair. _____

17. If one is short, they may want to choose a short skirt to make them look taller. _____

18. Neither the cold virus nor the AIDS virus have cures. _____

19.   Give a famous musician any song and they will make it popular!   _____

20.   The number of common-law marriages has risen.   _____

21.   All the languages that a person knows is an asset to their identity.   _____

22.   Going to the movies are fun except when one happens to sit beside or near people who talk too much, move a lot in their seats or block the view.   _____

23.   While one is downtown, they may wish to play a video game.   _____

24.   My sister will not let me borrow her things, because she is scared that I may ruin it for her.   _____

25.   Every résumé should have a brief covering letter which shows the company that you know something about them.   _____

26.   Travelling is a great way to learn about ourself.   _____

27.   For a few minutes of happiness in gambling, one can lose the fortune which they have built all their lives.   _____

28.   If anyone tried to wander from the camp, they were imprisoned or shot.   _____

29.   I take pride in my car. It's great to have my own transportation for my convenience.   _____

30.   Advertisers have realized that the consumer is getting older, and therefore advertisements are directed at them.   _____

31.   When an older person retires, his or her income is usually cut in half.   _____

32.   I was accepted at Windsor University for their social work program.   _____

33.   Once a student is streamed into general-level courses, they are often stigmatized by their peers and their teachers as lacking intelligence.   _____

34.   When I was younger I used to play in the park with my friends all day long, and you knew all the kids that you played with.   _____

35.   The gambler is always under tremendous stress and always promising to themselves that if they win they will quit.   _____

36.   I have a sister of my own height and shape, which means you can wear each other's clothing.   _____

37.   Each one of us are special within our own race and culture.   _____

38. Teens today need to learn that sex isn't the only way to show somebody how you truly feel about them. _____

39. There was once a time when it was rare that you didn't know your next-door neighbour in my neighbourhood. _____

40. One weekday morning I slept in, so I missed my school bus. After listening to my mother chastise me, I phoned a neighbour at 7:40 a.m. and asked if they could give me a lift. He jumped into his car, and drove me to school. _____

WORKSHEET

Agreement, Level 1

NAME _____

Though many of the choices below would sound natural and correct in conversation, circle or highlight only those most appropriate for the essay writer.

1. The government (*are/is*) cutting back programs right and left.

2. The benefits of knowing more than one language (*is/are*) incredible.

3. To avoid criminal attack, we must think of methods to reduce the chance of its happening to (*you/us/him or her*).

4. Sarah's family (*has/have*) a history of diabetes.

5. The rapid activity, unpredictable events, and exciting violence of hockey (*leaves/leave*) a spectator standing on the seat.

6. Neither money nor power (*provide/provides*) true happiness.

7. Lying is something that everybody does at some point in (*his/their/his or her*) life.

8. To me, friends are essential. Without them (*you/I*) would be lost.

9. The first term was coming to an end and I, like many other eager first-year students, (*were/was*) studying in the library on a Sunday night.

10. One benefit of the laser printer is (*their/its*) low maintenance.

11. You and I do not really know what starvation and poverty are, the way the developing world (*do/does*).

12. Satellites, telescopes, and other sophisticated equipment (*provide/provides*) a watchful eye into space, allowing us to detect or even prevent cosmic disaster.

13. Neither a husband nor a wife (*are/is*) free to break marriage vows.

14. Nobody wants to have a dump in (*his/her/their/his or her*) neighbourhood.

15. In Canada a criminal is eligible for parole after (*they have/he has/he or she has*) served one-third of (*their/his/his or her*) sentence.

16. The fastest-growing segment of the population (*is/are*) senior citizens.

17. Quebec just wants to be recognized for (*their/its*) importance in Canadian culture and tradition.

18. Across the street (*was/were*) an emergency hydro truck, two fire trucks, three police cars and an ambulance.

19. One's home is (*his/her/their/his or her*) private place.

20. The orchestra (*was/were*) playing quietly in the background.

21. The media (*likes/like*) to report crimes committed by members of minority groups.

22. High levels of UV radiation (*leads/lead*) to skin cancer in humans.

23. The rural population is known for (*their/its*) strong values.

24. Anyone who denies that (*he or she has/they have*) ever flirted just isn't telling the truth.

25. Across the border the merchandise, such as stereos, cameras and other electronic equipment, (*are/is*) cheaper than in Canada.

26. Today the cost of living makes me think twice. Should (*I/you*) move out, or stay with (*my/your*) parents?

27. In the big city, everyone (*is/are*) for (*themself/themselves/himself or herself*).

28. A series of accidents involving teenagers (*have/has*) led to the new procedures for licensing drivers.

29. The group of Canadians who sponsored us (*has/have*) been helpful from the very beginning.

30. In Winnipeg if people want to park their car, (*they/we/he or she*) (*have/has*) to pay over ten dollars.

W O R K S H E E T

Agreement, Level 2

NAME _____

Though some of these passages might be all right for conversation, all contain at least one fault in agreement that makes them too inexact for an essay. Wherever you find such a weakness, cross out the problem words and write your correction in the blank.

Example: The number of white-collar crimes h̶a̶v̶e̶ risen sharply.   *has*

1. I have several e-mail correspondents throughout the world. It seems so amazing that you can connect through the touch of a button.   _____

2. It's true the city never sleeps, but why can't they stop emptying the huge garbage bins at one o'clock in the morning?   _____

3. Gambling at places like charity casinos are for a good cause.   _____

4. I will be more careful in choosing a partner for my next relationship. I want someone who can take the initiative in telephoning me, showing their feelings about me and just showing they care.   _____

5. When one receives a parking ticket and wishes to attend court, they have the choice between a French or English procedure.   _____

6. All too often, either injury or death is the result of drunk driving.   _____

7. After some negative reports, the Metro Housing Authority decided to improve their security system.   _____

8. As soon as I open the machine shop door, the smell of burning steel and oil rushes into my nose and makes me cough. The constant harsh noises hit you like a car.   _____

9. At one end of the room is the tuner, speakers, CD player, and two shelves of CDs.   _____

10. A few years ago I joined the World Wildlife Federation, an international nature organization. They fight against the extermination of species.   _____

11. One can almost believe that they are actually part of the film, as the Dolby stereo sound of an explosion trembles right through your body.   _____

12. Postsecondary students tend to study in groups rather than alone. For them there are many benefits to studying within a group because of the help you can receive from your peers.   _____

13. Television is not the only media that reinforces society's obsession with being thin.   _____

14. Ryerson Polytechnic was once a college, granting only diplomas to its graduates. It was just a few years ago that they received recognition and established themselves as a university.   _____

15. The number of people wearing contact lenses are increasing.   _____

16. The next time you walk by a homeless person, do not treat them like an animal. Give them the dignity and respect they deserve.   _____

17. Is confidentiality and privacy no longer sacred?   _____

18. As I grew older and was very attracted to men, the idea of committing yourself to one person for the rest of your life still didn't turn me on.   _____

19. This country needs to focus on changing their priorities.   _____

20. Imagine asking someone over for dinner, meaning supper, and they show up at noon to have dinner with you.   _____

21. When I go out at night in Vancouver, I make sure to take a cab home rather than walk, because you are less likely to be attacked when locked within the safety of a moving vehicle.   _____

22. Trust me, never give your new boss your exact time schedule for school. They will put your work hours right after your school hours, literally giving you no time at all to do anything.   _____

23. Being a night person, I can't understand how anyone can function properly if they have been awake since 7 a.m.   _____

24. At Broadview and Gerrard there is a small Chinese community with many exotic specialty shops. Walking through this community, you are able to experience another culture and appreciate the many facets of their heritage.   _____

25. What makes hockey bloodier than other major sports is the fact that for 60 minutes of playing time, each of the players carries a large weapon in his hands, a stick that measures five feet in length and has a pointed tip, the better with which to jab your opponent in the gut.   _____

WORKSHEET

Agreement, Level 3

NAME _____

Revise all the weaknesses in agreement, either adding changes above the line, or, if you need to rework a whole passage, writing in the spaces below. See if you can identify the one passage that has no error at all.

Example: Everyone on the boat, including myself, w~~er~~e very nervous about the storm.
                                                                      was

1. Shouting was the band's idea of singing. They all sounded like they had sore throats.

   _____

   _____

2. The government is not concerned about us. They are not concerned about all the mothers, fathers and children who have to work ten hours a day to survive.

   _____

   _____

   _____

3. If an applicant wants to work in the airline industry, knowing more than one language will drastically enhance their chance of gaining employment. This industry is known for combining different cultures as a function of their business.

   _____

   _____

   _____

   _____

4. The passionate screams, the cries for help, the pushing and shoving, the smell of rubber and asphalt, the noise of horns and the impact of the crash stands out vividly in my mind.

   _____

   _____

   _____

5. With age and experience comes reason.

   _____

6. When a person comes home from work or school, the first thing they do is throw off their shoes and sit on the couch, with their zapper in their hand. When you turn the television on, you change from station to station and finally settle on a program. It could be a comedy or a drama, but how many times is it Canadian?

   _____

   _____

   _____

   _____

   _____

7. To obtain a handgun in the United States, a person undergoes only a quick police check to ensure that they are not already a wanted criminal. Then they can buy a handgun. The gun does not even have to be locked up. It can be stored in a drawer in your home or the glove compartment of your car, or even concealed on your body. It can be stored anywhere a person might need it in order to protect themselves.

---

8. Examples of students passing notes in class is very common. All kids like to do it. It proves that kids can write, when it is something they enjoy. But when you tell them to write about motifs and foreshadowing in *Hamlet* or *Macbeth*, the same student often blanks out and write poorly.

---

9. As a potential alcoholic walks down the street and sees the terrifying life of skid-row panhandlers, complete with their wine sores and filthy clothes, they confidently say that this would never happen to them because they are different. They do not realize that just a few years ago, the person they are looking at probably had a good job and a happy home life! Then something happened that they couldn't handle, and the drink which had always rescued them now turned out to be their worst enemy.

---

10. In a big city, pedestrians are aloof, and extremely guarded. When you approach a stranger on the street for directions they look at you for a few seconds trying to sum up your motive. For example, does this person want money, or are they trying to flirt with me? Unfortunately, with all the city crimes we hear about, a person must take extra precautions and therefore we lose a sense of togetherness.

Editing for Equality of the Sexes in Language

Language is always changing. During your own lifetime English has changed faster than ever, because society is changing faster than ever. For example, our vocabulary has shifted significantly to reflect the equality of males and females in modern society. For most people, seeking fairness in the way they refer to women and to men has become almost second nature.

© COREL PHOTOS.

Yet old habits die hard. Do you still write "policeman," when every day you see women, as well as men, patrolling the streets and driving squad cars? It is only natural that newspaper reporters, television newscasters and students writing essays now use the term "police officer." Language that conveys sexism is now widely regarded as a blunder, much like a grammar error but with social repercussions. Does it appear in your own writing? If so, consider and try out the following suggestions:

A. *Avoid terms that unnecessarily differentiate female from male:*

AVOID	TRY
actress	actor
businessman	business person, entrepreneur, manager
chairman	chairperson, chair, head
maiden name	birth name
mankind, man	humanity, humankind, humans, the human race, people
man-made	imitation, synthetic, artificial
policeman, patrolman	police officer
salesman	salesperson, clerk, sales clerk
waitress	server, attendant
woman doctor, lady dentist, woman lawyer	doctor, dentist, lawyer

B. *Use forms of address that reflect equality of the sexes.* Traditionally we have called a woman either "Miss" or "Mrs.," signalling whether she is single or married. By contrast, we have used the less specific term "Mr." for all men. Some women still prefer the traditional terms; in these cases respect their wish to be called "Miss" or "Mrs." But call other women "Ms.," so they will not resent the unnecessary scrutiny of their private lives.

In the past, a woman was often addressed by her husband's full name:

Mrs. Pierre Tremblay

Mrs. Albert Tsang

Avoid this practice, which implies that a woman's identity is derived only through a husband. Instead, use the woman's own first name, preceded by "Ms."—unless she prefers "Mrs":

Ms. Jocelyne Tremblay

Mrs. Elaine Tsang

(Of course specify her own last name if she does not use her husband's.)

C. *The pronoun "he" should refer only to males.* This idea may seem to be self-evident, but remember the old practice of using "he" for a person or persons of unspecified gender ("Everyone paid for *his* own dinner"). In cases like this, the "his" or the "he" implies that males are more important than females; in fact, it almost implies there are no females at all. Another example:

> A lawyer has little time for *his* family. (Unspoken assumption: lawyers are all men.)

One alternative is "his or her" (to be fair, use "her or his" half the time):

> A lawyer often has little time for *his or her* family.

One problem with this approach, though, is its clumsy repetition and wordiness:

> A lawyer has not only too little time for *her or his* clients, but also for *her or his* family.

In reaching for a style free of repetition, many people create new errors, this time in agreement (see pages 159–161):

> A lawyer has not only too little time for *his or her* clients, but also for *their* own family. (While "his or her" is singular, "their" is plural.)

A better solution is to use plurals all the way:

> *Lawyers* have not only too little time for *their* clients, but also for *their* own families.

An even cleaner solution to this and other pronoun problems is sometimes just to rewrite the sentence with no pronoun at all:

> A lawyer has too little time for either clients or family.

At first it may seem hard to free your prose of gender bias while still maintaining good style. But remember that there are almost always other ways to word your thoughts. Seek them through revision, as in these examples.

D. *Stereotyping the sexes is a form of bias. Avoid it.* Consider alternatives such as these:

BIASED	NEUTRAL
A welder must protect *his* eyes. (In other words, welders are men.)	Welders must protect *their* eyes. (Use plurals to avoid "his.")
A nurse must respect *her* patients. (In other words, nurses are women.)	A nurse must respect patients. (Remove the pronoun.) OR Nurses must respect *their* patients. (Use plurals.)
There were too many *guys* at the party and not enough *girls*. (In other words, females are only girls.)	There were too many *men* at the party and not enough *women*. OR There were too many *boys* at the party, and not enough *girls*. (Imply equality by using parallel terms.)

W O R K S H E E T

Equality of the Sexes in Language

N A M E _____

Most of the passages below contain expressions or attitudes that do not reflect the equality of men and women. Remove all sexism, either crossing out and replacing terms, or revising the whole passage in the space. Write "FAIR" under any passage that is bias-free.

1. All the executives and their wives came to the party.

   _____

2. Within a decade, man will be on Mars.

   _____

3. When I regained consciousness, a lady doctor was taking my pulse.

   _____

   _____

4. There are 23 girls in my class but only seven guys.

   _____

5. Our neighbourhood is crowded with young girls and boys.

   _____

6. The chairman tabled the committee's report.

   _____

7. The guests were Mr. and Mrs. Edward Turnbull, Mr. Peter Chen, Miss Nancy Donnelly and Mr. and Mrs. Antonio Santos.

   _____

   _____

   _____

8. A good foreman is fair to his workers.

   _____

9. A good secretary keeps her desk neat.

   _____

10. Forty police manned the roadblocks to catch the fleeing gunmen.

    _____

    _____

11. After a day on the oil rigs, you crave a man-sized dinner.

    _____

12. Are there limits to the amount of knowledge man can obtain?

_____

_____

13. If he studies each day's work on time, the student will have no trouble with exams.

_____

_____

14. It takes more than just size to be a policeman.

_____

15. No one chooses his destiny.

_____

16. How much should we tip the waitress?

_____

17. What was your mother's maiden name?

_____

18. The farmer often makes too little to cover his own costs, while the middleman in the city grows rich.

_____

_____

19. The candidates are Mr. Frank Johnson, Miss Lise Gagnon, Mr. Joseph Horvath and Mrs. Barry Rossiter.

_____

_____

_____

20. My neighbour is a police officer.

_____

21. Every soldier knows how to maintain his rifle.

_____

22. Any person who skips breakfast is endangering his health.

_____

_____

23. Most of Canada's top businessmen think federal taxation is out of control.

_____

_____

24. Man now has the capability to create human life by artificial means. Perhaps man has obtained more knowledge than he was ever intended to have. In his quest for knowledge, man must set limits in his journey, both for himself and for all of mankind.

---

25. The more time a person puts into developing his career, the richer his life experience becomes. He gets advancement in his job. He enjoys every day of his life. He gets full satisfaction out of his work experience and seems content and happy with his life. Advancement in his career also brings in more money and hence a luxurious life that everybody dreams of. He feels that he has got all that he ever wanted in life.

EDITING TO AVOID MISPLACED MODIFIERS AND DANGLING MODIFIERS

A MODIFIER is a word or word group that explains another word or word group. Place a modifier right next to what it explains. If you do not, it may seem to explain the wrong thing.

UNCLEAR

Most people like to relax after a hard day's work *in front of the TV.*

CLEAR

Most people like to relax *in front of the TV* after a hard day's work.

Often a misplaced modifier creates a ridiculous meaning, as above where people seem to do a hard day's work in front of the TV. Other times, a misplaced modifier just makes the passage hard to understand. The carelessly worded first sentence below was supposed to mean what the second one actually says:

UNCLEAR

I *only* eat out once a week.

CLEAR

I eat out *only* once a week.

See how, in the first version, "only" seems to explain the word "eat"—as if eating is all the person ever does. But in the second version, "only" now limits "once a week"—to correctly show that our author does not eat out every day.

"Only" is the most often misplaced modifier in our language. Note below how the meaning changes each time "only" moves to a new position:

Only I saw the robbery in Saturday. (No one else saw it.)

I *only* saw the robbery on Saturday. (I saw it but did not hear it.)

I saw *only* the robbery on Saturday. (I saw nothing else.)

I saw the *only* robbery on Saturday. (There was no other.)

I saw the robbery *only* on Saturday. (I did not see it any other day.)

A DANGLING MODIFIER is not connected at all to the word or word group it was meant to explain. Thus it seems to explain the wrong thing. Dangling modifiers are tough to fix: they can't just be moved, but instead, part of the sentence has to be rewritten to make the connection. In some parts of Canada, drivers are startled to see road signs that tell them "Slow down when flashing." It may take only a second to reject the ludicrous idea that motorists are "flashing" and to notice the warning lights that do "flash"—but during this moment of failed communication, the highway department has not exactly improved its image. How about adding a key word to say "Slow down when light is flashing"? Here are more dangling modifiers, this time from student compositions:

"NEARING THE TOP OF THE FLIGHT OF STAIRS, MY NOSTRILS DETECTED THE FAMILIAR STALE STENCH OF THE GYM"

© GREG DEVITT.

UNCLEAR

While reading this essay, 4 people will die of starvation and 24 babies will be born somewhere in the world.

If the author of this statement had specified a reader, the ridiculous idea of dying and newborn persons reading the essay would not occur to us.

CLEAR

While you read this essay, 4 people will die of starvation and 24 babies will be born somewhere in the world.

CLEAR

In the time it takes the reader to finish this essay, 4 people will die of starvation and 24 babies will be born somewhere in the world.

UNCLEAR

When driving, the most important part of the car is the brake. (Is the brake driving?)

CLEAR

To drivers, the most important part of the car is the brake.

Not all dangling modifiers are as silly as these; others are harder to detect and fix:

UNCLEAR

At home, *when doing my homework,* there aren't any noisy parties to bother me, as there are in the dorm.

Since the author has said "*my* homework" and "to bother *me*," we may not imagine a noisy party doing the homework. Yet the sentence gives an uneasy feeling that we are guessing at its meaning. If our author had openly used the word "I," and moved "the dorm" closer to the "noisy parties" that occur there, all would be clear:

When I am at home, the noisy parties at the dorm cannot distract me from my homework.

Misplaced and Dangling Modifiers

NAME _____

Write "MM" in the blank beside each sentence that contains a misplaced modifier, and underline the misplaced modifier.

1. Just like any other disease, we must wait for the cure to racism to be found. _____

2. I moved to Bayside with my parents when I was 13 years old from the city of Ottawa. _____

3. The waiter brought menus covered with Chinese writing to us. _____

4. If you are like most people, a mortgage will be the largest debt of your lifetime. _____

5. As a child, my father told me the world is a cruel place to be in alone. _____

6. When I was a kid I lived with my grandmother, a lovely lady who would let me do anything I wanted to, for a few months. _____

7. Preparing for an eight-hour ride, the motor of the car was the only noise. _____

8. We are only young once. _____

9. It takes my mother only three minutes to drive to work. _____

10. I have only been in Canada for one year. _____

11. Long-distance health care is only possible because of computers. _____

12. In the past, stores were only allowed open on Sundays during the holiday shopping season. _____

13. We have become a species that knows only how to sleep and turn on the TV. _____

14. Since I was an only child, my parents wanted to protect me. _____

15. After being hired, the manager teaches the newcomer his or her duties and responsibilities. _____

16. Drinking is said to be a bad habit by many doctors. _____

17. I was discouraged from speaking the truth by my lawyer. _____

18. In the past, even an unimportant disease could kill the victim such as measles, whooping cough or diphtheria. _____

19. Some children are forced to learn their first language by their parents. _____

20. I have been working to put myself through school for the last five years. _____

Write "DM" in the blank beside each sentence that contains a dangling modifier, and underline the dangling modifier.

1. Climbing back into the car, our lunch was half eaten. _____

2. When you are living as a family, housework needs to be done. _____

3. Dogs make good household pets because they are used for protecting the house while away for the day. _____

4. After eating a whole pizza, my stomach begins to feel strange. _____

5. After spending three hours shivering and trying to stay warm, the storm subsided and we quickly headed for camp. _____

6. Ever since seeing this film at age 12, the memory has been burned into my mind. _____

7. After waiting two hours in the lobby, the doctor spent less than two minutes on me. _____

8. Upon arrival in Canada, I experienced the language barrier. _____

9. By recycling paper, thousands of square kilometres of forest will be preserved. _____

10. Dressed in secondhand clothing with long messy hair, his appearance was anything but clean-cut. _____

11. When feeling lonely and depressed, a dog is always at your side wagging its tail. _____

12. Living on the farm in Alberta, winter tends to be cold and harsh. _____

13. Being an ESL student, I had a hard time understanding the teachers. _____

14. After writing tests and quizzes, the board of education agreed to let me attend grade twelve at York Memorial High School. _____

15. Parents have noted an increase in fights between siblings after watching certain programs on television. _____

16. After a few months of cleaning a dentist's office, the dentist recommended me to her bookkeeper, so I was able to clean the bookkeeper's office too. _____

17. Becoming more educated now, more interests entered my mind and engulfed it. _____

18. Loose bindings will cause the skis to fall off while standing up and skiing. _____

19. Going through grade twelve, the teachers began to demand more work. _____

20. When driving in a big city like Montreal, parking is always a problem. _____

WORKSHEET

Misplaced and Dangling Modifiers, Level 1

NAME _____

Revise these sentences, correcting all misplaced or dangling modifiers. If a sentence has no error, write "Correct" in the space.

Example: *When I was*
~~As~~ a teenager, Agatha Christie was my favourite novelist.

1. After working two months at minimum wage, my boss increased my pay to nine dollars an hour.

   My boss increased my pay to nine dollars an hour, after working two months at minimum wage

2. Now at the age of six months, we take the dog everywhere we go.

   we take the dog everywhere to go when it's six month old.

3. Having gone through a messy divorce, I was glad to see my sister find inner peace and happiness.

   My sister have gone through a messy divorce, I was glad to see my sister find inner peace and happiness

4. Entering the park, the smell of hot dogs and peanuts filled our nostrils.

   As I enter the park, the smell of hot dogs and peanuts filled our nostrills.

5. At the age of four, my parents separated.

   When I was at the age of four, my parents separated.

6. While downhill skiing, your expenses can run into the hundreds of dollars.

   When your downhill skiing, your expenses can run into the hundreds of dollars

7. Consumers are the ones who suffer from higher costs, not the producers.

   Consumers, not the producers are the ones who suffer from higher cost.

8. In living common-law, a child is considered illegitimate.

   When a couple live in common-law, any child they have is consider illegitimate.

9. Now old people are told by their children what to do.

   Correct

10. I only lost my first game.

    I lost only my first game

11. Standing on the beach, the water gently rippled over my toes.

    The water gently rippled over my toes, when I was standing on the beach.

12. Growing up, my brothers had a large influence on me.

I grew up with my brothers, they had a large influence on me

13. When raining, the motorcyclist can easily have an accident.

Motorcyclist can easily have an accident when it's raining.

14. I was almost doing every job in the shop.

_____

15. Many items we eat on a regular basis are full of empty calories, such as jam, mayonnaise and ketchup.

Many items we eat on a regular basis, such as jam, mayonnaise and ketchup are full of empty calories

16. Barrie is a quiet town when browsing through the main street.

When browsing through the main street Barrie seems like a quiet town.

17. Now we have only one system of weights and measures.

Correct.

18. By simply repeating commands, my dog eventually understood what I wanted him to do.

By simply repeating my commands, my dog eventually understood what I want him to do.

19. Walking along Robson Street, a major thoroughfare like Yonge Street but half the length, the trendy shops sell the latest fashions and souvenirs for tourists.

I was walking along Robson street, I notice a major thoroughfare like Yonge Street but half length, the trendy shops sell the latest fashions & souvenirs to tourists.

20. Basketball games can make people excited on TV.

People get excited by basketball games on TV.

21. Glasses can be a burden, especially when competing in hockey or football.

Glasses can be a burden, especally when I am competing in hockey or football.

22. I remember clearly, at the age of 18 my parents started to question me about getting my driver's licence.

_____

_____

23. Peering through the windows, the computer lab looked full.

_____

24. After finishing breakfast, the house is straightened up.

_____

25. As a child growing up in Jamaica, every Monday my aunt would cook us stewed peas and rice.

_____

_____

WORKSHEET

Misplaced and Dangling Modifiers, Level 2

NAME _____

Revise these sentences, correcting all misplaced or dangling modifiers. If a sentence has no error, write "Correct" in the space.

1. Having grown up on a tobacco farm, our horses assisted with the harvest.

   _____

2. When watching a one-hour show, as many as six food commercials can come on.

   _____

   _____

3. The bride had long white gloves made of lace on her hands.

   _____

4. My love of France was increased after my visit to the glorious palace of Versailles, which was built for King Louis XVI with its spacious garden.

   _____

   _____

5. Sitting in the waiting room, looking through an old coverless issue of *National Geographic,* the dentist approached me.

   _____

   _____

6. Going through high school, our families pay for most of our expenses.

   _____

7. Although too young to watch restricted movies, the government allows many young teenagers to drive a lethal machine.

   _____

   _____

8. Nearing the top flight of stairs, my nostrils detected the familiar stale stench of the gym.

   _____

9. After the man received his money, he rushed out of the bank and vowed that he would never return.

   _____

   _____

10. After talking to him for a while he asked me if I could work for him.

    _____

11. The diameter of a capillary is only large enough to accommodate one red blood cell.

12. Most students employed during the school break are able to work only three or four months.

13. Being a wealthy city, crimes such as mugging and robbing are rare.

14. I called the personnel manager on the phone, and by making a good first impression she called me for an interview.

15. With suburban car purchases increasing by the thousands annually, should the use of cars be reduced when commuting to the city?

16. In prison one is only allowed a certain amount of time to go outside into a yard surrounded by a fence, or else to sit and read in the cell.

17. Racing into a high-speed curve at 150 kilometres per hour on a motorcycle, many things are going through the biker's head.

18. Living in an age when fast information interchange is needed, the Net offers a helping hand with its vast services such as electronic mail.

19. Sitting on the bus, tears came to peoples' eyes as they thought back to the joyful life they had led before the rebels took over the country.

20. Many myths have surfaced through the years concerning rape which will be discussed later.

21. Academic streaming causes students to feel low self-esteem, because they are stigmatized as lacking in intelligence by their teachers and peers.

    _____

    _____

    _____

22. After living in the old-age home for six months, I began to see a change in my grandfather; he was getting weaker and weaker every day.

    _____

    _____

23. When you get bored with a particular CD, unlike an audio tape, you cannot record over it.

    _____

    _____

24. Being out of the house most of the day because of school, and evenings because of dancing, my parents became aware that I was growing up.

    _____

    _____

25. It seems that when reading the newspaper today, a story can always be found on a large company being caught for polluting the environment.

    _____

    _____

26. Reviewing the statistics, wife assault crosses all socioeconomic barriers.

    _____

27. The music on the album was both recorded on stage and in the studio.

    _____

28. While observing all the fascinating shapes of coral in the water, odd peeping fish began to crowd around my feet.

    _____

    _____

29. Living at the corner of Jarvis and Carleton, the growl of engines, screech of tires and shriek of horns blend together in a roar so loud that at times it shakes the windows.

    _____

    _____

    _____

30. Although growing up in a big family meant a lot of sharing, sacrifices and privations, I am more than happy about being a large family member.

    _____

    _____

EDITING FOR PARALLEL FORM

Closely related parts of a sentence should fit harmoniously together. Like a red fender on a blue car, the wrong kind of word or word group in a sentence can ruin the effect of the whole. Consider this example:

> My boss was furious. She wanted to know why I was late, why I hadn't phoned, *and you'd better get serious about this job*!

While we can guess that the person who must get serious about this job is the author, not "you" the reader, this sentence would be clearer and the style more harmonious if we made a change:

> She wanted to know why I was late, why I hadn't phoned, and *why I wasn't serious about this job.*

Now we have a series of three indirect questions, rather than the start of a series interrupted by an independent clause. We have a sentence written in *parallel form.*

A. *Items in a series should be parallel in form.* For example, if one is a noun they should all be nouns; if one is a verb they should all be verbs; if one is in past tense they should all be in past tense.

WEAK

> Three ways to control stress are having an active social life, eating a balanced diet and regular exercise.

BETTER

> Three ways to control stress are *having* an active social life, *eating* a balanced diet and *getting* regular exercise. (All present participles ending in "-ing".)

BETTER

> Three things that control stress are an active social *life*, a balanced *diet* and regular *exercise*. (All nouns.)

BETTER

> Three ways to control stress are *to socialize* often, *to eat* a balanced diet and *to exercise* regularly. (All infinitives beginning with "to".)

If the items of a series are *parallel in form*, they should also be *related in logic.* One person wrote this:

> Santa Claus, an old Christmas legend, is a reality to young children. He is an old gentleman in a red suit, black boots, white beard, a big belly and eight flying reindeer pulling a sleigh.

Well, Santa Claus may be an old gentleman *in* a red suit and *in* black boots, but is he *in* a white beard? Is he *in* a big belly? Is he *in* eight flying reindeer pulling a sleigh? Let's revise:

> He is an old gentleman *in* a red suit and black boots, *with* a white beard and a big belly. Eight flying reindeer pull his sleigh.

Split up a list, as above, if the items are not closely enough related to be parallel in form.

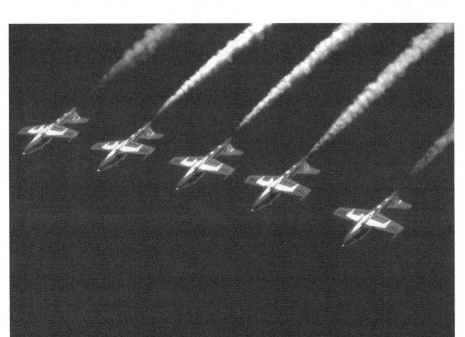

© COREL PHOTOS.

B. Word groups that are paired by *contrast*, *alternation* or *another relationship* are strongest when parallel:

WEAK

> I thought *I would save my money* but instead *a financial loss occurred.*

BETTER

> I thought *I would save my money* but instead *I lost it.* (Note that "it," a pronoun, parallels "money," a noun. Note also that putting a paired statement in parallel form can make it more concise as well as more direct.)

WEAK

> The advantages of public transit are *low fare* and *the environment is saved.*

BETTER

> Public transit helps us *to save* money and *to protect* the environment. (Both infinitives beginning with "to".)

BETTER

> Public transit *saves* us money and *protects* the environment. (Both verbs.)

C. "You can't compare apples and oranges," the old saying tells us. *In comparisons, parallel form is especially important.* Do you want to write "faulty comparisons" like this one found in a student essay?

> The heart of a child beats faster than an adult.

In other words, a *heart* is beating faster than a *person.* Let's add the pronoun "that" to parallel the noun "heart":

> The *heart* of a child beats faster than *that* of an adult.

When you look hard at this next comparison, does it really make sense?

> An airplane takes a shorter time reaching its destination than by driving a car.

In case we picture not humans but an airplane driving the car, let's cut out all the unparallel items:

> An airplane is faster than a car.

Finally, does this one, found in a student essay, make sense?

> What fascinates me about New York is the size of the buildings and the people.

Unless New Yorkers are giants, why not take "the buildings" and "the people" out of parallel so we will not compare them with each other?

> What fascinates me about New York is the people and the size of the buildings.

W O R K S H E E T

Parallel Form, Level 1

NAME _____

One item in each series is not parallel to the other items. Cross it out, then substitute an item that is parallel.

Example: eating
drinking
~~talked~~   *talking*
sleeping

1. hockey
football
~~playing~~ tennis
basketball

2. see
hear
taste
touch~~ing~~
feel

3. Toyota
Nissan
~~Harley-Davidson~~ Honda
Lexus

4. honesty
~~intelligent~~ly
integrity
loyalty

5. Monday
~~April~~ Friday
Wednesday
Saturday

6. ~~to skate~~ skating
skiing
swimming
dancing

7. Spain
France
Italy
Ireland
London

8. lying
~~murder~~ murdering
cheating
stealing

9. tall
wide
thick
~~heaviness~~ heavy

10. Wayne Gretzky
Gordie Howe
Maurice "Rocket" Richard
Bobby Hull
Babe Ruth

11. love
    hate
    jealousy
    ~~friendliness~~ _friendly_
    angry

12. newspapers
    books
    magazines
    ~~going to the movies~~ _movies_

13. lack of exercise
    drinking too much
    excess of food

14. bear
    ~~crow~~ _horse_
    deer
    moose
    wolf

15. accelerate
    ~~shifted gears~~ _gears._
    steer
    park

16. frying
    baking
    ~~to roast~~ _roasting_

17. to write
    ~~speaking~~ _to speak_
    to read

18. ~~to plough the soil~~ _ploughing the soil_
    planting the seeds
    cultivating the earth
    harvesting the crop

19. under the table
    ~~after dinner~~ _behind the door._
    in the closet
    behind the chair

20. British Columbia
    New Brunswick
    ~~Calgary~~ _Ontario_
    Prince Edward Island
    Alberta

W O R K S H E E T

Parallel Form, Level 2

NAME _____

Most of these passages, from actual student essays, violate parallel form. Edit them, using the method of revision that seems best for each. Make the improvements either by crossing out and adding, or by rewriting in the spaces. When you find a passage already parallel in form, write "parallel" in the blank.

take

Example: In my free time I listen to records, go to movies and long walks.
                                                                /\

1. My brother prefers luxuries like eating good food and nice clothing.

    _____

    _____

2. The cost of living in Saskatoon is not as high as other cities.

    _____

    _____

3. We have many stereotypes of "bike" riders: black leather jackets, big black boots, long thick chains and of course tough and mean.

    _____

    _____

4. Clearly, the speed and cost of using e-mail are much better than the traditional mailing system.

    _____

    _____

5. My favourite newspaper is the *Toronto Sun*: it is small, easy to read, the horoscope and the sports section.

    _____

    _____

6. Asia is the largest continent on earth, with many very old civilizations such as Thailand, Chinese and India.

    _____

    _____

7. My office position requires me to answer phone calls, filing charts, using the computer to assist me in reaching the information that I need, and to retrieve charts for nurses and doctors.

    _____

    _____

    _____

8. As a small child I was very spoiled: I was the only daughter, the only granddaughter and the only niece.

   _____

   _____

9. Unlike the United States, a Canadian cannot carry a gun in public.

   _____

   _____

10. The power of television to influence children is often greater than the parents, themselves.

    _____

    _____

11. The farmer's jobs included shovelling manure, feeding the cows, forking hay, field work, and not including the full day that he and I spent baling hay.

    _____

    _____

    _____

12. Having the luxury of your own car gives you many privileges: car radio, control of the temperature, and you may eat and smoke.

    _____

    _____

    _____

13. Men's shoes are made for comfort and made to last longer than women.

    _____

    _____

14. Alcohol is a drug that can profoundly affect thinking, distort emotion, and alters behaviour.

    _____

    _____

    _____

15. Like many of the schools in Trinidad, we all had to wear uniforms.

    _____

    _____

16. Narrow-minded people still look down on a woman who lifts weights, works on a car engine or speaking her thoughts freely.

    _____

    _____

    _____

17.   Some people feel that to lose their job is to lose their life.

_____

_____

18.   The population of New York City is much larger than Toronto.

_____

_____

19.   In Canada we have snow, rain, sun, cloudy, wind, warm and cold.

_____

_____

20.   It is no surprise that people turn to smoking, drinking, and consume so much coffee.

_____

_____

21.   Unlike the big city, people in a small city take time to talk to you and even bake you cookies.

_____

_____

22.   The rent of newer buildings is much higher than older buildings.

_____

_____

23.   Today there are three types of parents: permissive, strict and wealthy.

_____

_____

24.   Canadian society is a combination of many different cultures: East Indian, Chinese, Iranians, Greek, Italian, etc.

_____

_____

_____

25.   Salespersons of today have different attitudes toward customers. The three kinds include: pushy, people who do not care, and helpful.

_____

_____

_____

26. In Singapore, the pedestrians were actually walking faster than the cars.

   _____

   _____

27. In renting a condominium one is faced with certain restrictions: no pets, no overnight visitors, need for permission to do decorating and the noise level should be kept low at all times.

   _____

   _____

   _____

   _____

28. Many people leave their homeland in hopes of getting a better job and have a higher standard of living.

   _____

   _____

29. The price of brand-name computers is about 25 percent higher than clones.

   _____

   _____

   _____

30. Everyone looks for distinctive qualities in a career: how much money it brings, how long will it take to get, what are the benefits, is it compatible with one's lifestyle, and the list can go on forever!

   _____

   _____

   _____

   _____

EDITING FOR SPELLING AND RELATED MATTERS

A couple of generations back, many teachers and students believed spelling to be one of the major writing tasks. It seemed almost as important as the argument itself—despite the fact that some major authors, such as Keats and Hemingway, had been terrible spellers.

Today we view spelling as a relatively minor part of writing. After the main work of focussing and developing has been done in the early draft or drafts, we check over the spelling as a kind of "quality control"—much as the manufacturer of a well-engineered car looks over the paint job to make sure there are no scratches to mar the finish.

Another change is that often now we postpone attention to spelling until the *end* of the writing process. Why do the work right away, when you may end up deleting whole passages from your argument, and with them the effort you would have put into their spelling?

Or if you are computerized, like most people now, it may still make sense to use spell check to clean up the mess as soon as your discovery draft is done; with almost no effort on your part, this will make early drafts seem cleaner and easier to work with.

However, as we will see later on, spell check is not perfect. You still need to look over your spelling by hand, to catch what the relatively crude software missed. And that step is still best at the end of the writing process, for the same reason given above: so you don't waste your time on sections that may not make it into your final version.

Though it's obvious that spelling is less important than the quality of the argument, why do we still give it some quality attention? Partly because poor spelling is a public relations disaster: it can seem to ruin even the best of essays, by giving your audience a poor overall impression. Would you take seriously, for example, the sports essay one student wrote about the "Super*bowel*"? Or another that at one point stated "I couldn't comprehend what all the *fuzz* was about"? And how about these items found in still other essays?

bathtube	the Specific Ocean
drink a bear or two	suck-seed
escapegoat	supperpower
law biting citizen	toe truck
low self-steam	ultra-violent radiation
the Mid-Evil age	viscous circle
pair tree	well fear cheque
soup opera	who nose?

Whether such bloopers make readers laugh or cry, one thing is for sure: they will distract the audience from your message, and put into doubt anything else you may have to say.

"Strange how all six of your previous employers left the 'C' out of the word 'excellent.'"

Commonly Confused Words

Note that all the above cases occurred when one word was confused with another. Not every error is made this way, but the worst and most frequent are. Note also that only 3 of the 16 whoppers you have just read would be caught by spell check, since most are just combinations of words—the *wrong* words —that themselves are correctly spelled. *Make sure that you know the difference, then, between the following commonly confused words.* (The worst trouble-makers are **boldfaced**.) Definitions are not given here, because you have a dictionary:

accept/except	capital/capitol
advice/advise	clothes/cloths
affect/effect	coarse/course
are/our	council/counsel
bare/bear	desert/dessert
brakes/breaks	do/due
breath/breathe	emigrated/immigrated
buy/by	farther/further

hear/here	principal/principle
heroin/heroine	**quiet/quit/quite**
hole/whole	right/wright/write
its/it's	role/roll
know/no/now	sight/site/cite
lead/led	**than/then**
loose/lose	**their/there/they're**
moral/morale	thorough/threw/through
passed/past	**to/too/two**
peace/piece	weather/whether
personal/personnel	were/we're/where

W O R K S H E E T

Commonly Confused Words

NAME _____

Circle or highlight the one correct choice in the parentheses. Do not be afraid to use your dictionary.

1. A person must (*accept/except*) all that life has to offer, both good and bad.

2. Mom warned us not to eat all the candy, but we ignored her (*advice/advise*).

3. Oil slicks in the ocean have a devastating (*affect/effect*) on wildlife.

4. The presence of parental love can (*affect/effect*) a child's ability to love others.

5. How do dreams change (*are/our*) lives?

6. I am so attached to my cat that I cannot (*bare/bear*) to part with it.

7. Some people get all the (*brakes/breaks*).

8. When oil is applied to the water, increasing the surface tension, the mosquito larvae can no longer poke their tubes up into the air to (*breath/breathe*).

9. A beginner will go to the nearest sports shop and (*buy/by*) every piece of equipment in sight.

10. Saint John's is the (*capital/capitol*) of Newfoundland.

11. One of the most important preparations for cross-country skiing is selection of light (*clothes/cloths*) that can be worn in several layers.

12. By the time I finished high school, I had never had a (*coarse/course*) in art.

13. A municipal (*council/counsel*) tends to be divided into prodevelopment and antidevelopment factions.

14. Large parts of Africa are turning into (*desert/dessert*).

15. Let's give credit where credit is (*do/due*).

16. In 1997 my parents (*emigrated/immigrated*) to Canada.

17. I swam laps in the pool till I thought I could go no (*farther/further*).

18. Old people feel isolated because they cannot (*hear/here*) well.

19. Desdemona is a tragic (*heroin/heroine*).
20. My sister ate the (*hole/whole*) pizza.

21. A dog is faithful to (*its/it's*) owner.

22. You never (*know/no/now*) what can happen.

23. Through the example of their parents, children are (*lead/led*) to cheat in society.

24. To (*loose/lose*) a game is to learn a lesson.

25. Police associations say that even the most disciplined force cannot function well if the (*moral/morale*) is low.

26. A year (*passed/past*) before Stephen Leacock found himself teaching at Upper Canada College.

27. I wanted a (*peace/piece*) of the action.

28. Three days after I was hired, the (*personal/personnel*) manager called me to her office.

29. I was not one of those troublemakers who were always sent to see the (*principal/principle*).

30. The hours past midnight are best for studying, because everything is (*quiet/quit/quite*).

31. At university, students have to (*right/wright/write*) exams as long as three hours.

32. Professional athletes are (*role/roll*) models to thousands of children.

33. Many students lose (*sight/site/cite*) of their goals.

34. Ravers dress differently (*than/then*) others their age do.

35. (*Their/There/They're*) stood my husband with the knife firmly in his hand, waiting to plunge it into the intruder.

36. The police are hard workers. (*Their/There/They're*) not out on the streets slacking off.

37. My friends and I used to go on trips (*thorough/threw/through*) the wilderness.

38. More and more coaches and athletes take a friendly match of football (*to/too/two*) seriously.

39. (*Weather/Whether*) to take a part-time job depends on many factors.

40. When students (*were/we're/where*) asked to name the prime ministers of Canada, some of them mentioned John Kennedy.

Your Own Spelling List

If you are like most people, 90 percent of your spelling errors may be the same 20 or 30 words gone wrong every time you write them. While over the long term the best way to spell better is to read a lot, *the most direct way to improve your spelling right now is to list all words you get wrong in assignments, then study the correct spellings till you have made them automatic.*

Have a friend test you on your list, then again on the "short list" of those words that still give trouble. You may be surprised at how far your spelling performance goes up in your next paper.

_____

_____

_____

_____

_____

_____

_____

_____

_____

_____

_____

_____

_____

_____

_____

_____

_____

_____

_____

_____

_____

_____

A Hundred Words Often Misspelled

Every English teacher has observed the mysterious fact that the same words are misspelled by large numbers of people. Here are most of the culprits, with the worst troublemakers **boldfaced**. Before you start memorizing, have a friend test you on these words—then study only a "short list" of the 10 or 20 that may need attention.

accommodate	disappear	persistent
achievement	disappoint	piece
acquaintance	disastrous	playwright
acquire	dominant	possess
across	embarrass	predominant
adequately	emperor	preferred
a lot	**environment**	prejudice
all right	even though	prevalent
among	exceed	**privilege**
analyze	**existence**	pronunciation
argument	experiment	psychology
athlete	fascinate	quantity
attendance	fiery	**receive**
basically	**government**	resistance
beneficial	heroes	rhyme
category	imagination	rhythm
committee	**independence**	seize
compatible	knowledge	separate
completely	laboratory	similar
conceive	leisure	sincerely
condemn	loneliness	studying
conscience	maintenance	subtle
consistent	material	surprise
controversy	**necessary**	tendency
convenient	noticeable	tomorrow
deceive	obedience	tragedy
definite	**occasion**	truly
dependent	occurred	unnecessary
description	opponent	villain
desirable	perceive	weird
destroy	permanent	
dining	perseverance	

Canadian Spelling

Everyone who reads much knows that the British spell certain words one way, the Americans another, and that Canadians are torn between the two.

Many Canadians, especially in the middle and eastern provinces, continue to use the mainly British spellings they were taught in school. Thus they work in *centres* such as the Toronto Dominion Centre. They get paid by *cheque.* After they *labour* they watch their *colour* television set or perhaps go to a *theatre.*

Yet when some Canadian newspapers write the words as *center, check, labor, color* and *theater,* Canadians may not sense those spellings as foreign, even though they are American. Though some newspapers do use American spelling, the *Globe and Mail* has recently changed back to Canadian spelling, because readers wanted it. Most Canadian book publishers also continue to use Canadian spelling, and so does the federal government in its publications.

So what is the student writer to do? Though some teachers mark American spellings as errors, calling American spelling wrong is no more logical than saying English is better than French, or vice versa. Rather, the spelling you employ is mostly a cultural matter. Both systems are "correct," so the choice is yours.

If you are exceedingly concerned with saving a letter here and there (like managers of some newspapers who like to save a hundredth of a cent any way they can), then you may prefer the sometimes shorter American spellings. Even then, some equivalents, such as "centre" vs. "center," are the same length.

On the other hand, if tradition means something to you, and if Canadian spelling "feels" better just because you have always seen it, you will probably wish to stay with the usage you learned in school.

Many students who would like to do so complain that American spell-check programs used here actually show Canadian spellings as errors. If you experience this, you could write to the software company to protest this cultural oversight. In the short run, there is an easy and quick way to fix the problem: systematically enter into the "add" function of your spell-check all Canadian spellings that differ from American spellings (referring to our chart on page 200). Now "colour," "centre," etc. will be recognized as correct, along with "color" and "center." If you feel like taking things a step further, your software may also permit removing words (the American spellings) from its central list.

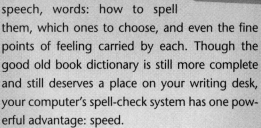

The dictionary has always been a key tool for writers, giving data on those building blocks of all speech, words: how to spell them, which ones to choose, and even the fine points of feeling carried by each. Though the good old book dictionary is still more complete and still deserves a place on your writing desk, your computer's spell-check system has one powerful advantage: speed.

Now that we can whip through the spelling of a thousand-word essay in a couple of minutes, we may even change the point at which we do the job; though parts may be chopped in later editing, the work is now so easy that some people spell-check even the first version—to make it cleaner and easier to work with. Software settings that underline misspellings in red as we make them encourage us to do so.

Yet despite the speed and convenience of spell check, you no doubt have noted a serious flaw in this still crude software: since spell check works by comparing your spellings to the spellings in its own word list, it can do only one main thing: point out a word it does not recognize.

Thus you need never again write "recieve" for "receive" or "enviroment" for "environment"—but if you confuse "to," "too" and "two," the software thinks you are right. *The fact is that you must still always check spelling by hand, near the end of the editing process.* (So that you can do so, be sure you can distinguish the "words commonly confused" earlier in this section.)

See also page 31 on using the electronic thesaurus, which also performs some functions of the traditional dictionary.

Whatever your view of this whole matter, remember that neither American nor Canadian spelling is "wrong": the only editing error is in mixing "correct" forms. *Be consistent: do not write* colour *and* color *in the same paper.* Here are three more principles to observe:

- Avoid the common error of extending Canadian forms to words in which they are not used, as in writing *authour* for *author* or *amoung* for *among.*

- Observe the limits to the *-our* form in Canadian usage: *honour, honourable* but *honorary*; *labour, labourer* but *laborious*; *vigour* but *vigorous* and *invigorate.* When you are in doubt, consult the list that follows.

- Although Canadian forms are based on British spelling, do not let avoidance of American forms lead you to use British forms that are eccentric in Canada. Avoid spellings such as these: *amongst, whilst, connexion, gaol, kerb, tyre* and *waggon.*

To help you apply consistently the system that you choose, here is a list of the most common differences between Canadian and American spelling. Try to use only one side or the other, and give some thought to your choice.

Canadian, Eh?

Several good Canadian dictionaries are out there in printed form. They not only help you use Canadian spelling accurately, but they also report words and expressions unique to our country. Try the *Gage Canadian Dictionary*, the *Nelson Canadian Dictionary*, and especially the newer and very complete *Canadian Oxford Dictionary*. Reviewing this one, the *Globe and Mail* pointed out that "Five full-time lexicographers and Oxford's formidable international resources have yielded a volume of about 130 000 entries, including 2000 Canadianisms, 5800 biographies (800 Canadian), 6000 geographical entries (1200 Canadian), and 4000 entries on flora and fauna." Among the many terms used only in Canada you will find the "brown cow," "Canadian Tire money," "bumbleberry pie," "panzerotto," "Steeltown," "cube van" and "seat sale." Consider buying this excellent resource for your writing desk.

CANADIAN USAGE	SHARED USAGE	AMERICAN USAGE
armour		armor
behaviour		behavior
colour, colourful		color, colorful
favour, favourite		favor, favorite
fervour		fervor
flavour, flavourful		flavor, flavorful
harbour		harbor
honour, honourable	honorary	honor, honorable
humour, humourless	humorist, humorous	humor, humorless
labour, labourer	laborious	labor, laborer
neighbour, neighbourhood, neighbourly		neighbor, neighborhood, neighborly
odour, odourless	odoriferous, odorous	odor, odorless
rigour	rigorous	rigor
vapour	vaporize	vapor
vigour	vigorous, invigorate	vigor

CANADIAN USAGE	SHARED USAGE	AMERICAN USAGE
calibre	calibration	caliber, calibre
centre	central	center
fibre	fibrous	fiber, fibre
litre		liter
lustre	lustrous	luster, lustre
manoeuvre		maneuver
metre	metric	meter
spectre	spectral	specter, spectre
theatre	theatrical	theater, theatre

CANADIAN USAGE	SHARED USAGE	AMERICAN USAGE
mould (for casting), moulding, moulded		mold, molding, molded
mould (fungus), mouldy		mold, moldy
smoulder		smolder

CANADIAN USAGE	SHARED USAGE	AMERICAN USAGE
defence, defenceless	defensive	defense, defenseless
offence	offensive	offense

CANADIAN USAGE	SHARED USAGE	AMERICAN USAGE
cheque, cheque book, chequing account		check, check book, checking account

CANADIAN USAGE	SHARED USAGE	AMERICAN USAGE
plough, ploughing		plow, plowing

Five Spelling Rules

Although at first the study of individual words is the fastest and most direct way to fix your spelling, the technique works less well once you have cut out the most frequent errors. You simply use too many words to study them all.

A partial solution is rules. Some languages, such as Spanish, have a logical system whose universal principles ensure correct spelling of almost any word, even a new one. We are less fortunate. English is such a mixture of other languages that some spelling rules contradict each other, and most have exceptions. Learning the rules may improve your spelling—but not very much. Besides, the task of applying lengthy principles to every tenth or twentieth word will probably not help you finish your essay by midnight.

In hopes that they may help, though, here are five of the clearest spelling rules. If you would like more, whole books about spelling can be found in any bookstore. You would do better, though, to take seriously the advice on page 212 about reading being at the heart of improvement in spelling.

A. Put *i* before *e*, except after *c*
Or when sounded like *a*
As in *neighbour* or *weigh*.

Examples of *i* before *e*:

belief, chief, piece, priest, relief

Examples of *e* before *i*:

ceiling, deceive, eight, receive, their

Exceptions to the rule:

either, foreign, height, neither, seize, weird

B. When you add a *prefix*, do not change the spelling of the root word:

dis	+	appear	=	*dis*appear
dis	+	satisfy	=	*dis*satisfy
im	+	possible	=	*im*possible
im	+	moral	=	*im*moral
mis	+	lead	=	*mis*lead
mis	+	spell	=	*mis*spell
un	+	afraid	=	*un*afraid
un	+	noticed	=	*un*noticed

C. When you add a *suffix* beginning with a vowel to a word root that is accented on the last syllable or that has only one syllable, and if the root ends in a single consonant preceded by a single vowel, then double the final consonant of the root:

bat	+	*ed*	=	batt*ed*
begin	+	*ing*	=	beginn*ing*
control	+	*ed*	=	controll*ed*
occur	+	*ence*	=	occurr*ence*
omit	+	*ing*	=	omitt*ing*
prefer	+	*ed*	=	preferr*ed*
rap	+	*ed*	=	rapp*ed*
run	+	*ing*	=	runn*ing*

D. Drop the final *e* when the suffix begins with a vowel:

lose	+	*ing*	=	los*ing*
come	+	*ing*	=	com*ing*
use	+	*ing*	=	us*ing*
imagine	+	*ary*	=	imagin*ary*
separate	+	*ion*	=	separat*ion*
ice	+	*y*	=	ic*y*

Exceptions (to keep *c* or *g* soft):

advantageous, changeable, enforceable, outrageous, noticeable

Exceptions (to avoid mispronunciation):

eyeing, hoeing, mileage

Keep the final *e* when the suffix begins with a consonant:

achieve	+	*ment*	=	achieve*ment*
excite	+	*ment*	=	excite*ment*
live	+	*ly*	=	live*ly*
lone	+	*ly*	=	lone*ly*
sincere	+	*ly*	=	sincere*ly*
use	+	*ful*	=	use*ful*

Exceptions:

argument, probably, truly, wholly

E. A plural is normally formed by adding *s*, but *es* is added when another syllable results:

ONE SYLLABLE

tree	tree*s*
lake	lake*s*
cloud	cloud*s*
star	star*s*

ONE SYLLABLE	**TWO SYLLABLES**
ash	ash*es*
branch	branch*es*
fox	fox*es*
match	match*es*

Apostrophes

We'll discuss the apostrophe here, because, although it is a punctuation mark, its misuse feels like a spelling error. Hardly an essay is written that does not contain one such error, and some contain dozens. Remember these principles:

A. Use the apostrophe to show *contraction*:

I am	=	I'm
you are	=	you're
he is	=	he's
we are	=	we're
they are	=	they're

it is	=	it's
do not	=	don't
cannot	=	can't
should not	=	shouldn't
I would	=	I'd

B. Use the apostrophe to show *possession*:

- In a singular possessive, the apostrophe goes *before* the final *s*:

  The single parent*'s* responsibility is doubled.

- In a plural possessive, the apostrophe goes *after* the final *s*:

  Most parents*'* greatest concern is for their children*'s* happiness.

  Note how the word "children" above is already plural without an *s*. In such cases the apostrophe follows the plural ending, and an *s* comes last to show how the word is pronounced: *children's*. Two more common words that work this way are *women* (*women's*) and *men* (*men's*).

- To show possession with a name already ending in *s*, place an apostrophe alone after the *s*:

  The party was at James*'* house.

- The possessives *its* and *whose* never take an apostrophe, although the contractions *it's* and *who's* do. Many errors are made by people who ignore the difference:

  POSSESSION

  The snake reared *its* head.
  Not: The snake reared *it's* (*it is*) head.

  I know *whose* work this is.
  Not: I know *who's* (*who is*) work this is.

  CONTRACTION

  It's snowing (*It is* snowing.)
  Who's there? (*Who is* there?)

C. The apostrophe is *not* used with every word that ends in *s*. Avoid the knee-jerk reaction of thinking that, since the apostrophe sometimes goes with final *s*, it always does.

- The apostrophe does not form a plural:

  ERROR

  Student*'s* from high school*'s*, college*'s* and university*'s* were looking for summer job*'s*.

  CORRECTION

  Students from high schools, colleges and universities were looking for summer jobs.

- The apostrophe does not form a third-person verb:

  ERROR

  A politician make*'s* new promises whenever election time roll*'s* around.

  CORRECTION

  A politician makes new promises whenever election time rolls around.

To Contract or Not to Contract ...?

Finally, should contractions be used at all in academic writing? You surely had high school teachers who said to avoid them all. Were those teachers right or wrong?

Like most pieces of advice, this one contains some truth but not the whole truth. Yes, in the kind of formal research essay explored in our final chapter, you should avoid all contractions—such as "didn't" or "wouldn't"—because they are too informal, too conversational. For the reader to believe in your scholarship, not only should your quotations and referencing be good, but your tone should be dignified and objective—not like a lunchtime conversation in the cafeteria. Even in other kinds of writing where a formal tone is expected (a literature paper, a business report, a lab report), contractions should be avoided.

On the other hand, in informal personal essays and certainly in things like letters to friends, a total absence of contractions would be too formal, too stuffy, too intimidating. In much of this everyday writing a contraction here and there is a good thing, a device to make language more direct and natural. Do continue to avoid contractions in academic writing, but in less formal assignments try to "feel" the style: if writing something out seems awkward or stuffy, then go ahead and use the contraction.

WORKSHEET

Apostrophes

NAME _____

Whenever you see an apostrophe error in these passages from student essays, write the correction, with the word in which it occurs, in the blank at the right. Write "C" after any sentence that is correct.

Example: The sun's r~~ay~~'s become more direct in spring.   _____*rays*_____

1. All pet's should receive more sympathy than they do.   _____

2. For entertainment Oshawa has movie theatres, ice rinks, roller arena's, night clubs and all sorts of gym's to work out at.   _____

3. The Beatles influence and popularity will live as long as rock and roll exists.   _____

4. The present art of producing with an assembly line system has come a long way since it's introduction.   _____

5. As I plunged into the water, its cold temperature chilled every bone in my body.   _____

6. Its exciting to see a great horse thundering down the track.   _____

7. The only way to reduce student's financial problems is to increase their grants and loans.   _____

8. Students who are 18 and over are the one's who need money the most.   _____

9. Thousands of people fish Quebec's lake's and river's each year, but how many will take a minute to consider the result's of fished-out waters?   _____

10. Driving a motorcycle give's one a sense of independence, because the rider know's people are watching.   _____

11. People who have no confidence in their own work will try to use others ideas.   _____

12. Politic's is what get's everyone talking and moving in this world.   _____

13. Parent's moral values are passed on to the next generation.   _____

14. My parent's emigrated from Bosnia.   _____

15. The Rolling Stones' music was unique for its time. _____

16. After each goal the team that was scored against get's possession of the ball behind it's net. _____

17. Its a holiday to escape from work and see who can catch the most fish. _____

18. It's my parent's duty to take care of me; they are legally required to. _____

19. She see's only his good qualities. _____

20. What drains peoples' energy is the accelerating rate of change. _____

21. Solar system's have a sun and various numbers of planet's. _____

22. Are Canadian's ashamed of their own country? _____

23. A person who's on LSD may see the ceiling of the house crash in. _____

24. There are many owner's club's for most sport cars. _____

25. Newtons Second Law of Motion helps the swimmer to conserve energy. _____

26. Illness can be the minds expression to withdraw from lifes stress's and strains. _____

27. We'd go to my grandparents house each year. _____

28. With it's small and friendly society, it's rain forest attractions like the wildlife, it's breathtaking waterfalls and it's easy-going life, Guyana is my favourite holiday spot. _____

29. When Nick sees the Buchanan's reaction to Myrtle's death, he develops a sense of moral responsibility. _____

30. Animals such as rabbit's, monkey's and cat's are being used for meaningless experiments. _____

31. The arteries' main function is to carry oxygenated blood. _____

32. It was Labour Day when all the delayed thought's of moving from my parents finally hit home. _____

33. When children see their favourite player's using sticks to jab and spear other players, the next thing you know, the children are imitating. _____

34. Anyone who has run for a few year's on the road has no doubt experienced a deterioration of the knee's. _____

35. Elizabeth realized the faults of her parent's marriage.   _____

36. At colleges and universities, drinking has become part of the system.   _____

37. True punk rockers wear safety pins through their nose's or cheek's.   _____

38. A newborn child see's the light for the first time.   _____

39. My mothers parent's don't travel at all.   _____

40. All over the world we are confronted with the same problems in womens lives. _____

Capitals

Since capitals, like apostrophes, tend to be sensed as an aspect of spelling, we'll discuss them here.

Though everyone knows the main uses of capital letters, some fine points are not so well known—or may just be forgotten in the rush to finish assignments. Look over the principles below, in case there are any you have been ignoring.

A. Use a capital to *begin a sentence, a word group standing for a sentence*, and *a line of regular poetry*:

> Our big cities are no longer safe.

> Yes. Of course. No doubt about it.

> Western wind, when will thou blow?
> The small rain down can rain.
> Christ, that my love were in my arms,
> And I in my bed again.
> —Anonymous

B. Capitalize the beginning of a *direct quotation* if it is a sentence or a word group standing for a sentence:

> According to Aristotle, "Poverty is the parent of revolution and crime." (The quotation is a sentence.)

> He shook his head and said, "Over my dead body." (Though the word group is not a sentence, it is meant to function as one.)

> "I'll have roast duck," she said, "with fried rice." (The "with" is not capitalized, because it does not begin a new sentence.)

> Ben Jonson wrote that Shakespeare knew "small Latin and less Greek." (The "small" is not capitalized, because the quoted words are only part of Jonson's original sentence.)

C. Capitalize *proper nouns*:

▪ Names of persons, nationalities and languages:

Shania Twain	Scottish
Michael Ondaatje	Spaniard
Canadian	speak French
Australian	an English course

▪ Academic courses whose names are not derived from languages are normally not capitalized:

psychology		English
history	BUT	French
calculus		Latin

▪ Specific places:

Calgary	Yonge Street
Saskatchewan	Cabbagetown
Canada	the Maritimes
the Fraser River	the North (referring to
the Rocky Mountains	a region, not just a
	direction)

▪ Names of organizations:

Georgian College
Mennonite Brethren Church
Wilderness Canoe Association
Parliament
Nortel Networks

BUT

a community college
went to church
a canoeing club
parliamentary procedure
a high-tech corporation

▪ Days of the week, months, and holidays, but not seasons:

Tuesday	Chinese New Year
Saturday	Ramadan
January	spring
August	winter

▪ Titles of books, magazines, newspapers, plays, films, musical compositions, poems, short stories, articles and essays. Capitalize the first word and all others except for connecting words (such as *a, an, the, and, or, but, in, on, by*) that have no more than five letters:

Book: *Anil's Ghost*
Magazine: *Maclean's*
Newspaper: *The Vancouver Sun*
Play: *Hamlet*
Film: *King Kong*
Song: "Yesterday"

Poem: "As the Mist Leaves No Scar"
Short story: "The Painted Door"
Article or essay: "Exaggeration as a Comic
    Device in the Novels of Mordecai Richler"

(Note that names of periodicals and titles of books, plays and other *long items* are symbolized by italics or underlining. On the other hand, titles of *short items* such as songs, poems, short stories, articles and essays, are not italicized or underlined, but are put in quotation marks as above.)

■ Words of family relationship when used as names or with names:

    I congratulated Mother.
    There was Father.
    Uncle Ivan
    Aunt Mary

    BUT

    I congratulated my mother.
    There was our father.
    My uncle is named Ivan.
    Mary is my aunt.

■ Titles appearing before a name, or used alone as a form of address:

    Professor Serrano
    Doctor Vaudouris
    Captain Tremblay

    Hello, Professor.
    Thank you, Doctor.
    I agree, Captain.

    BUT

    a professor
    my doctor
    an army captain

W O R K S H E E T

Capitals

NAME _____

Add the missing capitals wherever necessary, but avoid creating unnecessary ones.

1. a friend of mine, frank, once told me that he had been behind a mac's store smoking a cigarette when all of a sudden a police officer approached and asked him where the pot was hidden.

2. during the hockey game, the mother of one of the opposing players stood up from her seat and yelled as loudly as she could, "kill that little worm!"

3. in the first year of the program, students have to take accounting, economics, geography, mathematics, english, management, business law and psychology.

4. canadians have long been concerned with developing the north, but only recently with protecting it.

5. my parents bought a house north of the business district, within a five-minute walk of an elementary school, a middle school, a high school, a mac's milk store and a shopping centre.

6. on a bright summer morning, the first monday of july, we got in our canoe and started down the missinaibi river.

7. who has seen the wind?
       neither you nor i;
    but when the trees bow down their heads
       the wind is passing by.
                —christina rossetti, 1872

8. in high school one of my english teachers spent two months on *hamlet*.

9. in addition to containing beef and/or pork, wieners may contain water, flour, milk solids, salt and preservatives such as sodium nitrite, which has been known to cause cancer in laboratory animals.

10. cruise ships have many facilities such as bedrooms, swimming pools, lawn tennis courts, dancing halls, movie theatres and bars.

11. lady macbeth, a strong-willed character who was capable of influencing macbeth to murder his king, brought about her breakdown and death by her own ambitions.

12. john osborne was born on december 12, 1929, in london, england.

13. in today's modern society, people's morals and values are changing, so divorce, birth control and abortion are more easily accepted.

14. j. d. salinger's best short story, "for esmé—with love and squalor," shows how destructive war is to human feelings.

15. when i began high school i really got involved in soccer.

16. i arrived in trinidad on monday and began my search for a job on tuesday.

17. stephen leacock once wrote, "the essence of humour is human kindliness."

18. in his *biographia literaria*, coleridge refers to "that willing suspension of disbelief for the moment, which constitutes poetic faith."

19. mackenzie king said, "the promises of yesterday are the taxes of today."

20. blaise pascal called humans "the glory and the shame of the universe."

21. the driver stopped the bus to jump out and take a look. he was immediately followed by the spaniard, two mexicans, hugh, geoffrey and yvonne.

22. when the canadian dollar sank in value, foreign automobiles such as the volvo, volkswagen, toyota, subaru and honda rose sharply in price.

23. the national hockey league rules committee brought in new rules which prohibited players from being overly aggressive.

24. my mother speaks french, portuguese and english.

25. i have noted that math teachers do not dress as well as english teachers.

26. to depict their toughness, hockey players are given names such as "hammer," "battleship," "tiger" and "bulldog."

27. one of the fastest-growing religions in the world is islam.

28. in each of mordecai richler's earlier novels, *the acrobats, son of a smaller hero* and *a choice of enemies*, the hero is an artistically inclined canadian with a deep dislike of canadian culture and a conviction that the society he lives in is a fraud.

29. as a faithful expression of the theme found in the play, the movie *fortune and men's eyes* was the epitome of success.

30. "well, doctor," i said, "since you agree with the other doctors, i suppose we had better go ahead with the operation."

Abbreviations

Don't overdo the abbreviations. When you write "a.m." and "p.m." instead of "*ante meridiem*" and "*post meridiem*," you help your readers by saving their time. But when you cram into your essay every abbreviation you can think of (Can., Alta., N.S., Tues., Feb., GT, CB, ASA, LCBO, PC, etc.), you are only confusing them. Figuring out all these letters takes much longer than reading the full-length words.

See if you can put the words to the following common abbreviations into the blanks. If this activity gives you trouble, you can see how abbreviations would also give your reader trouble.

1. CPI _____

2. MBA _____

3. GIC _____

4. GST _____

5. ICU _____

6. CFA _____

7. RAM _____

8. R&D _____

9. RN _____

10. SASE _____

Do use abbreviations to avoid repetition. For example, after naming the United Nations Educational, Scientific and Cultural Organization in your first paragraph, have mercy on your reader by referring to it the next 10 or 20 times as UNESCO.

Also, if you are writing a technical report for specialists to read, such as "Shear Flow in Closed Single-Cell and Multi-Cell Systems," do use any abbreviations customary in the field, especially in tables and charts.

But in the kind of general classroom writing expected in courses such as English, history and philosophy, use abbreviations only where you can hardly avoid them. Here are some principles to guide you:

A. Abbreviate these titles before a name: *Mr., Mrs., Ms., Dr., Rev.*

    Mr. Violi
    Ms. Vasquez
    Dr. Chen
    Rev. Sung

Such titles are spelled out, though, when used in place of the name:

    Well, Doctor, what are my chances?

Other titles are usually not abbreviated, even before a name:

    Mother Theresa
    General Montcalm
    Sir Nigel
    Professor Beauchemin

B. Abbreviate names of private or public organizations if the abbreviation is well known and customarily used. Do write out the full name, though, the first time you mention an organization, with the abbreviation just after in parentheses.

RCMP	UN
ITT	INCO
TSE	BBC
CIA	YMHA
NAFTA	CBC

C. Abbreviate academic degrees:

B.A.	B.S.
M.A.	M.B.A.
M.S.W.	M.D.
D.Ed.	Ph.D.

D. You may abbreviate certain geographical names:

    U.K.   U.S.A.

Other geographical names (countries, provinces, counties, cities) are not abbreviated except in addresses.

E. Abbreviate certain terms from the Latin:

■ Words that specify time periods:

a.m.	p.m.
B.C.	A.D.

■ Certain terms used in academic writing:

cf. (compare)	i.e. (that is)
e.g. (for example)	q.v. (which see)

■ That overused term, *etc.* Use *etc.* only to signal actual items that you know but choose not to include—never to hide what you do not know. Avoid abuses like this:

> The major crops of British Columbia are apples, etc.

Symbols and Numbers in the Metric System

Although the traditional Imperial system of weights and measures is still used in some areas of our daily lives—as when we tell our height in feet and inches, or our weight in pounds—the metric system has become the norm in Canada for most other uses. Even when we write an essay, we may need to know the standard metric abbreviations, officially called "symbols," and how to use them.

When numbers are spelled out, terms of measurement used with them are also spelled out; when numbers appear as figures, the terms of measurement appear as symbols.

Thus in technical writing or in any charts and tables where a great many numbers are used, you will probably use figures and symbols. But where numbers occur less frequently, as in most essays, you will probably write out both numbers and terms of measurement:

> A piece of steel 0.25 cm thick, 1.75 m wide and 3.15 m long is welded to the frame.

> The average fingernail is about one centimetre wide.

The following table gives the most common metric terms and the symbols for them. The symbols are identical in both singular and plural uses, and, unless they occur at the end of a sentence, are written without a period.

LENGTH

kilometre	km
metre	m
decimetre	dm
centimetre	cm
millimetre	mm

AREA

square kilometre	km^2
hectare	ha^2
square metre	m^2
square decimetre	dm^2
square centimetre	cm^2

VOLUME

cubic metre	m^3
cubic decimetre	dm^3
cubic centimetre	cm^3
kilolitre	kL
litre	L
millilitre	mL

MASS

tonne	t
kilogram	kg
gram	g
milligram	mg

TEMPERATURE

degree Celsius	^oC

Our traditional 24-hour day and its parts are of course not metric, but are wisely being retained:

TIME

day	d
hour	h
minute	min
second	s

The metric system specifies certain principles for the use of numbers:

■ A zero is put before a decimal fraction:

> 0.9144 m

■ A space, rather than a comma, separates groups of three digits. Numbers of only four digits are not separated:

> 1 000 000 g   1000 g

■ Only numbers 10 and over are expressed in figures:

> five kilograms   75 kg

Reading: The Key to Spelling

On the average, North Americans read less than one book a year, perhaps because they watch four hours a day of television. By the time they graduate from high school they have spent more hours in front of "the tube" than in the classroom. They may know a great deal about how to catch a bank robber, apply a half nelson or estimate the price of a refrigerator, but one thing they may not know well at all is how to spell.

By contrast, people who have read a book or two a month (or an hour or two a day of magazines or newspapers) from childhood to adulthood have seen each word so many times that, with rare exceptions, their own spelling is automatically correct.

Reading is the long-term solution to spelling problems and to most other writing problems as well. The great majority of people who read regularly will eventually become much better in spelling, grammar and style than those who do not.

Though the process takes several years, it is the only way to profoundly improve your writing. Therefore, *if you do not have the reading habit, consider acquiring it now.*

Subscribe to a magazine or two in a field that interests you. Read a newspaper every day. Keep a couple of good books by your TV chair. If you don't have the time now, start during the holidays or the summer break. And if you have not enjoyed reading in the past, don't let that stop you. With every hour you read, you are a better reader; and as you improve, the reading will become more fun.

Some Good Canadian Books

(Novels except where noted otherwise)

Alias Grace, Margaret Atwood

Barney's Version, Mordecai Richler

Black Robe, Brian Moore

The Book of Secrets, M. G. Vassanji

A Casual Brutality, Neil Bissoondath

A Discovery of Strangers, Rudy Wiebe

A Dream Like Mine, M. T. Kelly

The English Patient, Michael Ondaatje

Fall on Your Knees, Ann-Marie MacDonald

My Father's House (memoir), Sylvia Fraser

Fifth Business, Robertson Davies

A Fine Balance, Rohinton Mistry

Fugitive Pieces, Anne Michaels

In Transit (stories), Mavis Gallant

La Guerre, Yes Sir!, Roch Carrier

Klee Wyck (autobiographical sketches), Emily Carr

Lives of the Saints, Nino Ricci

The Love of a Good Woman (stories), Alice Munro

Microserfs, Douglas Coupland

Never Cry Wolf (semi-autobiography), Farley Mowat

Nuk Tessli: The Life of a Wilderness Dweller (memoir), Chris Czajkowski

Obasan, Joy Kogawa

The Stone Angel, Margaret Laurence

The Stone Diaries, Carol Shields

Touch the Dragon: A Thai Journal (memoir), Karen Connelly

Travels with the Poor (social reporting), John Stackhouse

Volkswagen Blues, Jacques Poulin

The Wars, Timothy Findley

PART FOUR

The Research Essay

The process of writing a research essay is both like and unlike the process of writing the "short essay" which we have already discussed. A research essay rests on the same foundations, but of course has a larger and more detailed structure.

One difference can be length. Though a research paper is sometimes as short as five or six pages, it's often 10 or 12 or even longer. Another difference can be the level of objectivity. While a "short essay" often relies on our own thoughts or experiences, a research essay is a more objective and formal argument—a methodical sifting of evidence to arrive at a valid conclusion. And in referring to this sifted evidence, it uses the scholarly devices of quotations, name-page references, and list of works cited.

Yet these differences do not change the fact that both the "short" and "research" essays need original ideas, a thesis statement that gives focus and direction, unified development by example and argument, and some serious revision. Since these foundations underlie the process of writing both essays, we won't go through the whole thing again here. Instead, we'll focus mostly on the special challenges and special rewards of the research paper.

If you haven't already studied "Process in Short Essays" (pages 1–40), you might want to look those pages over now, as preparation for the more specialized essay we are investigating here.

SELECTING AND FOCUSSING THE TOPIC

What will you write about? Often a teacher makes it clear by giving a very specific assignment: you will analyze the imagery of water in the novel *Fugitive*

Pieces by Anne Michaels, or evaluate the role of the Family Compact in causing the 1837 Rebellion, or describe how a hamburger chain selects a certain corner for a business site.

When you are given a ready-made and specific topic like one of these, part of your work has already been done. You may not know much about the subject, but you do know the direction your research will take, and you'll waste no time on side issues.

More troublesome at first—but often more rewarding in the end—are the more open assignments meant to be narrowed down so they fit limits of scope and size. For example, Amy, a student in Communication 210, has a teacher who is giving a list of very broad subjects so students will get practice shaping their own topics. "I don't want anybody writing on what you see here," he is saying, pointing to the list on the assignment page. "These subjects are only the beginning."

Looking at the page, Amy sees that to do her research essay she could investigate "pollution," "family violence," "health," "language" or "employment." The last one almost gives her a shiver, because her brother, who graduated two years ago with a degree in geography, is still slinging hamburgers in a fast-food restaurant and always talking about his "McJob."

"I don't want that one," she thinks, "It's scary." But a minute later she is still looking at it on the page, and thinking: "So it's scary. Maybe that's *why* I should do it. This might teach me something, because someday *I* want to be employed."

Now Amy also realizes that both she and her brother are fans of the Canadian writer Douglas Coupland, who in novels like *Generation X* and *Microserfs* describes the frustrations people in their twenties have these days in finding a meaningful job and career. In fact, it was Coupland who thought up the word "McJob" which her brother always uses. "Maybe," Amy thinks, "I've already begun my research."

Before writing the first word, Amy already sees that an important aspect of doing her research paper is present: **motivation.** To increase your own writing performance, be sure to give some thought to the relative importance and interest of topics on a list, and make sure, like Amy, to choose one significant to *you.*

At this point Amy has picked her subject, but how is she to cut down its size so she can write, as her instructor says, "**more about less**"? The possibilities are mind-boggling. A person could write on factors like job training, education, the booms and busts of the economy, the expanding or contracting of business sectors, NAFTA and world trade, or for that matter on totally different employment-related issues such as safety on the job or even the techniques of a particular occupation. The approach of a research paper on employment could be historical, psychological, geographic, technical, economic ... you name it.

In fact, Amy *does* have to name it.

Certainly she could write a few pages on a couple of dozen matters related to employment and claim she had discussed the topic. But a superficial treatment is worthless: why should anyone read generalizations that everyone already knows? To be satisfying, to be interesting, to teach the reader something—an essay must reach a certain depth. And unless we write an essay as long as a book, that depth is reached only by focussing the topic. To write about employment, then, Amy needs to **select *one* little piece of the subject and explore it in detail.**

But how will she choose? She still can't stop thinking of her brother, an intelligent and popular guy who got decent grades, who graduated—but then with all the budget-cutting and layoffs taking place, could not find a job in his field. The whole family often sits around at dinner analyzing why, and trying to come up with solutions. "Isn't this the real heart of the matter?" Amy asks herself. "What can students actually do to move from school into a decent job? *This is what I want to know, and if I want to know it, then my readers will want to know it too.*"

> #### Taking Time, to Save Time
>
> *Remember: When the topic is general, take time to find the right subtopic.* Later, as you write the essay, your heightened interest and motivation will repay you that time as well as increase the quality of your writing.

GATHERING AND ORDERING INFORMATION

Most of us can write "short essays" on topics we already know, without any research at all. But the major essay in a course is often a research paper meant to teach us about subjects we're just now learning. This means some library work and probably some Web research before the writing begins.

The trouble is that libraries can have a paralyzing effect. Surrounded by more books and magazines and microfilms and CD-ROM disks than they could read in a lifetime, people feel their heart beating faster and they ask themselves, "Where do I begin?" If you don't have the answer, try this plan of action:

1. **Read just enough to focus the subject.**

2. **Try a tentative thesis statement.**

3. **Do the main research, taking notes.**

4. **Try a short outline.**

5. **Write the essay.**

Now let's follow Amy through each of these steps.

STEP ONE: READ JUST ENOUGH TO FOCUS THE SUBJECT

Amy believes she already knows something about her subject of how a student moves on from school to a decent job. "After all," she thinks, "why do people go to college or university? Why do we go to guidance counsellors? Why did I read that article just last weekend in the *Globe and Mail* on this very subject?"

That night Amy gets the old *Globe* out of the recycling box in her dad's garage, and reads the article again. "Good material," she thinks, "but how about more?"

Back at the library the next day, she goes to the reference section and looks up her topic in the hardbound *Readers' Guide to Periodical Literature*. Then she moves to a CD-ROM terminal to check out the *CPI.Q Canadian Periodical Index Fulltext*, which covers the contents of some 400 Canadian and international periodicals. Her library also has several more electronic indexes if she needs them. (For a fuller list of these, as well as print sources, see pages 217–221.)

In these and other general indexes Amy finds the dates and page numbers to locate a half-dozen promising articles recently published in periodicals that her library has, and she prints off a few more from her even more current electronic sources.

Now Amy spends a couple of hours skimming these articles for ideas that relate to her subject. But today she takes very few notes. After all, once she nails down her exact approach, some of this preliminary material may turn out to be off-topic.

As she checks these articles, and later at the gym as she is working out, a preliminary concept takes shape in her mind. Four or five pieces of advice she has seen in her readings really do make sense, and she would like to explore them further. In fact, a couple of them sounded like things her family had already said around the table. Now she could recommend them to her own readers—that is, after investigating further to make sure the advice makes as much sense as it seems to today.

"Is this the way to narrow down the topic? Will my instructor think I have focussed enough, by concentrating on four or five good ways to get into a career?" she asks herself.

As you focus your own topic, you also will ask yourself questions like this. You do not want to be like the horseman who Canadian writer Stephen Leacock said "rode madly off in all directions."

On the other hand, is it possible to focus *too far*, saying too much about too little? A sociologist writing about, say, cults, might send off an article entitled "The Practice of Exorcism Among Upper-Middle-Class Social Groups in Southern California." Who knows, a scholarly journal for other sociologists might publish it. "That's not my situation at all, though,"

thinks Amy. "I want this essay to give practical, useful advice about how students like me can actually get a real job."

STEP TWO: TRY A TENTATIVE THESIS STATEMENT

At first this step bothers Amy. Will her argument come across as just a few miscellaneous suggestions, like a how-to-get-a-job article in a magazine, or will it hang together and be organized? We have seen, on pages 8–10 of our chapter on the short essay, that a thesis statement needs to do two things, *limit the scope* and *focus the purpose*. But how can the writer choose just the right thesis now, before having done all the main research? What if the later research contradicts the thesis? What if the thesis Amy thinks up right now will later seem totally off?

Sure, that could happen, but look at the alternative: with no thesis at all, Amy would be the horseman who "rode madly off in all directions." Better to make a good guess at a thesis, then use it as a guide to doing the main research. Better to have a tentative thesis than no thesis; after all, even the scientist in the lab follows a hypothesis, and a hypothesis is nothing more than a well-informed guess.

As Amy considers her subject, she realizes now that her advice will not be comfortable or easy to follow. It will be a challenge. This is the common thread in her argument. Realizing this way of "limiting the scope" and "focussing the purpose," Amy finds her thesis. Here it is (in the more polished version that ends up later in her final draft):

> The answer to the new employment questions is flexibility. Only by letting go of old certainties, only by welcoming new tactics for new times, can today's students move more surely toward a real and satisfying career.

STEP THREE: DO THE MAIN RESEARCH, TAKING NOTES

Amy's school library and most others have excellent online catalogues to their holdings. At a computer terminal Amy can find what books are available in the stacks, can see more details about the ones that look good, can find out where they are in the library, can see whether they are checked out right now or are on the shelf, and if one is out right now she can reserve it. This system is so easy to use, fast and complete that Amy goes straight to it to start her main research, *making a list of sources to consult.*

Instructions are normally posted by the side of these terminals, and librarians should also be around for help. The online system catalogues library books in three ways: by **author**, **title** and **subject**. Since Amy does not yet know authors or titles, she looks up subjects, trying out such terms as "employment," "unemployment" and "jobs." She quickly passes over titles of books that seem off her topic, or that seem overly technical, or that are old. For each book she does intend to consult, she accurately copies down these facts:

1. *author's full name*
2. *full title of the book (including number of edition, if any)*
3. *city of publication*
4. *publisher*
5. *year of publication*

After trying to locate books through the online catalogue, Amy realizes that her library has only a couple of promising books on her topic, since the whole subject is so recent. So now she goes back to the *Readers' Guide to Periodical Literature* and *CPI.Q Canadian Periodical Index Fulltext*, to look more carefully and find more current sources.

Each time she finds an article that looks promising, she carefully notes down all these facts:

1. *author's full name*
2. *title of the article*
3. *name of the magazine or newspaper*
4. *volume number and date of the issue*
5. *inclusive page numbers of the article*

(All the sources she actually uses must appear in a list of "works cited" at the end of the essay. If she does not have these facts with her then, her carelessness may cost her a last-minute trip to the library.)

It does not take long to gather a list of sources: perhaps 5 or 10 for a short paper and 20 or 30 for a long one. If you have a long list, you may want to record each source on a separate filing card, for ease of organization. A short list like Amy's, though, is more easily kept on one page.

Amy's topic is familiar enough that she is able to locate numerous sources. For more specialized topics, though, keep these research tools in mind:

- *Interlibrary loans*: Your librarian will supply you with request forms, or will show you how to order online. You give the title, author and other information about a book or a magazine article that you need but that your own library does not have. The library will then use its database system to see which other libraries do have the resource, and will order it for you. There may be a small fee. Large research projects can hardly be done without the resources of additional libraries, but remember that for books the process takes a week or two. (Journal articles may arrive sooner, if your library is part of a system that sends these electronically.)

- *CD-ROM* (compact disk—read-only memory): Almost everyone has used CD-ROM resources on personal computers, whether at home or at a school lab. As you know, one disk can store huge amounts of data, such as a whole encyclopedia, or a whole year of text from a newspaper.

Most postsecondary and large public libraries have many useful CD-ROM indexes and other databases, which students can quickly learn to use. For example, one favourite is *ERIC*, which indexes and abstracts (summarizes) the articles of hundreds of journals in the fields of education and the social sciences. Through a user-friendly menu and through dialogue boxes, the user chooses from a vast array of possibilities.

For example a "descriptor" (key word) such as "employment" can be entered, to call up a list of all publications that include this subject. To narrow down the search, more descriptors such as terms that specify *where* or *when* or *who* may then be entered. For example the key words "youth" and "Canada" might be added. The result is a "Boolean search," which identifies only those sources in which the descriptors overlap—in this case articles about "employment" for "youth" in "Canada." (Since search techniques for online indexes are not standardized, we will not attempt to give all the details here. Instead, study the directions that your library makes available next to the computers.)

The bibliographical data and the descriptions of articles on screen can then be downloaded onto the student's own floppy disk, to be printed out at home. Some libraries provide printers to do this on the spot. But if you want the full text of articles that a database only abstracts, then you will need to request an interlibrary loan—and this means starting the research early enough to leave time.

Many other databases, as you will see on pages 217–221, contain the actual full text of articles. Thus you either print at the library, or download to your own floppy disk, to study the articles at your leisure (see Seyed's story in the computer text box).

A True Story: How Seyed Researched His Essay

One student, Seyed, was fascinated by the return of Hong Kong to the People's Republic, and by the effects this historic change is now having on the city and its citizens. To research his essay on the subject, he went directly to his library's CD-ROM full-text versions of two newspapers, the *Toronto Star* and the *Globe and Mail*, and got most of his material there (after all, current topics show up in newspapers before books have time to cover them).

First Seyed located about 500 articles on Hong Kong. Trying to sort these rapidly by just looking at the titles, he downloaded what seemed like about the best 50 onto his own floppy disk, then took it home to read on his own computer screen. But there was nothing on the disk! Back at the library, this time he asked the librarian exactly how to download from these resources, did the whole thing over, and this time got it right.

At home again, he now read his 50 articles on screen, and printed out the best in draft form. Next he highlighted the most useful passages in yellow, and, finally, from this information and these potential quotations, developed his essay.

Reference Sources

The online library catalogue, the *Readers' Guide to Periodical Literature*, and a couple of electronic indexes such as *CPI.Q Canadian Periodical Index Fulltext*, led Amy to all the sources she needed for her essay, especially since most articles and books that she consulted referred her to further writings on the subject.

In researching longer essays, though, or any essay on a more specialized topic, you may need to look further. Thousands of other reference sources cover almost any field you can imagine. These are a few that students have found useful. **Electronic sources are identified with a bold asterisk (*).**

General Sources

The New Encyclopaedia Britannica. Detailed and authoritative.

The Encyclopedia Americana. More popular than scholarly.

**The Canadian Encyclopedia*, Deluxe Edition (CD-ROM). Also *The Canadian Encyclopedia*, 2000 edition (in print form). Covers Canadian history, culture, geography, commerce and public life.

**Microsoft Encarta Encyclopedia* (CD-ROM). Has 42 000 articles and links to 8000 Web sites.

**Compton's Encyclopedia* (CD-ROM). The complete contents of the 26-volume set, with 8000 Web links.

*World Book (CD-ROM).

**Microsoft Infopedia* (CD-ROM). Includes the complete *Funk & Wagnall's Encyclopedia*, *Roget's Thesaurus*, the *Merriam-Webster's Dictionary of Quotations*, the *Hammond World Atlas*, etc.

**Canadian Newsdisc*. CD-ROM full-text edition of the *Toronto Star*, the *Ottawa Citizen*, the *Montreal Gazette*, the *Calgary Herald*, the Halifax *Daily News* and the *Vancouver Sun*. Find stories through key words in the headline or text.

Canadian Periodical Index. Index to articles in hundreds of English- and French-language periodicals in many fields.

CPI.Q Canadian Periodical Index Fulltext. The full electronic version of the *Canadian Periodical Index*, covering over 400 Canadian and international periodicals.

Lexis/Nexis. An extremely useful full-text database with over two billion records, focussing on business, current events, law and news.

The Globe and Mail (Toronto). Full-text edition available on CD-ROM.

World Almanac and Book of Facts. Annual collection of statistics and other facts on many subjects worldwide.

Canada Year Book (CD-ROM). A review by Statistics Canada of economic, social and political developments in the country. Many statistics.

Canadian Sourcebook. Annual collection of facts about Canada.

The New York Times Atlas of the World. Maps of all parts of the world. Gives facts on geography, agriculture, industry, business and society.

The New York Times Index. Lists news articles of the *New York Times*, classified by subject, person and organization. The annual index shows when a story broke. Then use that date to find articles on the subject from other periodicals as well.

The Canadian Index. A major research tool. Indexes articles from over 180 Canadian business magazines, over 100 general Canadian magazines, and seven Canadian daily newspapers. *The CD-ROM version is called *CBCA*.

Canadian News Facts. An "indexed digest of Canadian current events."

Newscan. Gives full text of articles, columns and features in major Canadian and European newspapers and magazines.

Essay and General Literature Index. Author and subject index to books of collected essays "with particular emphasis on materials in the humanities and social sciences."

Book Review Digest. Excerpts from reviews of books.

Books in Print. Lists most books now in print in the United States.

Books in Print Plus—Canadian Edition. Database lists over 1.6 million books produced and distributed in Canada and the United States.

Academic Search FullText Elite. Database gives full text of a thousand journals, and indexes over 3000 scholarly journals.

Proquest Digital Dissertations. Abstracts 1.5 million doctoral dissertations and master's theses from 1000 North American and European graduate schools.

Periodical Abstracts Research II Edition Full Text (Proquest). Indexes, abstracts, and gives full text of hundreds of journals and magazines in many fields.

Canadian Research Index. Indexes Canadian federal and provincial research publications.

Bartlett's Familiar Quotations. Indexed collection of quotations on many subjects, from ancient to modern times. *Available also on the Internet: <http://www.columbia.edu/acis/bartleby/bartlett>.

Colombo's Canadian Quotations. Indexed quotations by Canadians.

Dictionary of National Biography. Biographies of important persons in Great Britain, to 1900.

Dictionary of American Biography. Biographies of prominent Americans no longer living.

Dictionary of Canadian Biography. Biographies of prominent Canadians.

The International Who's Who. Short biographies of important people worldwide.

Who's Who in Canada. Concise biographies of prominent Canadians.

Science and Technology

*Biotechnology Abstracts. Summaries of articles published in the field.

Chemical Abstracts. A mammoth international work summarizing conference papers, books and articles. Indexed in several ways. Both paper and *CD-ROM versions.

*Computer Select. On CD-ROM, contains articles from a hundred periodicals in computer, technology and business fields. Most of these are full-text.

The Engineering Index. A much-used monthly index to conference papers and the major articles of hundreds of periodicals in all engineering fields.

Compendex Plus. A database in numerous aspects of engineering.

Index to IEEE Publications. Annual index to articles in many areas of electronics.

The McGraw-Hill Encyclopedia of Science and Technology (7th edition, 1992). Twenty volumes on the physical, natural and applied sciences. Index.

Pollution Abstracts. Published six times a year, it indexes and summarizes "world-wide technical literature on environmental pollution." *Also an electronic version under the same name.

Science Citation Index. Multidisciplinary index to the world's scientific literature.

*Telecommunications. Full text of articles in the field.

Social Sciences and Psychology

The Social Science Encyclopedia. In one volume, surveys the major social sciences.

*Contemporary Women's Issues. Full text information from 600 sources published by 100 organizations worldwide. Also gives full text of 100 journals.

Psychological Abstracts. Summarizes articles from scholarly journals of many countries and indexes them by author and subject. Read the summaries to find which articles are worth looking up. *A similar version, PsycLIT, is available on CD-ROM.

Sociological Abstracts. Summarizes articles from the scholarly journals of many countries and indexes them by author and subject. Read the summaries to find which articles are worth looking up.

*Sociofile. Produced by Sociological abstracts, this is an enormous electronic database for sociology, social science and political science. It summarizes articles from over 2000 journals.

Social Sciences Citation Index. "An international multidisciplinary index to the literature of the social sciences."

Social Sciences Index. Author and subject index to English-language articles from many publications in anthropology, economics, geography, law and criminology, public administration, political science, psychology, social work and sociology.

*ERIC. On CD-ROM, this is the U.S. national bibliographic database for education literature, indexing over 700 periodicals in the field.

Business and Economics

*Business and Industry. A global database covering over 900 trade and business publications. Sixty percent is full-text and the remainder is summarized.

Business Periodicals Index. Monthly subject index to articles in a great many English-language business periodicals.

*Canadian Business and Current Affairs (CBCA). Contains the full text of 130 Canadian periodicals and other sources of information. Also indexes some 600 periodicals and nine daily news sources.

The Canadian Index. Indexes articles from Canadian business magazines, general magazines and newspapers.

*Canadian NewsDisc. Gives the full text of columns, articles and features published in Canada's major newspapers.

Globe and Mail. Complete text of Canada's major national newspaper, as well as the *Winnipeg Free Press*, *Victoria-Times Colonist*, and the *Lethbridge Herald*.

Lexis/Nexis. See entry under "General Sources."

The Journal of Economic Literature. An international quarterly that has articles, book reviews, summaries of articles from other sources, and an index. Geared to theoretical economics rather than companies and trends.

The Humanities (Excluding Literature)

Humanities Index. International index to articles in hundreds of periodicals in the humanities. Includes language and literature, philosophy, politics, history, literary criticism and music.

Canadian Music Periodicals Index (CMPI). Database indexes entries from almost 500 Canadian music journals, newsletters and magazines.

Music Index. International author and subject index of articles in music periodicals, including reviews of books and records.

The New Grove Dictionary of Music and Musicians. Illustrated multivolume work on composers, instruments, musical works, etc.

International Film Archive. Indexes on CD-ROM over 200 journals worldwide, covering film and television.

The Oxford Companion to Film. Discusses directors, actors, critics, individual films, techniques, etc. Illustrated.

Film Literature Index. A well-used author and subject index to many film periodicals.

New York Times Film Reviews. Reviews beginning 1913. Indexed.

Art Abstracts. Indexes and summarizes more than 260 periodicals worldwide, including foreign-language journals.

Art Index. Much-used international author and subject index to many periodicals in all major fields of art. *Also on CD-ROM.

McGraw-Hill Dictionary of Art. A concise five-volume study of world art from its beginnings. Heavily illustrated.

The Encyclopedia of Philosophy. Authoritative articles about philosophy and philosophers from the beginnings, worldwide.

The Routledge Encyclopedia of Philosophy (CD-ROM).

The Encyclopedia of Religion. Published 1987 in 15 volumes.

The Cambridge Ancient History, The Cambridge Medieval History, The New Cambridge Modern History. Detailed and authoritative coverage of these periods.

Literature

A Dictionary of Literary Terms. A good first source for research on genres or on technical aspects of literature.

The Oxford Companion to Canadian Literature. A concise and authoritative first source for most topics in the field. Revised 1997. Covers authors, literary works, genres, criticism and more. Strong emphasis on Quebec.

Literary History of Canada, 2nd edition, eds. Carl Klinck et al. Comprehensive and authoritative.

The Oxford Companion to English Literature, 1998 revision. Also in this series are *The Oxford Companion to American Literature* and *The Oxford Companion to Classical Literature*.

Literary History of the United States, eds. Robert Spiller et al. An authoritative examination of the subject from its beginnings.

The Feminist Companion to Literature in English, 1 volume, 1990.

MLA International Bibliography. The basic reference for serious scholarly research in literature worldwide and in modern languages. Now on CD-ROM.

Canadian Literary Periodicals Index. Twice yearly from 1992, with annual accumulation.

Index to Canadian Literature. Yearly index to the important quarterly *Canadian Literature*.

Canadian Writers and Their Works. Large series of volumes with sections on many Canadian writers.

Contemporary Literary Criticism. Multivolume work that gives excerpts from criticism of current literature.

Contemporary Authors. Multivolume guide to current authors in all fields, including film and television.

The Oxford English Dictionary, 2nd edition. The largest and most complete dictionary of English, now on CD-ROM. Gives the fullest information on meanings, spellings and origins of words, illustrated by quotations from many periods.

The Concise Oxford Companion to the Theatre (1992). Briefly covers playwrights and their works, major movements in the theatre and technical aspects of theatre. Illustrated.

Researching with Internet Sources

You've probably noticed how many sources given on these pages are electronic. Going beyond CD-ROMs and online services, though, let's look at the Internet itself—how to conduct a search for information, and how to decide if that information is reliable enough to put in your essay.

For many people these days, the first step to investigating a topic—whether buying a car, planning a holiday or writing an essay—is the World Wide Web. After all, some 200 million people, including more than 8 million Canadians, are online these days, and the Web, with many millions of sites, is a kind of mega library to the world. Its already vast information is increasing by over a million pages a day, and over a billion hyperlinks already bind it together.

But how good is this information? Your own surfing has no doubt uncovered vast amounts of garbage, from thoughtless chat groups to sites with a political or social axe to grind, to pushy hard-sell businesses, to sites that seem antisocial or even illegal. Much of the writing itself is weak, since almost anyone can open a site. (By contrast, writers appearing in print have to be screened by editors and publishers, and articles for scholarly journals are judged by specialists in the field.) And what about the accuracy of statistics or other factual claims made by Internet authors? These questions are so troublesome that many postsecondary teachers—for example in the History Department of McGill—do not accept in their students' essays materials from the Web at all.

Yet good information can certainly be found there. You have no doubt visited sites that are carefully constructed, well written, authoritative with documented facts, and from a balanced and fair point of view. Is it any accident that most of these are created not by individuals or corporations, but by universities and governments? When Citizenship and Immigration Canada explains in its official Web site at <http://cicnet.ci.gc.ca> what the steps are to become a citizen of our country, you can probably have full confidence in the accuracy of the data—because this is the ministry that writes the rules to begin with. You can even print off the official application forms. Surely, then, you can quote all this information with confidence, in your research paper.

But how about, for example, the Web site of the National Rifle Association? At <http://www.nra.org> this American group of hunters and other gun owners argues for its own political purpose, which is ease of gun ownership. In its news releases and position papers it uses biased language to criticize any person or government that tries to control gun ownership. So do you quote the NRA in your essay on gun control? Not on the same factual level as you could with Citizenship and Immigration Canada. Certainly you could quote, to show what the hunters are saying, but always trying to assess the worth of those arguments, and always thinking twice before using NRA data to prove points. If you keep your eyes open, you will realize that the same is true of the vast majority of Web sites. Choose carefully!

Still another problem is timeliness. Since many Web sites are constructed and later abandoned, make sure to check, among other things, when the site was last updated. An argument to support or fight gun legislation is not exactly timely a year after the bill has been passed.

Web Portals

Once you do set out to research a topic on the Web, where do you begin? The following "portals" (Web sites that search other Web sites) are most peoples' choice. The main thing to remember, though, is that they are all different. Where one will fail to find your topic, another may well do the job. So don't just rely on one favourite. Put them all into a bookmark folder, so you can move easily from one to another as you search your topic. (Much of the information in this section comes from a useful book, *Internet Directory 2000: A Canadian Guide to the Best Web Sites and Tools*, by Scott Michell and Darren Wershler-Henry.)

Northern Light <www.northernlight.com>: This relatively new search engine will check over 150 million Web pages for you. It is a good place to start if your topic is large or general, because it gathers results into "folders" of related sites.

Hotbot <www.hotbot.com>: Has a database almost as big as that of Northern Light and AltaVista, and is updated often. Its search options are more numerous and sophisticated than those of other portals.

AltaVista <www.altavista.com>: Has a huge database, and offers Boolean search capabilities as well as searching in "natural language" mode (you put normal sentences or questions into the search box). Fast, but may dilute your search by finding many items not really related to your topic.

Yahoo! <www.yahoo.com>: As a "directory," rather than a search engine, its structure of categories permits fast focussing down to your desired topic.

Canoe <www.canoe.ca>: As the name suggests, a Canadian portal offering data on a wealth of topics.

Canada.com <www.canada.com>: Canada's largest search engine, with Boolean search capability and access to the Southam newswires.

MetaCrawler <www.go2net.com/search.html> or **Dogpile** <www.dogpile.com> or **All-in-One Search Page** <www.allonesearch.com>: These "metasearch engines" will organize searches through other search engines and databases all at once. While they search broadly, though, they search less deeply.

Finally, check this Web site for much more on search engines: <www.kcpl.lib.mo.us/search/srchengines.htm>.

Conducting a Simple Search

The most basic techniques of online searching are really easy, and you probably know them already:

- In some search engines, such as Northern Light or AltaVista, just type into the search box a question in "natural language"—that is, in everyday language just as if you were speaking.

- Or, in all engines, type a key word into the search box and hit "search" or Enter. Results will be listed each containing the word. You then look these over, before selecting those that seem most fully on your topic.

- Or type more than one word into the search box; the system will search for all those words. If the words have the most meaning together, though, enclose the group of words in double quotation marks. For example asking for "Wayne Gretzky" all in quotation marks will prevent the system from finding pages about other people named Gretzky.

These simplest kinds of searches are sometimes all you need, but many major engines also support searches that use a more sophisticated logic. The best thing to do is print off the "help page" of the site you prefer and study it. However, let's look at a fairly standard set of procedures for more-advanced-level searching. Named after the logician George Boole, these are techniques of the "Boolean search."

COURTESY OF CANOE, www.canoe.ca

Boolean Search

Most major engines support the Boolean search, which works through the logic of inclusion and exclusion. Here is a brief summary of techniques, drawing to some extent on suggestions found on the help page of Northern Light, at <www.northernlight.com/docs/search_help_optimize.html>.

■ Use of **AND**: A query for War AND Peace will return documents that include the word "war" and documents that include the word "peace". On the other hand, putting quotations around these words ("War AND Peace"), as mentioned above, will find documents such as the book of this title by Tolstoy, which will contain the whole phrase.

The advantage of Boolean techniques is their power to focus your search. For example, at the time this edition was being written, the word "employment" entered into the Northern Light search engine turned up 4 551 610 hits. Imagine checking that list over! But

using AND to add the term "youth" reduced the documents found to 283 059. Then using AND again to add "Vancouver" brought the number down to 10 622 —still enough to keep you reading for a few weeks. So using AND once again to add "fast food" brought the total down to 1554. The following is the total "string" of search terms:

employment AND youth AND Vancouver AND "fast food"

(*Note:* "Fast food" is in quotation marks so that the two words will be searched as one unit. If there were no quotation marks here, Northern Light would search both for "fast" and for "food," totally wrecking this investigation.)

The system is not perfect. Only a few of the documents listed may really be about youth summer employment in the fast-food industry in Vancouver. But if such documents do exist in the Northern Light database, you will see them, and the logic of the search engine software puts the most likely documents toward the top of the list. Still another way to sort is of course to skip over any document more than a few months old—and some found by this search were two or even three years old.

(*Note:* Instead of AND, some systems use the mathematical symbol "+.")

■ *Use of OR*: OR will tell the system to find documents containing any of the search terms. Example:

encryption OR cryptography

■ *Use of NOT*: This specifies a term that must *not* appear in documents found. For example:

dolphins NOT NFL (This researcher is interested in the ocean, not the playing field.)

(*Note:* Instead of NOT, some systems use the mathematical symbol "-.")

■ *Wildcards:* To include any possible form of a root word you are searching, key in the main part of the word and then an asterisk. For example, "Canad*" will find both the terms "Canada" and "Canadian," as well as company names that begin with those five letters.

These techniques are a start. If we went much further here, we would encounter serious differences between the ways various search engines operate.

Again, as you find your favourite systems, invest some time in studying their help pages and practising their advice, to make good search moves automatic. As with any other tools, the way to master them is to use them.

(*Note:* See the very end of this book for techniques of documenting Internet sources in your essays.)

Now let's return to Amy, who is writing a research essay on employment. Having gathered her list of sources, she then conducts her main research, using the following guidelines given by her instructor.

As you begin the main research, be efficient. A couple of minutes spent checking a book's table of contents and index, and leafing through the relevant chapters, may save hours. There is nothing more aggravating than laboriously collecting facts that are scattered through one book, only to find them collected in a few pages of the next book or even reduced to a graph or chart. Another waste of time is to collect facts from an old issue of a magazine or newspaper, only to find a newer issue (or a newer database) with more current facts that make your notes obsolete.

When you have selected the most likely sources, begin taking notes:

■ The bulk of your notes should be *summary* of facts or ideas you think you'll need. Don't just jot down isolated facts, but give some of their context, too, so later you can make sense of them.

■ When you find a key idea stated so forcefully or eloquently that you couldn't possibly word it as well yourself, copy it exactly, putting quotation marks where the quoted words begin and end.

> As many as half the quotations given in student essays contain one or more errors: spelling, words left out, punctuation changed, etc. Teachers notice carelessness, and don't like it. Help yourself proofread better by putting a straightedge, such as a ruler or a three-by-five card, under the line in the book or periodical, and another under the line you copied. Now move your eyes back and forth from one to the other, to make sure the two versions are identical.
>
> Of course errors in recording notes can be avoided if you have downloaded full-text database articles onto your own floppy and printed them out at home, where you can select your quotations and highlight them for use in your own essay. But later, when you insert these into your paper, you still need to guard carefully against errors in transcription, using the techniques given above.

Take steps now to save time later:

■ Accurately record the page numbers of all summaries and quotations, because youíll need them later for the references. *If you don't get them now, you'll be back the night before the essay is due, leafing furiously through books and magazines.*

■ As you take notes, mark the items that seem most important, perhaps with an asterisk (*) in the margin, or by highlighting in yellow. Later this step will help you to select more easily the main points of your outline.

■ Though the main outline comes after the research, put together a *rough outline* of five or ten lines as soon as you can. It may save you hours by channelling your reading and note-taking into exactly those areas that you will cover in the essay.

■ Use one of these systems for getting notes into order for an outline:

1. *For very long essays:* Write notes on file cards, one side only, with each subject labelled at the top. Don't waste time in recording all the reference information with each entry, but do list the author, the title—if you use more than one article or book by the same author—and the page number(s). Later, when writing the list of "works cited," you can look up the other data in your list of sources. When all the cards are eventually placed in the order required by your outline, you write the essay from them.

2. *For shorter essays:* Write notes on sheets of paper, one side only. As above, record the author, title and page number(s) with each entry, and write a subject label above or in the margin. Later you can cut each item apart from the others with scissors, and arrange the items like note cards according to your outline.

STEP FOUR: TRY A SHORT OUTLINE

Amy knows that a research essay, like a house, is made from a plan. An outline, though, is not a blueprint. While almost every detail of a house is decided in advance, so the builder won't put things like doors or windows in the wrong places, the writer of an essay sometimes gets the best ideas in the middle of the job.

Of course, the outline of a research essay is somewhat longer and more detailed than the brief and tentative outline of the "short essay" discussed in our opening chapter. But even this longer outline should not be so complete that it paralyzes Amy's imagination as she writes, or so final that she cannot improve it if her discovery draft awakens valuable new ideas.

To begin forming her outline, Amy divides her notes into groups that seem to fit together. (She actually moves them into different combinations on the desk in front of her, like the pieces of the puzzle which they are.)

Now she looks at them. Are there two main groups, one pro and the other con? Or does one group *cause* the material in the other group? Are there three groups, and therefore three branches of her subject? Or are there four? Do her notes flow onward in time order from first to last, with divisions wherever one time period ends and the next begins? Or is a clear background needed for the actual points to be given?

If you examine your notes with an open mind, you will usually "find" rather than "choose" the form of your outline. Amy finds, for example, that first she needs a good dose of background information to show why the workplace today is difficult, before she can then give her solutions to the problem one by one.

OUTLINE FOR AMY'S RESEARCH ESSAY

I. Introduction
   A. Background: the security of many jobs in past decades
   B. Contrast: problems on the job market today
      1. layoffs because of technology
      2. underemployment
   C. Thesis: New challenges require new approaches

II. Body: five ways for students to use flexibility in the quest for worthwhile employment
   A. Get a co-op education
   B. Develop computer expertise
   C. Diversify
   D. Put liberal arts in your education
   E. Begin to invest

III. Conclusion: playing it safe vs. taking risks

Amy's outline is indeed short, still tentative, leaving room for development rather than trying to blueprint every single detail to come. It does rough out an introduction, a body and a conclusion, the three traditional parts of an essay. It also attempts (successfully, it turns out) to predict the main points to come.

Now before we discuss the last step of actually writing the essay, please read "Students and the New Workplace" on the pages that follow, so we can refer to it as an example.

Sung 1

Amy Sung

Professor Giuliani

Communication 210

5 April ____

Students and the New Workplace

The world of employment is in rapid change. When many students look back at their grandparents' careers, they see nine-to-five jobs, years and years with the same employer, holidays and health benefits—and at the end of the road a pension. Even many parents of today's students still live this secure and steady life of decades past.

Today, though, more and more Canadians, both older and of student age, see around them a society that is casting off its employees like dead leaves from a tree; a society in which too many people have no job, while many who do are working far too hard at thankless and repetitive tasks. Canadian Douglas Coupland, in the title of his widely read novel *Generation X*, named a whole generation enduring the underemployment of what he calls the "McJob: A low-pay, low-prestige, low-dignity, low-benefit, no-future job in the service sector" (5).

It is true that the characters of his later novel *Microserfs* are the lucky graduates with "good" jobs in the computer software industry. Are they really that much better off, though? These talented "geeks," as they label themselves, have to spend 371 pages fighting their way out of the isolation and repetition of their workaholic jobs and into real life.

The "Xers" and "geeks" Coupland writes about are some years older than today's high school, college or university student, but their younger brothers and sisters face the same challenges. How in fact do today's students plan a decent career? How

Sung 2

can they enter today's "lean and mean" workplace and succeed?

5

The overall answer to the new employment questions is flexibility. Only by letting go of old certainties, only by welcoming new tactics for new times, can today's students move more surely toward a real and satisfying career. The rest of this essay first examines the new challenges, then explores five ways to overcome them through flexibility.

6

It is clear that present employment trends are not good. Why have corporations such as banks and manufacturers been making hefty profits for their management and shareholders, while at the very same time laying off thousands of employees? Why does a company's share price often jump when new "downsizing" of workers is announced? Why do we now do our banking by machine, talk with voice mail instead of humans, and drive cars built by robots?

7

Jeremy Rifkin, president of the Foundation on Economic Trends in Washington, D.C., captures these new realities in the very title of his book, *The End of Work.* In his view,

> The Information Age has arrived. In the years ahead, new, more sophisticated software technologies are going to bring civilization closer to a near-workerless world. In the agricultural, manufacturing, and service sectors, machines are quickly replacing human labor and promise an economy of near automated production by the mid-decades of the twenty-first century. The wholesale substitution of machines for workers is going to force every nation to rethink the role of human beings in the social process. (xv)

In other words, in the ever more competitive world economy, corporations keep trimming expenses to boost the balance sheet, relying on their new electronic "employees"—and of course hoping that their former human employees still have some money to continue buying the products.

8

The future envisioned by Rifkin is one in which a few highly paid "knowledge workers" organize all the computers to profit corporations and shareholders, while former workers are left in a vacuum of inactivity and poverty. Unless good solutions are found, he concludes, social unrest and even violence will result.

9

At the same time that many jobs are being eliminated, others are diminishing in desirability. According to Edward Greenspon,

> almost half the jobs created in Canada in the past 20 years
> have been non-standard jobs (part-time, temporary or contract)
> without pensions or security [. . .] . They also pay about $150
> less than the same work done by non-temporary employees
> [. . .] . (A12–13)

To show where she has left out less important words or phrases, Amy uses ellipses (three dots, with a space between and enclosed in square brackets). Where she omits the end of a sentence, she adds a fourth spaced dot outside the brackets, which is the sentence period.

10

As for the growing numbers of temporary workers, the jobs of 75 percent last less than six months, according to Chris Clark, policy analyst for the Canadian Council on Social Development. In the same vein, Andrew Jackson, senior economist for the Canadian Labour Congress, points out that these days only around 60 percent of Canadians work full-time all year long for one employer (Wells 15).

Since the author of the article is not mentioned in the text, her name is given with the page number in the parentheses.

11

Finally, in the new economy it may be women who face the hardest challenges of all. Social critic Heather Menzies, in her book *Whose Brave New World? The Information Highway and the New Economy*, points out that

> More and more women are being ghettoized in the new permanent
> part-time workforce, with few if any benefits, including training, and
> with a skills, credentials, and silicon ceiling preventing their mobility.
> They are also part of the growing trend towards home-based work,
> particularly in the female ghettos of clerical, sales, and service. (34)

Each page is numbered at the upper right, with your last name just before it.

Sung 4

12   If high-quality employment is indeed threatened, as these critics are saying, and if a new, leaner world of underemployment and unemployment is taking its place, what, then, can today's students do to meet the challenge? What new attitudes and tactics are of more use than the rosy assumptions of the past? What will work right now and in the years to come?

13   One overall personal trait seems to lie behind the best answers given by analysts: flexibility. When times change, people must change. Only by shaking off the old assumptions, the old patterns and the old habits, can people begin to seize new opportunities. Only by rethinking business as usual can the new generation meet the new challenges.

14   The following pages explore five concrete ways for today's student to bring this flexibility to the quest for worthwhile employment.

Here Amy clearly announces her organization for the rest of the essay.

Get a Co-op Education

15   One path to job success in today's world can be choosing a co-op program at college or university. "The most important thing," writes Gordon Betcherman, a leading Canadian authority on the future of work, "is to encourage forms of education that mix schooling with work experience—internship, co-op programs and work-term efforts. These methods have been shown to be very successful." He points out that students in such programs "make connections with potential employers," that they "learn what is required to sell [themselves] to employers," and that they "learn how to do the work" (D2).

Here Amy fits choice bits of a longer quotation into her own sentence structure. The whole thing should sound natural, as though she had written all the words herself.

16   Many of these students also speak to so many employers that eventually a job interview seems like an everyday thing. Many co-op students on job placement also make a salary, which helps pay for their education, and

then after graduation many are invited back to work for the same employer. Naguib Oman, of the University of Waterloo, is an example. As a computer science major, he had a work term with a small software company, and even before graduation was making so much money that he bought a new car. Since then he has held down a well-paid job with the same company, writing software for a wireless communication program that uses satellite data to map locations and destinations for automobile drivers (Oman).

There is nothing like a concrete example—such as this case study of Naguib Oman—to help readers "see" your point.

17   A co-op education truly demands the recommended trait of flexibility: the student alternates frequently between school and work, leaves friends every few months, moves to other cities and finds housing, then takes a year longer to graduate. However, for many students the effort brings great rewards.

If you are computing, set your margins to be "justified left," leaving a ragged right-hand margin as if the paper had been typed.

Develop Computer Expertise

18   This path is probably the easiest for most students: become fluent in computing, including use of the Internet and its rapidly expanding World Wide Web.

19   Not that these skills automatically translate into a good employment life. A great deal of computer-related work is low-level drudgery: for example data entry, or many service-sector applications such as food order systems in fast-food restaurants. Even some "good" computer jobs, as Coupland shows in *Microserfs*, can oppress the individual. On the other hand, those who rise to the ranks of programmers, systems analysts and other "knowledge workers" will in many ways be the winners of the future; they will create and manipulate the artificial intelligence that will then displace other workers who did not make it to the top.

20   Heather Menzies underlines the growing role of computer skills in the

workplace:

> In mid-1995 Statistics Canada reported that nearly half of all
>
> workers (48 per cent) were working with or on computers,
>
> three times the figure of 1985. It also found that "the most
>
> elite class of workers, managers and professionals," were
>
> the most computer literate—with 75 per cent of the men and
>
> 61 per cent of the women in that group working with computer
>
> systems. (47)

21   As for the Information Highway, though many students see it as

entertainment, mastering its ever-increasing functions can help the

individual's larger goals come true. Consider the example of one student

at York University, who used the Internet to find a summer job in Italy.

This experience then led to a new career choice in design (which, these

days, also exploits computer skills). As she puts it, "The whole thing was

so easy. I just made the initial contact by e-mail, then sent the documents

and references the company asked for, and in two months I was there

working" (Friedman).

Another student example makes Amy's point more concrete.

Since Friedman had sent these comments to Amy by e-mail, there is no page number to include in the reference. Her last name is given, though, because it does not appear above in the text. Note in the "Works Cited" how an e-mail message is listed.

22   Another Ontario student, Dan Jordan, is studying International

Business at Seneca College and expects to work in that field, but in the

meantime his computer skills have helped him create home pages for

companies. His advantage: instead of charging the $4000 that a commercial

firm does for company home pages, he charges $400. Even at one-tenth

the fee, he makes $100 an hour because he can usually do the job in four

hours (Jordan).

23   Through their computer skills, these students gain in career flexibility.

They are on their way to the future.

Sung 7

Diversify

24

A quick transition moves readers from the previous section to this one.

The example of Jordan leads into another technique of flexibility in today's job world: diversification. It is said that, in medieval times, fathers tried to teach their sons more than one trade. Then if demand for the one diminished, the son could change to the other and still put bread on the table. Have things really changed? Jordan may think he is heading into international business, but who really knows? What if it, like so many other fields, falls victim to automation and consequent downsizing of employees? He can then shift to his other option, the world of computers. Each student should look around, asking himself or herself what the options are. These are usually seen first in hobbies, pastimes, or part-time or seasonal areas of employment. Which of these excite the person? Which relate to real tasks done in the real world?

25

More examples help us "see" Amy's point.

Often these alternative areas are entrepreneurial. Does the person enjoy working outside? Then someday, with a used pickup truck and some lawn mowers, the person could start a landscaping company. Is the person adventurous? Has he or she explored Latin America and learned Spanish in the process? Then the future may be some kind of international business. Does the person like to write? Then someday the scribbling might turn into manuscripts for romances or crime fiction, or for that matter company proposals and annual reports. The flexibility of diversification is the essence of being an entrepreneur, and in a time of unemployment and underemployment, being an entrepreneur may be the shortest path to a career.

26

In a 1995 address on youth unemployment, Al Flood, CEO of the Canadian Imperial Bank of Commerce, summed up his view: "The overall task is to show more of the new generation, new to the workforce or not

Sung 8

yet in it, how to be entrepreneurs" ("Business and Education Must Join Forces to Combat Youth Unemployment, CIBC Chairman Says").

Put Liberal Arts in Your Education

27   Ironically, an important path toward success in the new economy is an old-fashioned, well-rounded liberal arts education—the kind society has been devaluing for years in its quest for the bottom line. Who are the people who rise in a company? Is it possible that they are the ones who wrote good essays in school?

28   Demographer David Foot believes that "The decline of literacy has enhanced the value of the small minority who can write well and who are able to make effective oral presentations." He adds that "the successful worker of the future needs the kinds of skills that an old-fashioned liberal-arts education still provides very well—the ability to assemble information, analyze it and think about it" (Foot and Stoffman D2).

29   The student who seeks future success would do well to take courses in literature and in writing, to read some philosophy, to know some history—to systematically gain exposure to a wide variety of subjects. English teachers often complain that few people write well. Students who aim high in the world of employment might well want to join these few.

30   English may be important, but is it enough? Tim Reid, president of the Canadian Chamber of Commerce, himself an anglophone who mastered French to further his career, believes that today's students need other languages:

> Business dealings today have moved beyond our backyards and into the global arena. The status quo of education requirements of our

Sung 9

generation mean nothing in a job market filled with applicants from around the world, not just around the corner. Our children need every advantage we can give to them so they can go out and create their own opportunities for success. (1)

31   With the emergence of our global economy, and with the North American Free Trade Act drawing Mexico, the United States and Canada closer together, many future employees will indeed have to know languages. This means taking French or Spanish in school. It means going to Quebec on a language bursary, to Mexico on a student exchange, or anywhere else that gives real-life experience in major languages and cultures. It means openness to other lifestyles and values—a difficult thing for those who have never yet left home. For those who grew up speaking another language, it also means practising and protecting their skill in it, and making sure they can write it as well as speak it. The rewards can be great: when equally good candidates compete for a job, the one who knows other languages will more often be chosen.

Amy does not document this information, because it is from her general knowledge, not her essay research.

Begin to Invest

32   The fifth path to success in the new economy demands even more flexibility and sacrifice than the others. It seems a cruel hoax to urge those lucky graduates who are finally making money in their first real job to delay buying the long-awaited sound system or car—and instead write cheques to the mutual fund company or stockbroker. What few realize is that the painful act of saving money early in life begins an economic snowball effect which can eventually augment and even replace salary. In a time of

Since the fifth "path" is hardest, it is put last where it will form a climax.

Sung 10

government cutbacks and a Canada Pension Plan that many believe will disappear, it is the ultimate safety net.

33   Suppose the new employee manages to save $2500 a year for four years. With this $10 000, he or she then invests in stocks (probably at first through the easier and safer means of a stock mutual fund managed by a professional). Suppose also that the investment gains the long-term stock market average of 12 percent a year. Anyone who can figure compounding on a scientific calculator will see that in 10 years the $10 000 will on average grow to over $30 000, in 20 years to almost $100 000, in 30 years to almost $300 000—and in 40 years to almost a milliion.

Amy does not document these figures, since they come from her own calculator, and since her readers will come up with the same figures if they double-check.

34   This is not the place to discuss the many fine points an investor must learn, such as the differences in taxation between an RRSP (registered retirement savings plan) and a regular investment account, or the many techniques involved in choosing good mutual funds and good stocks, or the economic cycles that influence markets, or the art of diversifying kinds of investment for safety. The person who wants to set the snowball rolling must invest a great deal of study time, as well as some money. One place to start is *Gordon Pape's Investing Strategies 2000: Mutual Funds and Beyond*, a Canadian book by financial authors experienced in writing for the general public.

To keep the essay moving, here Amy refers readers to another source, rather than getting bogged down in a mass of specialized details.

35   After the sacrifice of saving and the work of financial study should come the benefits: once the snowball really gets going, the investor can cash in stocks to start a business, to boost a low salary, or to pay bills when between jobs. Ironically, if in the new economy the corporation is gaining power over the employee, the employee can also gain power over the corporation—by owning it.

36

Most research essays have a summary near the end, leading into the conclusion. Keep your summary short, like Amy's, so the reader is not bored by repetition.

The closing should pack a punch, to send readers off inspired. This one ends on an ironic contrast, concluding that in our times, safety can be more dangerous than risk.

As with the other paths to success in the new economy—getting a co-op education, developing computer expertise, diversifying, and studying liberal arts subjects like writing and languages—achieving financial security through investment takes flexibility, openness, and the ability to take risk. These are new times. To some people they seem risky times. The highest risk, though, to today's students planning a career, is to follow the comfortable old path of playing it safe.

Sung 12

Works Cited

Betcherman, Gordon. "What Government, Business and You Can Do to

Brighten the Job Future." *Globe and Mail* [Toronto] 27 Apr. 1996: D2.

"Business and Education Must Join Forces to Combat Youth Unemployment,

CIBC Chairman Says." 21 Sept. 1995. *Canada NewsWire.* CD-ROM.

Coupland, Douglas. *Generation X: Tales for an Accelerated Culture.* New York:

St. Martin's Press, 1991.

---. *Microserfs.* Toronto: HarperCollins, 1995.

Foot, David K., and Daniel Stoffman. "The Great Canadian Job Funk." *Globe

and Mail* [Toronto] 25 May 1996: D1–2.

Friedman, Jana. E-mail to the author. 21 Mar. 2000.

Greenspon, Edward. "Economy Changing Faster Than People." *Globe and

Mail* [Toronto] 20 Apr. 1996: A1+.

Jordan, Dan. E-mail to the author. 17 Mar. 2000.

Menzies, Heather. *Whose Brave New World? The Information Highway and the

New Economy.* Toronto: Between the Lines, 1996.

Oman, Naguib. Telephone interview. 25 Mar. 2000.

Pape, Gordon, Richard Croft, and Eric Kirzner. *Gordon Pape's Investing

Strategies 2000: Mutual Funds and Beyond.* Scarborough: Prentice Hall

Canada, 1999.

Reid, Tim. "International Thinking Is a Reality of Our Youth." *CPF National

News* 71 (1996): 1+.

Rifkin, Jeremy. *The End of Work: Technology, Jobs and Your Future.* New York:

Putnam, 1996.

Wells, Jennifer. "Jobs." *Maclean's* 11 Mar. 1996: 12–16.

Where the author is not named, start the entry with the title.

Where you list two works by the same author, the second entry begins with three hyphens instead of the name.

Where there are two authors, only the first is presented in reverse name order.

Only the first line of each entry is at the left margin, so readers can more easily see the alphabetical order of references.

Amy can add her own primary research to the list: telephone or personal interviews, or (see above) e-mail messages.

Put no punctuation between name and date of a periodical.

STEP FIVE: WRITE THE ESSAY

Since the research essay is longer and more fully planned than the "short essays" discussed in our opening chapter, it is written in a less experimental way. We might still call the first version a "discovery draft," because the act of writing does trigger new ideas. Yet the major reading, note-taking and organizing done before the writing begins will strongly shape even the first draft.

Amy finds herself writing more slowly and deliberately than in the "short essays" earlier in her course. Now she takes fewer risks, staying closer to her outline, because any big shift of direction now would mean new planning and new research.

Yet if while writing she senses that the facts are working *against* her tentative thesis statement, showing it to be wrong, like a scientist's experiment disproving the hypothesis, the only honest response would be to interpret those facts all over, throw out the old outline and write a new one.

As Amy writes her first draft, she follows these guidelines suggested by her instructor:

- **Put your thesis statement into an introduction.** An essay about a very familiar subject might have a short introduction with the thesis statement in the first paragraph, while one on a less familiar subject might begin with several paragraphs of introduction. Amy's falls in between: she gives a moderate amount of introduction to the new problems of the new workplace, then at the end of paragraph 4 places her thesis statement.

  In your introduction, whatever its length, try to *interest and prepare your readers*. Amy's references to two current novels widely read by people her age, and the threats to her generation's professional life which she presents in paragraph 4, are designed to involve her readers and get them thinking about the topic.

  Other introductions use a quotation from a famous person, an amusing story, a scary statistic, or whatever else the author thinks will interest and prepare readers.

- **Connect the parts.** Just as the sentences of a paragraph are connected by transitions, so are the paragraphs of an essay. Use the transitions we examined

on page 46, especially at the beginning and end of paragraphs. Note, for example, how the opening sentence of Amy's paragraph 24 moves us onward from the point just ended to the point just beginning: "The example of Jordan leads into another technique of flexibility in today's job world: diversification." You may even use a whole paragraph, like Amy's paragraph 12, as a bridge between longer sections.

Finally, larger organizational devices can connect the parts and keep them moving on. For example, Amy uses a natural and logical time order, looking first at traditional employment in past decades, then at the problems of employment now. Then once she is giving her suggestions to solve the problems, she saves the hardest for last, rising to the momentum of a climax.

- **Write a meaningful conclusion.** Do not end with a mere summary, although most research essays, like Amy's, do have one near the end. Instead, try for a larger effect, as in musical compositions that rise at the end to a climax. (Note the rising order in the placement of her suggestions, just discussed.) Also the very end should convey some kind of power, to leave the reader moved. Amy reaches for this through a contrast or paradox: she claims that in today's employment world, trying to be "safe" is actually more dangerous than taking risks.

  Above all, end with a punch, not with some minor matter. Imagine the effect if Amy had closed on a sentence like this: "Finally, when a job interview does occur, it can often be important to polish your shoes, press your clothes, and not chew gum."

- **Revise from one draft to another,** as the author of our "short essay" did on pages 26–29. Since we have already seen the whole process at work on those pages, we will not repeat it all here. What you have just read is a final draft, revised, edited and proofread—the product of Amy's most careful work. It may still have flaws, but its writer sought to polish the argument as thoroughly as possible by "reseeing" it through several drafts.

  In the last of those drafts, Amy scrutinized all suspicious-looking sentences and all words that just might be misspelled (since spell check doesn't catch everything!). It is in this final stage that she reaches for her guide to style and usage. (Why do this in the early stages, when paragraphs or even whole pages may later be cut?)

Putting the editing and proofreading last does not take away from their importance. Some readers pounce on punctuation or spelling errors like a hawk pouncing on a mouse. They are happy that you were wrong and they are right. Don't let this happen: why distract a reader with bloopers when what you want that reader to do is pay attention to your argument?

Since research papers are long and are revised through several drafts, word processing is a powerful tool in writing them. A first draft can be stored, retrieved at any time for further work, or printed out in "hard copy" where you can see it better and edit on paper. Why not save all drafts, under different file names such as "draft 1," "draft 2," etc.? Then if a newer version doesn't work out, you can go back to use part or all of an earlier one.

Notes and potential quotations can of course be put into their own files as well. Keeping a running copy of the bibliography, in its own file, is especially useful; at any time you can check it so far, add new items, delete items that were not used, or print.

As to format, the Modern Language Association of America (MLA) advises "justifying" left, leaving a ragged right-hand margin as in typed copy. As for underlining in-text titles, it now advises that either the traditional underlining or the equivalent symbol of italicizing is acceptable.

Especially when writing a long assignment such as a research paper, be sure to save drafts onto a backup floppy disk; otherwise you could lose a week or more of work if your hard drive crashes (and every hard drive eventually does crash). For any project over 20 pages or so, it is also good to make a second backup disk to keep in another building—in case of theft or fire.

FINAL FORM OF THE RESEARCH ESSAY

Few things are agreed upon by everyone, and essay format is no exception. If your teacher does not specify a particular style, though, follow the form of our sample research essay, which is based on the name-page method of referencing recommended by the Modern Language Association of America (MLA) in its *MLA Handbook for Writers of Research Papers* (5th edition).

This widely used way of documenting replaces the old footnote or endnote system. Now brief references in parentheses, in the text of the essay, refer directly to items in a list of "works cited" (formerly called the "bibliography") at the end of the essay. Footnotes or endnotes, now called "content notes," are used only for explanations too minor to appear in the essay itself. (Amy didn't use any at all in her paper.)

Title Page?

Though some teachers still ask for a title page, the MLA no longer recommends it. See whether your own teacher wants one, and if so, what should be on it. Otherwise follow MLA format, which replaces the title page with the following facts on the upper left of the first page of the essay:

> your name
> teacher's name
> course designation
> date

The title appears just below this information, centred, and below it comes the first line of the essay. (See page 1 of Amy's essay for format and spacing.)

Page Format

Use standard-size paper, one side only, and leave standard margins so your teacher will have room to write comments. If you type or use word processing, double-space. If you write by hand, ask your teacher whether single- or double-spacing is preferred. If the teacher requires a title page, do not repeat the title at the top of page 1. In the upper right corner of each page, put your last name and the page number (see Amy's essay for exact format). Indent the first line of each paragraph five spaces if you type (or, in word processing, one "tab"), and further if you write by hand.

Quotations

Of course, whenever you repeat someone else's exact words, you must signal that fact so the reader will not think the words are yours. **Quotations up to four lines long are put in quotation marks and incorporated into the body of your text. Quotations longer than four lines, though, are indented ten spaces all along the left margin, and are double-spaced.**

Note that quotation marks are not used in a passage of more than four lines, because the indented format already identifies the passage as a quotation.

■ **A quotation and the sentence in which it appears must make grammatical sense together.** Avoid constructions like this:

> The author refers to the snow "It would fill the tracks in half an hour."

To correct this fused sentence, let's integrate the quotation with what comes before:

> The author says that the snow "[. . .] would fill the tracks in half an hour."

Note how the final quotation marks come after the period, not before. They would also come after a comma:

> The author says that the snow "[. . .] would fill the tracks in half an hour," making the search more difficult.

(See also more explanation and examples of this matter on page 121 of the section "Editing Out the Comma Splice and Fused Sentence.")

■ **Where one quotation occurs inside another, enclose the inner one in single quotation marks:**

> Then I said, "If this is what you call 'natural food,' I'll go back to TV dinners."

■ **You may omit unimportant material from the beginning, middle or end of a quoted sentence by** substituting an ellipsis (three dots with a space between each) in square brackets—to show that the act of omitting material is your own, and that the dots were not written by the author of the quotation itself.

> They also pay about $150 less than the same work done by non-temporary employees [. . .] (A12–13).

Note the spacing of the dots, in this example from paragraph 9 of Amy's essay. See also how a fourth dot, the sentence period, ends the whole thing just after the reference. If there were no reference, this sentence period would come right after the last bracket, with one space between:

> They also pay about $150 less than the same work done by non-temporary employees [. . .] .

Even with omissions, the quotation as it appears in your essay must make sense. Don't attempt to save time by just quoting the beginning and end ("With a . . . it"), assuming your reader will find the rest in the book. Instead, the reader will just get lost!

Fairness to your source is equally important. An unscrupulous publisher might place on the back cover of a new paperback a quotation from a reviewer who said the novel is " . . . an excellent book . . . ," when unfortunately the critic's full comment was " . . . an excellent book to throw in the garbage." An essayist who quotes out of context is falsifying as surely as if he or she had written the whole passage in the first place.

■ **You can sometimes make a quotation clearer by adding or substituting your own words in square brackets** (see the example in paragraph 15 of Amy's essay, where the added word "[themselves]" replaces the pronoun "yourself," which made less sense in her more formal, third-person style). Use such square brackets sparingly.

Name-Page References

Quotation marks tell your reader when you are using another person's words, but not whose words they are or where the reader can find them in order to check the accuracy of the quotation or find more information on the subject. In a short, informal essay it may be enough to introduce a quotation with a few facts: "As Margaret Atwood points out on page 75 of *Survival...*." Your teacher will let you know if this is all the documentation expected.

But in a longer, formal research essay, you need a fuller system of giving credit for quotations. The standard used to be footnotes or endnotes, followed on the last page by a bibliography. This system did the job, but wasted time: arranging and typing footnotes was laborious, and the notes and bibliography repeated too much of the same information.

For some years now, the MLA has recommended a modernized system that delivers all the same information but in streamlined form. If your teacher prefers this approach, as most now do, study the following directions and see Amy's research essay for examples of their use.

The main feature of the name-page reference system is the way you now refer briefly, in the body of the essay, to sources used. Instead of adding a numeral that refers to a note elsewhere, you simply place, after a quotation or other borrowed material, the author's last name and the page or pages where the information can be found. Note how both facts are put in parentheses, as in this example from paragraph 10 of Amy's paper:

(Wells 15)

This brief reference is one part of your documentation of sources; the other is the corresponding entry in your list of works cited (formerly called the "bibliography") at the end of the paper. When we look there under the name "Wells," we find all the other facts we may need: the rest of the author's name, the title of her article, the fact that it appeared in *Maclean's*, the date and year, and the page numbers:

Wells, Jennifer. "Jobs." *Maclean's* 11 Mar. 1996: 12–16.

Now we can look up the original article to check Amy's accuracy, or to find more information.

The exact form of the name-page reference and the form of the entry in our list of works cited will both vary sometimes, depending on several factors. Study

the guidelines that close this chapter, as well as the examples in Amy's essay, so you know what to do in each case. But first let's discuss the main question of documentation more fully.

When Do We Reference?

Some people worry about documentation, gloomily expecting to make a mistake and be accused of plagiarism. But most teachers can easily tell the difference between accidental and intentional plagiarism. The few students who deliberately present others' words or ideas as their own, in order to avoid the work of thinking, are often caught and harshly punished—perhaps by failure in the course or even expulsion from school.

Realize that teachers now have a new tool: several search engines have been developed to help them catch plagiarized material. These services can identify whole essays quite quickly, and even segments of material available online. One teacher found 12 serious cases of plagiarism out of a class of 32. (The search took only a few moments.) All the cheaters were then given a failing grade in the course.

As for the honest majority of essay writers, observing the following principles should cover most cases of documentation. Even if your performance is not perfect, your teacher will note your honesty and will probably recommend improvements rather than blame you for "stealing" information.

■ **Reference whenever you quote an author's words or copy visual information such as a chart.** If the borrowed passage is only part of a sentence, or even just a key word or two, it is still put in quotation marks and referenced.

■ **Reference whenever you summarize or paraphrase a source.** In high school some students think that doing "research" means finding good passages in the encyclopedia and copying them out into their essay, shuffling a few words around to avoid plagiarism. What they fail to see is that not only words, but also ideas, can "belong" to the person who wrote them.

For example, James Higgins, in his essay "Gabriel García Márquez: *Cien años de soledad*," published in Philip Swanson's 1990 book *Landmarks in Modern Latin American Fiction*, states the following on page 157:

The character with the acutest sense of life's futility is the disillusioned Colonel Aureliano. After undertaking thirty-two armed uprisings he comes to the conclusion that he has squandered twenty years of his life to no purpose and withdraws to his workshop, where he devotes himself to making the same little golden ornaments over and over again.

Suppose that a student doing an essay on the novelist García Márquez would write the following:

Colonel Aureliano is the character who shows the most acute sense of life's futility. After his 32 armed uprisings he realizes that he has squandered 20 years to no purpose and retreats to his workshop, where he spends all his time making the same little ornaments of gold over and over.

Do these thoughts still "belong" to Higgins? Despite the shifting of phrases and substituting of synonyms, a comparison of the two passages shows the whole progression of thought to be unchanged. A name-page reference should obviously follow the new version. Furthermore, small groups of words such as "thirty-two armed uprisings" are identical in both passages. The essayist must either change all such passages, to produce a total paraphrase, or put the borrowed parts in quotation marks to show who wrote them.

■ **Reference whenever you take from your source a particular idea or fact that is not common knowledge and that does not appear in other sources.**

For example, the year of Shakespeare's birth is not such common knowledge that most people could give it when asked. But since it can be found in thousands of sources, do not reference it. However, if critic X discovers an old trunk in an attic, filled with mouldy documents that prove the year of birth to be not 1564 but 1565, and publishes an article about it, you must reference this information because it is the intellectual property of the author.

Kinds of Name-Page References

Reference to a Single Author

As for the growing numbers of temporary workers, the jobs of 75 percent last less than six months, according to Chris Clark, policy analyst for the Canadian Council on Social Development. In the same vein, Andrew Jackson, senior economist for the Canadian Labour Congress, points out that these days only around 60 per cent of Canadians work full-time all year long for one employer (Wells 15).

Note how the period ending the sentence is placed *after* the reference. Note also that no comma appears between the name and page number, and that the word "page" or "p." is not used before the page number. This name-page reference leads us to the alphabetized entry under "Wells" in the list of works cited, where more information is given. Finally, although the above passage is not a quotation from Wells, it is documented because it is Amy's close paraphrase of Wells' information.

Here is a common variation on the kind of basic name-page reference shown above. If you give an author's name in the text of your essay, then you need give only the page number in the reference:

"The most important thing," writes Gordon Betcherman, a leading Canadian authority on the future of work, "is to encourage forms of education that mix schooling with work experience—internship, co-op programs and work-term efforts" (D2).

Note how often Amy does name her source in her own text; this procedure helps her essay "flow" by giving readers enough context that they are not tempted to interrupt their thoughts by always turning to the list of works cited.

A variation on the above mode of documentation is placing the page reference directly after the author's name in the text:

Social critic Heather Menzies (34) believes that women are even more victimized than men by the spread of part-time work.

When Two or More Titles by the Same Author Are Listed in the "Works Cited"

Suppose the following sentence occurred in Amy's essay:

Recurving is "Leaving one job to take another that pays less but places one back on the learning curve" (Coupland, *Generation X*, 24).

Since another of Coupland's novels, *Microserfs*, is also listed in the works cited, Amy avoids confusion in the above reference by naming the novel quoted. She also names the author, since he is not mentioned here in the text.

(By the way, see how in paragraph 2 of Amy's essay Coupland is quoted, but the reference gives only the page number. The reasons: his name is not needed because it was given a few lines earlier in Amy's essay, and the title does not appear in the reference either, because it, too, is mentioned above; thus we would not mistakenly go to Coupland's other book listed in the works cited.)

Documentation procedure may seem complicated, as in this case, but it is all based on reason: references give only the facts we really need to know.

A Work That Has Two Authors

In the future, successful employees may well need the skills fostered by an education in liberal arts (Foot and Stoffman D2).

Titled but Unsigned Sources

In a 1995 address on youth unemployment, Al Flood, CEO of the Canadian Imperial Bank of Commerce, summed up his view: "The overall task is to show more of the new generation, new to the workforce or not yet in it, how to be entrepreneurs" ("Business and Education Must Join Forces to Combat Youth Unemployment, CIBC Chairman Says").

List of Works Cited

Book

Rifkin, Jeremy. *The End of Work: Technology, Jobs and Your Future.* New York: Putnam, 1996.

(Note how only the first line of the entry is at the left margin, while the rest is indented. This helps the reader find the right entry, because the last name of the author is the item alphabetized.)

Newspaper Article

Greenspon, Edward. "Economy Changing Faster Than People." *Globe and Mail* [Toronto] 20 Apr. 1996: A1+.

(Note where periods are used or not used. Also note that months are abbreviated. Finally, if an article appeared on more than one page, and the pages are not consecutive, you may just specify the beginning page and add a plus sign.)

Magazine Article

Wells, Jennifer. "Jobs." *Maclean's* 11 Mar. 1996: 12–16.

(Note how the month is abbreviated. Note also how the inclusive page numbers are given, since in Wells' source the article continued on consecutive pages.)

A Work by Two Authors

Foot, David K., and Daniel Stoffman. "The Great Canadian Job Funk." *Globe and Mail* [Toronto] 25 May 1996: D1–2.

(The first and last names of the second author are not reversed, since the last name of only the first author appears in the alphabetical order of the list. Also see how the month is not abbreviated, since the word "May" is already very short.)

Electronic Sources

A Telephone Interview

Oman, Naguib. Telephone interview. 25 Mar. 2000.

An E-Mail Source

Friedman, Jana. E-mail to the author. 21 Mar. 2000.

A CD-ROM

The Oxford English Dictionary. 2nd ed. CD-ROM. New York: Oxford UP, 1992.

(In this example cited by the *MLA Handbook for Writers of Research Papers*, 5th edition, note how "Oxford University Press" has been abbreviated to "Oxford UP." In general, documentation aims for conciseness.)

An Internet Online Posting

Jerrold, Alice. "Getting That Job in the New Millennium." Online posting. 22 Jan. 2000. 12 Mar. 2000 <news: comp.work.employment>.

(The first date is when the posting was made; this information can be important because material on the Internet is often updated and therefore changed. The second date is when the essay writer found the piece online. Finally comes the online address.)

A Work from an Online Service

Fox, Justin. "What in the World Happened to Economics?" *Fortune* 15 Mar. 1999: 90–102. *ABI/INFORM Global*. ProQuest Direct. Regional Community Coll. Lib., Little Rock. 2 Mar. 1999 <www.umi.com/proquest/>.

(This last example is given in the *MLA Handbook for Writers of Research Papers*, 5th edition. For many more examples of how to document CD-ROM, online, and Internet sources, consult this definitive guide, for sale in most college and university bookstores. A brief version of MLA guidelines for electronic sources can also be seen online at: <www.mla.org/style_top_index.htm>.)

Answer Key

Using a Little Craziness to Overcome Writer's Block: Worksheet (p. 9)
This activity is of course open-ended.

Limiting the Scope: Worksheet (p. 11)
This activity is open-ended.

Making Thesis Statements: Worksheet (p. 13)
This activity is open-ended.

Relating to Your Audience: In-Class Role Playing (p. 17)
This activity is open-ended. Done very spontaneously, in the spirit of dramatic "improvisations," it has strong potential to turn fun into learning.

Relating to Your Audience: Worksheet for In-Class Group Exploration (p. 19)
This activity is open-ended.

The "Main" Paragraph: Worksheet (p. 47)
Answers to the first set of five questions are of course open-ended. The topic sentence answers to the next set of five will probably be close to these in theme:

1. Going online can waste large amounts of a person's time.
2. Car ownership can be costly.
3. Fast food is not nutritious.
4. Clearcutting forests harms the environment.
5. Contact lenses can be more trouble than they are worth.

Topic Sentences: Worksheet (p. 51)

1.	C	2.	A	3.	C	4.	C	5.	A
6.	B	7.	C	8.	B	9.	C	10.	B
11.	A	12.	C	13.	C	14.	C	15.	A
16.	C	17.	A	18.	A	19.	B	20.	B

There could, of course, be alternatives to these answers, depending on how the topic sentences might be developed.

Unity in "Main" Paragraphs: Worksheet (p. 53)
The revisions are open-ended. Note that there are many tempting ways to go off-topic, or even to shift from one point or topic to another in the middle of a paragraph. Not that all this is to be condemned. Such shifts can be a sign of thinking while writing, of "discovering" in the middle of the task. Do encourage students to determine which of these examples seem to show new and better ideas arriving, and in such cases whether the topic sentence should be changed rather than new content removed.

Coherence in "Main" Paragraphs: Worksheet, Level 1 (p. 55)
This is a very easy exercise to begin working with coherence; rather than soliciting new material, it just asks for identification of what is already there.

Coherence in "Main" Paragraphs: Worksheet, Level 2 (p. 56)

This one is a little harder. It will be best not to be rigid about which expression goes where, in case students see other connections that also make sense. As a starting point, though, here is the paragraph with all the blanks filled with what seem the most obvious choices of transitions:

Note that some of the transitions begin with a capital, a hint as to their position in the exercise.

> Good planning is the key to a good holiday. Little did my sister and I know, when we decided to spend three weeks cycling in New Zealand, <u>that</u> the friends planning our trip did not know what they were doing. <u>A long time ago</u> they had driven, not cycled, through these mountains. <u>When</u> we arrived with our touring bikes, everything seemed good. The cyclists were all excited. The sun was shining. <u>In fact</u>, it was shining too hard: <u>since</u> the ozone layer of that southern latitude has almost disappeared, we had to cover ourselves with sunscreen <u>constantly</u> to avoid skin cancer. <u>Soon</u> we learned what it was to bike up a steep mountain, in first gear all the way. Semis roared past, <u>and</u> the wind <u>sometimes</u> pushed us into the ditch. A panel truck got too close and hit two bikers. One is <u>still</u> in hospital with a broken leg. <u>After</u> a day of such extreme effort, the camping was too much work. <u>Finally</u> several people quit and rented a car for the rest of the holiday. My sister and I were glad to get home <u>at last</u>. We were happy to be alive. <u>From now on</u> we will be very careful planning holidays.

Coherence in "Main" Paragraphs: Worksheet, Level 2 (p. 57)

Unlike the preceding worksheet, this one is open-ended. Some answers may be obvious, such as a "Now" before the final sentence, while others will be discretionary.

Coherence in "Main" Paragraphs: Worksheet, Level 3 (p. 58)

A good activity here would be for students to share their freewriting in pairs or small groups, for help in deciding if the freewriting has uncovered material good enough to develop in the paragraph.

Improving "Thin" Paragraphs: Worksheet (p. 63)

Why not do one of these paragraphs together, on the blackboard or word processing with video display, as an example, before the students choose another and do it on their own? The activity could be very entertaining and therefore motivating.

Economy: Diagnostic (p. 71)

Only these items are free of wordiness or undesirable repetition: 8, 16, 24, 31, 39.

Economy: Worksheet, Level 1 (p. 73)

Here are the most obvious corrections of these self-repeaters:

1. astounded	2. in the future	3. industrial products	4. the result
5. advantages	6. feelings	7. cheap	8. fascinating
9. a fact	10. at that moment	11. unique	12. share
13. 8 a.m.	14. in the future	15. our environment	16. crucial
17. deaths	18. confidence in myself	19. etc.	20. $150
21. obvious	22. fascinating	23. miserable	24. self-esteem
25. reappear	26. moisture	27. obvious	28. 600 students
29. sure	30. crucial	31. rectangular	32. light green
33. impossible	34. in June	35. in 1998	36. light brown
37. unique	38. no alternative	39. competition	40. in my opinion

Economy: Worksheet, Level 2 (p. 75)

Only number 9 is "correct." Revisions, of course, could vary so much that there is no point in presenting them here.

Economy: Worksheet, Level 3 (p. 77)

No item is "correct." The revisions are open-ended.

Clichés: Worksheet (p. 81)

Only number 3 is "correct."

Euphemisms: Worksheet (p. 87)

The answers are open-ended.

Euphemisms and Their Opposite: Words Biased Pro or Con: Worksheet (p. 89)

All answers are open-ended. Encourage students to use the dictionary where necessary.

Jargon: Worksheet (p. 93)

This activity has no one set of correct answers.

Slang and Colloquialisms: Worksheet (p. 98)

These items are "appropriate": 10 and 23.
The revisions are open-ended.

Completing Sentences: Worksheet (p. 103)

This one is open-ended. Since the last edition, several items have been replaced, to reduce joke answers.

Complete Sentences: Diagnostic (p. 110)

Only the following items contain no sentence fragment: 4, 10, 18, 22, 26, 31.

Complete Sentences: Worksheet, Level 1 (p. 113)

Items 6, 15 and 19 are complete. Also complete are items 4 (first word group), 8 (first word group), 20 (first word group), 21 (first and fourth word groups), 23 (first word group), 24 (first word group), and 25 (first word group).

Complete Sentences: Worksheet, Level 2 (p. 115)

Items 11 and 17 are complete. Also complete are items 1 (second word group), 3 (first and third word groups), 5 (first word group), 7 (first word group), 10 (first and third word groups), 12 (first word group), 14 (first word group), 15 (first and second word groups), 16 (first word group), 19 (first and fourth word groups), and 20 (first word group).

Complete Sentences: Worksheet, Level 3 (p. 117)

These items are complete: 3 (first and second word groups), 6 (first and second word groups), 7 (first word group), 8 (first two word groups), 9 (first word group), 10 (first and second word groups), 12 (first and second word groups), 13 (first word group), 14 (first, third and fourth word groups), 15 (first word group).

Comma Splice and Fused Sentence: Diagnostic (p. 122)

1. CS	2. CS	3.	4. CS	5. CS	6. FS
7. CS	8. FS	9. FS	10. CS	11. CS	12.
13. CS	14. CS	15. CS	16. FS	17. FS	18.
19. CS	20. CS	21. FS	22. CS	23. CS	24. FS
25.	26. FS	27. CS	28. CS	29. CS	30. FS
31. FS	32.	33. CS	34.	35. CS	36. CS
37. CS	38. CS	39. CS	40. CS		

Comma Splice and Fused Sentence: Worksheet, Level 1 (p. 125)

Items 3, 8, 17, 22 and 27 are "correct." The revisions are open-ended.

Comma Splice and Fused Sentence: Worksheet, Level 2 (p. 127)

Items 2, 8, 14 and 21 are "correct."

Commas: Worksheet (p. 132)

1. As I put my coat on, the dentist and receptionist had a brief discussion.
2. Sharon flirted outrageously with Michael, and Kenny and Jason flirted with her. OR:
   Sharon flirted outrageously with Michael and Kenny, and Jason flirted with her.
3. My brother, grandfather and I had been going to the races since before I could remember.
4. North Americans believe in eye contact.

5. The fastest sports are soccer, hockey, football, rugby and basketball.
6. Some researchers say that the few precious moments after birth are critical in forming a strong bond between parent and child.
7. O. J. Simpson, the famous athlete, a hero to many, was an abusive husband.
8. Once I placed a couple of lines on the paper, some thoughts began to appear.
9. The Chinese way of life stresses education.
10. Our media, especially television, are to blame for sexism in society.
11. If you can, use cash or make your payments promptly.
12. While Dad was putting the lights on, my brothers and I started to place the star on the Christmas tree.
13. Adoption is an event that dramatically changes a child's life.
14. Children who were victims of their parents' violent outbursts may undergo mental illness or personality disorder when they grow up.
15. Our diet should contain dairy products rich in protein, and vegetables.
16. Correct.
17. Clinging to their old culture gives immigrants a sense of security.
18. Marriage is a big commitment.
19. Hard work can pay off.
20. For hundreds of years English Canada had social and political control over Quebec.
21. Although stubborn, Hagar is one of Margaret Laurence's most admirable characters.
22. As I mentioned before, Ontario has a low level of education.
23. When planning your holiday, visit or phone the tourist information centre in your city.
24. Correct.
25. A student such as myself, who has a part-time job while attending university full-time, is bound to sooner or later pay the price.
26. Once the needle is in, the plunger is retracted to check for blood.
27. One thing that really bothers me is the idea of a large dog being kept in the city.
28. I love to play hockey, but studies come first.
29. Alcohol has become a problem for our schools, and teachers are deeply concerned.
30. The truth is that many alcoholics never seek help, resulting in their own destruction.
31. Correct.
32. Ham radio has become my obsession.
33. Correct.
34. Harsh lighting produces harsh photographs.
35. Correct.
36. One of my math teachers helped me learn to achieve my goal in the subject, by spending a great deal of time working with me.
37. When rivers lose their velocity, suspended particles of clay and silt are deposited, creating fertile soils in river deltas.
38. Brian McDonald, a youth worker in Vancouver, says one of the major reasons for school violence is the "slow response of a clogged court system."
39. The last step is to record the time, drug and dosage on the patient's chart.
40. I love to cook, myself, and eat at home.

Semicolon, Colon, Question Mark and Exclamation Point: Worksheet (p. 137)
These items are "correct": 9, 15, 22, 31.
The revisions are open-ended, since there is often more than one way to improve the punctuation.

Run-on Sentence: Diagnostic (p. 141)
Only the following items are not run-ons: 1, 6, 9, 13, 16, 21, 24.

Run-on Sentence: Worksheets, Levels 1 and 2 (pp. 143 and 146)
There are no "correct" items in these exercises. The revisions are open-ended.

Pronoun Reference: Diagnostic (p. 151)
Only the following items do not have a fault in pronoun reference: 4, 10, 15, 21, 31, 35.

Pronoun Reference: Worksheet, Level 1 (p. 153)
These items are "correct": 7 and 14.

Pronoun Reference: Worksheet, Level 2 (p. 155)
No items at all are correct all the way through.

Agreement: Diagnostic (p. 162)
The following items are "correct": 5, 11, 15, 16, 20, 29, 31.

Agreement: Worksheet, Level 1 (p. 165)

1. is	2. are	3. us	4. has
5. leave	6. provides	7. his or hers	8. I
9. was	10. its	11. does	12. provide
13. is	14. his or her	15. he or she has, his or her	16. is
17. its	18. were	19. his or her	20. was
21. like	22. lead	23. its	24. he or she has
25. is	26. I, my	27. is, himself or herself	28. has
29. has	30. they, have		

Agreement: Worksheet, Level 2 (p. 167)
Number 6 is the only "correct" item.

Agreement: Worksheet, Level 3 (p. 169)
Number 5 is the only "correct" item.
The revisions are of course open-ended.

Equality of the Sexes in Language: Worksheet (p. 173)
These items are "fair" (unbiased): 5 and 20.
The revisions are open-ended.

Misplaced and Dangling Modifiers: Diagnostic (p. 178)
Write "MM" in the blank beside each sentence that contains a misplaced modifier, and underline the misplaced modifier.

1. <u>Just like any other disease</u>, we must wait for the cure to racism to be found. MM
2. I moved to Bayside with my parents when I was 13 years old <u>from the city of Ottawa</u>. MM
3. The waiter brought menus covered with Chinese writing <u>to us</u>. MM
4. If you are like most people, a mortgage will be the largest debt of your lifetime. _____
5. <u>As a child</u>, my father told me the world is a cruel place to be in alone. MM
6. When I was a kid I lived with my grandmother, a lovely lady who would let me do anything I wanted to, <u>for a few months</u>. MM
7. <u>Preparing for an eight-hour ride</u>, the motor of the car was the only noise. MM
8. We are <u>only</u> young once. MM
9. It takes my mother only three minutes to drive to work. _____
10. I have <u>only</u> been in Canada for one year. MM
11. Long-distance health care is <u>only</u> possible because of computers. MM
12. In the past, stores were <u>only</u> allowed open on Sundays during the holiday shopping season. MM
13. We have become a species that knows only how to sleep and turn on the TV. _____
14. Since I was an only child, my parents wanted to protect me. _____
15. <u>After being hired</u>, the manager teaches the newcomer his or her duties and responsibilities. MM
16. Drinking is said to be a bad habit <u>by many doctors</u>. MM
17. I was discouraged from speaking the truth <u>by my lawyer</u>. MM

18. In the past, even an unimportant disease could kill the victim <u>such as measles, whooping cough or diphtheria.</u>   MM

19. Some children are forced to learn their first language <u>by their parents.</u>   MM

20. I have been working to put myself through school <u>for the last five years.</u>   MM

Write "DM" in the blank beside each sentence that contains a dangling modifier, and underline the dangling modifier.

1. <u>Climbing back into the car,</u> our lunch was half eaten.   DM

2. When you are living as a family, housework needs to be done.   ———

3. Dogs make good household pets because they are used for protecting the house <u>while away for the day.</u>   DM

4. <u>After eating a whole pizza,</u> my stomach begins to feel strange.   DM

5. <u>After spending three hours shivering and trying to stay warm,</u> the storm subsided and we quickly headed for camp.   DM

6. <u>Ever since seeing this film at age 12,</u> the memory has been burned into my mind.   DM

7. <u>After waiting two hours in the lobby,</u> the doctor spent less than two minutes on me.   DM

8. Upon arrival in Canada, I experienced the language barrier.   ———

9. <u>By recycling paper,</u> thousands of square kilometres of forest will be preserved.   DM

10. <u>Dressed in secondhand clothing with long messy hair,</u> his appearance was anything but clean-cut.   DM

11. <u>When feeling lonely and depressed,</u> a dog is always at your side wagging its tail.   DM

12. <u>Living on the farm in Alberta,</u> winter tends to be cold and harsh.   DM

13. Being an ESL student, I had a hard time understanding the teachers.   ———

14. <u>After writing tests and quizzes,</u> the board of education agreed to let me attend grade twelve at York Memorial High School.   DM

15. Parents have noted an increase in fights between siblings <u>after watching certain programs on television.</u>   DM

16. <u>After a few months of cleaning a dentist's office,</u> the dentist recommended me to her bookkeeper, so I was able to clean the bookkeeper's office too.   DM

17. <u>Becoming more educated now,</u> more interests entered my mind and engulfed it.   DM

18. Loose bindings will cause the skis to fall off <u>while standing up and skiing.</u>   DM

19. <u>Going through grade twelve,</u> the teachers began to demand more work.   DM

20. <u>When driving in a big city like Montreal,</u> parking is always a problem.   DM

Misplaced and Dangling Modifiers: Worksheet, Level 1 (p. 180)

These items are "correct": 9 and 17.

The revisions are open-ended.

Misplaced and Dangling Modifiers: Worksheet, Level 2 (p. 182)

These items are "correct": 9 and 12.

The revisions are open-ended.

Parallel Form: Worksheet, Level 1 (p. 187)

1. playing tennis	2. touching	3. Harley-Davidson	4. intelligent
5. April	6. to skate	7. London	8. murder
9. heaviness	10. Babe Ruth	11. angry	12. going to the movies
13. drinking too much	14. crow	15. shifted gears	16. to roast
17. speaking	18. to plough the soil	19. after dinner	20. Calgary

Parallel Form: Worksheet, Level 2 (p. 189)

These items are "parallel": 8 and 17.

The revisions are open-ended.

Commonly Confused Words: Worksheet (p. 195)

1. accept	2. advice	3. effect	4. affect	5. our
6. bear	7. breaks	8. breathe	9. buy	10. capital
11. clothes	12. course	13. council	14. desert	15. due
16. immigrated	17. farther	18. hear	19. heroine	20. whole
21. its	22. know	23. led	24. lose	25. morale
26. passed	27. piece	28. personnel	29. principal	30. quiet
31. write	32. role	33. sight	34. than	35. there
36. they're	37. through	38. too	39. whether	40. were

Apostrophes: Worksheet (p. 203)

1. All pets should receive more sympathy than they do.
2. For entertainment Oshawa has movie theatres, ice rinks, roller arenas, night clubs and all sorts of gyms to work out at.
3. The Beatles' influence and popularity will live as long as rock and roll exists.
4. The present art of producing with an assembly line system has come a long way since its introduction.
5. C
6. It's exciting to see a great horse thundering down the track.
7. The only way to reduce students' financial problems is to increase their grants and loans.
8. Students who are 18 and over are the ones who need money the most.
9. Thousands of people fish Ontario's lakes and rivers each year, but how many will take a minute to consider the results of fished-out waters?
10. Driving a motorcycle gives one a sense of independence, because the rider knows people are watching.
11. People who have no confidence in their own work will try to use others' ideas.
12. Politics is what gets everyone talking and moving in this world.
13. Parents' moral values are passed on to the next generation.
14. My parents emigrated from Greece.
15. C
16. After each goal the team that was scored against gets possession of the ball behind its net.
17. It's a holiday to escape from work and see who can catch the most fish.
18. It's my parents' duty to take care of me; they are legally required to.
19. She sees only his good qualities.
20. C
21. Solar systems have a sun and various numbers of planets.
22. Are Canadians ashamed of their own country?
23. C
24. There are many owners' clubs for most sport cars.
25. Newton's Second Law of Motion helps the swimmer to conserve energy.
26. Illness can be the mind's expression to withdraw from life's stresses and strains.
27. We'd go to my grandparents' house each year.
28. With its small and friendly society, its rain forest attractions like the wildlife, its breathtaking waterfalls and its easy-going life, Guyana is my favourite holiday spot.
29. When Nick sees the Buchanans' reaction to Myrtle's death, he develops a sense of moral responsibility.
30. Animals such as rabbits, monkeys and cats are being used for meaningless experiments.
31. C
32. It was Labour Day when all the delayed thoughts of moving from my parents' finally hit home.
33. When children see their favourite players using sticks to jab and spear other players, the next thing you know, the children are imitating.
34. Anyone who has run for a few years on the road has no doubt experienced a deterioration of the knees.
35. Elizabeth realized the faults of her parents' marriage.
36. C

37. True punk rockers wear safety pins through their noses or cheeks.
38. A newborn child sees the light for the first time.
39. My mother's parents don't travel at all.
40. All over the world we are confronted with the same problems in women's lives.

Capitals: Worksheet (p. 208)

1. A friend of mine, Frank, once told me that he had been behind a Mac's store smoking a cigarette when all of a sudden a police officer approached and asked him where the pot was hidden.
2. During the hockey game, the mother of one of the opposing players stood up from her seat and yelled as loudly as she could, "Kill that little worm!"
3. In the first year of the program, students have to take accounting, economics, geography, mathematics, English, management, business law and psychology.
4. Canadians have long been concerned with developing the North, but only recently with protecting it.
5. My parents bought a house north of the business district, within a five-minute walk of an elementary school, a middle school, a high school, a Mac's Milk store and a shopping centre.
6. On a bright summer morning, the first Monday of July, we got in our canoe and started down the Missinaibi River.
7. Who has seen the wind?
   Neither you nor I;
But when the trees bow down their heads
   The wind is passing by.
                —Christina Rossetti, 1872
8. In high school one of my English teachers spent two months on *Hamlet*.
9. In addition to containing beef and/or pork, wieners may contain water, flour, milk solids, salt and preservatives such as sodium nitrite, which has been known to cause cancer in laboratory animals.
10. Cruise ships have many facilities such as bedrooms, swimming pools, lawn tennis courts, dancing halls, movie theatres and bars.
11. Lady Macbeth, a strong-willed character who was capable of influencing Macbeth to murder his king, brought about her breakdown and death by her own ambitions.
12. John Osborne was born on December 12, 1929, in London, England.
13. In today's modern society, people's morals and values are changing, so divorce, birth control and abortion are more easily accepted.
14. J. D. Salinger's best short story, "For Esmé—with Love and Squalor," shows how destructive war is to human feelings.
15. When I began high school I really got involved in soccer.
16. I arrived in Trinidad on Monday and began my search for a job on Tuesday.
17. Stephen Leacock once wrote, "The essence of humour is human kindliness."
18. In his *Biographia Literaria*, Coleridge refers to "that willing suspension of disbelief for the moment, which constitutes poetic faith."
19. Mackenzie King said, "The promises of yesterday are the taxes of today."
20. Blaise Pascal called humans "the glory and the shame of the universe."
21. The driver stopped the bus to jump out and take a look. He was immediately followed by the Spaniard, two Mexicans, Hugh, Geoffrey and Yvonne.
22. When the Canadian dollar sank in value, foreign automobiles such as the Volvo, Volkswagen, Toyota, Subaru and Honda rose sharply in price.
23. The National Hockey League Rules Committee brought in new rules which prohibited players from being overly aggressive.
24. My mother speaks French, Portuguese and English.
25. I have noted that math teachers do not dress as well as English teachers.
26. To depict their toughness, hockey players are given names such as "Hammer," "Battleship," "Tiger" and "Bulldog."

27. One of the fastest-growing religions in the world is Islam.
28. In each of Mordecai Richler's earlier novels, *The Acrobats*, *Son of a Smaller Hero* and *A Choice of Enemies*, the hero is an artistically inclined Canadian with a deep dislike of Canadian culture and a conviction that the society he lives in is a fraud.
29. As a faithful expression of the theme found in the play, the movie *Fortune and Men's Eyes* was the epitome of success.
30. "Well, Doctor," I said, "since you agree with the other doctors, I suppose we had better go ahead with the operation."

Abbreviations (p. 210)

1. CPI = consumer price index
2. MBA = master's in business administration
3. GIC = guaranteed income certificate
4. GST = goods and services tax
5. ICU = intensive care unit
6. CFA = certified financial analyst
7. RAM = random access memory
8. R&D = research and development
9. RN = registered nurse
10. SASE = self-addressed stamped envelope

INDEX